Journalism Research That Matters

T0355444

JOURNALISM AND POLITICAL COMMUNICATION UNBOUND

Series editors: Nikki Usher, The University of Illinois Urbana-Champaign, and Daniel Kreiss, University of North Carolina at Chapel Hill

Journalism and Political Communication Unbound seeks to be a high- profile book series that reaches far beyond the academy to an interested public of policymakers, journalists, public intellectuals, and citizens eager to make sense of contemporary politics and media. "Unbound" in the series title has multiple meanings: It refers to the unbinding of borders between the fields of communication, political communication, and journalism, as well as related disciplines such as political science, sociology, and science and technology studies; it highlights the ways traditional frameworks for scholarship have disintegrated in the wake of changing digital technologies and new social, political, economic, and cultural dynamics; and it reflects the unbinding of media in a hybrid world of flows across mediums.

Other books in the series:

Reckoning: Journalism's Limits and Possibilities
Candis Callison and Mary Lynn Young

Imagined Audiences: How Journalists Perceive and Pursue the Public
Jacob L. Nelson

Journalism Research That Matters

Edited by

VALÉRIE BÉLAIR-GAGNON AND NIKKI USHER

UNIVERSITY PRESS

OXFORD
UNIVERSITY PRESS

Oxford University Press is a department of the University of Oxford. It furthers
the University's objective of excellence in research, scholarship, and education
by publishing worldwide. Oxford is a registered trade mark of Oxford University
Press in the UK and certain other countries.

Published in the United States of America by Oxford University Press
198 Madison Avenue, New York, NY 10016, United States of America.

© Oxford University Press 2021

All rights reserved. No part of this publication may be reproduced, stored in
a retrieval system, or transmitted, in any form or by any means, without the
prior permission in writing of Oxford University Press, or as expressly permitted
by law, by license, or under terms agreed with the appropriate reproduction
rights organization. Inquiries concerning reproduction outside the scope of the
above should be sent to the Rights Department, Oxford University Press, at the
address above.

You must not circulate this work in any other form
and you must impose this same condition on any acquirer.

Library of Congress Cataloging-in-Publication Data
Names: Bélair-Gagnon, Valérie, editor. | Usher, Nikki, editor. |
Minnesota Journalism Center Workshop (2019 : University of Minnesota)
Title: Journalism research that matters / edited by Valérie
Bélair-Gagnon, Nikki Usher.
Description: New York : Oxford University Press, 2021. |
Series: Journalism and political communication unbound |
Includes bibliographical references and index.
Identifiers: LCCN 2020058466 (print) | LCCN 2020058467 (ebook) |
ISBN 9780197538470 (hardback) | ISBN 9780197538487 (paperback) |
ISBN 9780197538517 (Online) | ISBN 9780197538500 (epub)
Subjects: LCSH: Journalism—Research.
Classification: LCC PN4784.R38 J68 2021 (print) | LCC PN4784.R38 (ebook)
| DDC 070.43—dc23
LC record available at https://lccn.loc.gov/2020058466
LC ebook record available at https://lccn.loc.gov/2020058467

DOI: 10.1093/oso/9780197538470.001.0001

1 3 5 7 9 8 6 4 2

Paperback printed by Marquis, Canada
Hardback printed by Bridgeport National Bindery, Inc., United States of America

Contents

PART III. JOURNALISM RESEARCH'S HIDDEN CHALLENGES

PART IV. JOURNALISM PRACTICE MATTERS

Acknowledgments

This book started as an outgrowth of the Minnesota Journalism Center workshop on engaged Journalism Studies held in May 2019 at the University of Minnesota. The Center, which one of the co-authors directs, was established in 1979 by a gift to the University of Minnesota from the late John Cowles, Sr., chairman of the Minneapolis Star and Tribune Company, and his wife, the late Elizabeth Bates Cowles. Housed in Murphy Hall at the University of Minnesota's Hubbard School of Journalism and Mass Communication, the Center's goal is to bring research into practice. We also want to thank a generous host, Dr. Elisia Cohen, who attended the whole workshop and provided critical feedback and support to the workshop's participants.

We are indebted to the talented workshop participants of this book who agreed to share some of the genuine challenges they were facing as junior and mid-career faculty members in bridging research with practices. Thanks to Jane Yeah-In Pyo, Jesse Holcomb, Matthew S. Weber, Benjamin Toff, Lindsay Palmer, Melissa Tully, Stephanie Edgerly, Margaret Ng, Rachel R. Mourão, Soo Young Shin, Jan Lauren Boyles, Brian Ekdale, Danielle Kilgo, Jennifer Moore, Damon Kiesow, Mark Poepsel, and Matt Carlson. We also want to thank media professionals Chase Davis from the *Star Tribune* and Derek Willis from *ProPublica,* who accepted to critique what *Journalism Research That Matters* can do better to bridge research with practice.

We are also thankful to the two anonymous peer reviewers who helped with their useful insights. And we want to thank Daniel Kreiss, co-editor with Nikki Usher of the *Journalism and Political Communication Unbound* series at Oxford University Press, Stacy Trager who helped us think through the design, and Angela Chapko, who helped us shepherd this project to the end. Brinton Layser kept it real with his six-year-old precocity and dimpled smile. Finally, we are grateful for our respective spouses and family who supported us during the finalizing of the project in a time of global pandemic.

Contributors

Valérie Bélair-Gagnon, Assistant Professor, University of Minnesota

Jan Lauren Boyles, Associate Professor, Iowa State University

Matt Carlson, Associate Professor, University of Minnesota-Twin Cities

Chase Davis, Senior Digital Editor, *Star Tribune*

Stephanie Edgerly, Associate Professor, Northwestern University

Jesse Holcomb, Assistant Professor, Calvin College

Damon Kiesow, Knight Chair in Digital Editing and Producing, University of Missouri, Missouri School of Journalism

Danielle K. Kilgo, Assistant Professor, University of Minnesota

Yee Man Margaret Ng, Assistant Professor, University of Illinois Urbana Champaign

Rachel R. Mourão, Assistant Professor, Michigan State University

Lindsay Palmer, Associate Professor, University of Wisconsin-Madison

Mark Poepsel, Associate Professor, Southern Illinois University

Jane Yeahin Pyo, Graduate Student, University of Illinois

Soo Young Shin, Graduate Student, Michigan State University

Benjamin Toff, Senior Research Fellow, Reuters Institute for the Study of Journalism at the University of Oxford, and Assistant Professor, University of Minnesota-Twin Cities

Melissa Tully, Associate Professor, University of Iowa

Nikki Usher, Associate Professor, University of Illinois

Matthew S. Weber, Associate Professor, Rutgers University

Derek Willis, Journalist , *ProPublica*

Journalism Research That Matters

Introduction: Improving Journalism with Academic Research

Valérie Bélair-Gagnon and Nikki Usher

A journalist, a business consultant, and a journalism professor are sitting at a sports bar. They are chatting about the latest update to the latest social media platform.

The journalist exclaims, "Oh no, did my job just get harder?!"

The business consultant says, "This seems like the kind of innovation that might save journalism."

The academic opines, "Wow, how can we study this? What are we going to teach journalism students now?"

A sports fan comes into the bar to catch the end of the baseball game playing on the bar's TVs. She overhears the trio talking, and groans, audibly, "Really, more fake news?"

This people-walk-into-a-bar joke may not be as funny as your favorite "dad joke" rendition. But this story highlights the reason why this book exists. For news producers and news consumers alike, this is a confusing time, thanks to a myriad of disruptions that have fundamentally altered our experiences with the news and information environment. We live in a high-choice media environment, meaning that there are countless choices available for us to turn to for news and entertainment. Big technology companies have massive influence on people's ability to learn about the world around them. What counts as quality news and information is in the eye of the beholder, with professional journalism's claim to authority and expertise much undermined. Technological innovations are moving so fast that it can seem like it is impossible to keep up.

Similar to authoritarian regimes elsewhere in the world, the Trump administration was not been shy about calling formidable news institutions "fake news" to discredit unfavorable news coverage. Around the world, the right-wing news ecosystem has reached a state of digital maturity. In the

Valérie Bélair-Gagnon and Nikki Usher, *Introduction: Improving Journalism with Academic Research* In: *Journalism Research That Matters*. Edited by: Valérie Bélair-Gagnon and Nikki Usher, Oxford University Press. © Oxford University Press 2021. DOI: 10.1093/oso/9780197538470.003.0001

United States, for example, distrust in journalism follows sharply partisan lines, with 75% of Republicans reporting that they do not trust the media.[1] Talking about journalism has now become an "off limits" topic for the holidays and social gatherings. As with politics, there is no predicting how tempers might flare. Regardless of whether "fake news" is just another moral panic or a pernicious threat to democratic countries, it is clear that the partisan trolls, the propagandists, and other digital miscreants have been successful in seeding information disorder.

This situation is enough to inspire cynicism rather than action. As academics, we refuse to let that happen. In this book, we are concerned with rethinking how we can do journalism research that matters. Journalism research that matters is critical to helping various stakeholders navigate what is happening to news, explain *why* it is happening, and help chart a way forward. It matters in contexts such as news and data literacy, journalism's financial sustainability, diversity and inclusivity, and trust in journalism. Though most members of the public report not being concerned about the economic fate of local journalism, most of us closer to the reality of the news industry see that the uncertain economic model for journalism demands our attention. Rigorous journalism research should not just live in the academy. Rigorous journalism research also needs to question its own internal assumptions and power dynamics to strengthen academic contributions to public knowledge. By virtue of reading this book, you are a stakeholder in the future of news: you might be a concerned member of the public, a scholar, an entrepreneur, a philanthropist, a technologist, working at a think tank, a journalist or aspiring journalist, or a student assigned this book.

Journalism Research that Matters is both a call to action and a guide. As an orienting framework for scholarly inquiry, journalism research that matters is driven by four key questions: How can we use research to improve journalism? What are the most important areas of contributions from the field? How can we do our research better? What barriers exist to doing journalism research that matters? This book provides an overview of some of the most important conversations and areas of research within the academy. In this book, we interrogate our research tradition to call for research that is not extractive or exploitative. We also acknowledge the importance of thinking across audiences and hierarchies, and consider journalism and its connections to democracy, education, policy, race and inequity, and beyond. Finally, we open ourselves up to critique. In fact, the final section of the book features short commentaries from professional journalists, who offer their perspectives on how journalism scholars and journalists can work together.

The contributors to this edited volume share an intellectual commitment to pragmatism and applicability in our research. We are a collection of early career and mid-career scholars who are working in large, mostly public universities in the Midwest. These universities were home to the beginnings of formal education *and* research in journalism and mass communication in the United States. We take this historical legacy as a clarion call for a renewed spirit of journalism research that matters. We have been inspired by the legacy of our institutions to contribute to public knowledge, but this tradition does not simply live in slogans engraved on buildings or in historical memorabilia. Recovering this tradition of Midwest practicality and the ethos of the land-grant university allows journalism scholars to move beyond a guide for how to do public scholarship or applied scholarship. It allows us to discuss a way of thinking about research that has an endpoint that betters the academy, the experiences of the audience, and the industry. We hope to add to this ethos a commitment to interrogate power, diversity, and inclusivity.

Research beyond the "Ivory Tower"

Scholars have long sought to connect research with practice in order to inform practice, influence the way organizations operate, and set public policies. However, this approach to scholarship often lives outside the boundaries of traditional academic scholarship, which means it is not always recognized by universities as part of a scholar's research portfolio and is likely not to be part of formal tenure and promotion requirements. Despite the lack of institutional incentives, a tradition of public scholarship has emerged. There are different approaches for connecting beyond the Ivory Tower to inform public discourse, from open forums to collaboration with intermediary groups to working with journalists to connect with the general public.[2] These approaches aim to tackle real-life problems with insight and solutions informed by research. When research connects to practice, the success can be attributed to the questions selected, the significance of the findings and their connections to public concerns, and often, the scholars' own smart publicity strategies and their connections to influential funders and public figures outside the academy.

Universities have woken up to the importance of public engagement as part of their institutional missions. Across the world, universities have deployed public engagement initiatives. At the center of these considerations are inquiries about how to make "scholarship socially relevant and meaningful to the public by translating our findings into practice and targeting relevant professional communities to disseminate this information."[3] These are concerns shared across the academy that are salient in Journalism Studies, where our main object of study, journalism, faces both real and existential threats to its continuation.

Journalism research can help address these challenges and, in turn, improve journalism itself. Especially now, journalism lacks a clear definition, and scholars are often hesitant to make normative claims about what they believe journalism ought to be. This volume focuses on professional journalism, which refers to journalism created with the purpose of reaching mass audiences that follows a fairly standard set of norms, ethics, and practices that structure newsgathering and news production. Traditionally speaking, professional journalism legitimates other social institutions, provides knowledge to people beyond their immediate contexts, and links a broader public in a shared civic imaginary. Normatively, we believe that journalism can be better than it is now, and we believe that journalism stands to play an important role in society.

Journalism needs to be more equitable, inclusive, and transparent. Journalism at its best provides a check on the powerful, informs the public not just about politics but also with information to guide daily life, and perhaps most important, can foster a sense of shared history, purpose, and cultural identity. Better journalism builds a stronger society with more responsive, democratic, and inclusive political and social institutions. Professional journalism is riddled with problems, but that does not mean these normative aspirations are not worth striving toward.

Practically speaking, professional journalism faces distinct financial challenges, which are particularly acute for newspapers and digital-first news outlets. This financial uncertainty creates an infuriating question for scholars in the academy: should we devote our attention to solving the news industry's financial problems? Certainly, many other fields, from finance to marketing to education to public policy, focus their attention on scholarship that can have direct, applied benefits. In the past, journalism scholarship has often faced critiques that it is detached from the needs of the news industry. While scholars like us don't want professional journalism to go belly up, we also do not serve at the behest of the news industry. We care about the research–practice gap, but our interests go beyond finding a way for the commercial news industry to retain its profitability.

Researchers in this book take their position as industry outsiders seriously. Making journalism better requires research to understand the ways in which news production, consumption, distribution, and content have (or have not) changed. This book provides a guide to some of these changes. Scholars in this book also offer insight into how journalism can be more equitable and inclusive as an institution and in coverage. We push for a broader understanding of news consumers, including those who *don't* regularly consume news, and offer suggestions for equipping news audiences and journalists alike with better skills to understand news and data.

This book also engages in self-critique. All too often, that same research tradition that draws from an intellectual commitment to pragmatic research brings with it the ugly side of history. All too often, as scholars, we apply a Western gaze, fail to take note of our own power and privilege relative to research participants, and omit thinking about questions of diversity, equity, and inclusion. Journalism scholars often think people notice their work beyond the academy, but this may not be the case. If researchers want to commit to conducting research that matters, they not only have to do research better but also have to make sure this research is translated to those outside the academy. Journalism research that matters is also a way of doing research that is not extractive or exploitative to the people we study, and recognizes the importance of using scholarship to critique power.

Academics possess the time, the methodological training, and, in most cases, the independent perspective to make sense of what journalism can offer. However, doing research that matters is difficult. The expectations and the conventions that reside in the larger culture of academia do not always make it possible to connect journalism research to journalism practice. In fact, these expectations and conventions can disincentivize research that matters. The research published and presented in academic settings often involve big, theoretically complicated words or phrases with nuanced meaning that most members of our families would not recognize. Those of us contributing to this book have even coined or popularized a few of these on our own (among them include "metajournalistic discourse," "interloper," "boundary work," "news avoiders," and "information brokers").

Then why create these terms and publish in obscure journals if we say as scholars that we care so much about doing journalism research that matters?

One answer is our own subfield's academic imposter syndrome. Journalism is often regarded as vocational training, and journalism research itself associated with a narrow set of applied, industry-oriented questions. If you look at top universities, you will find that with a few exceptions, the Ivies, small liberal arts colleges, and even some of flagship state universities offer no formal training for journalists, especially at the undergraduate level. Journalism Studies scholars, then, are nested in an academic field fighting for legitimacy within the academy against more established disciplines with long-standing theoretical and empirical traditions. Aside from associated centers, there is little space for the formal academic study of journalism itself in these elite institutions, though this is slowly changing. Journalism is still demanding to be taken seriously within the academy.[4] To be taken seriously, we as scholars have to perform seriously as academics, too. If you are a journalism scholar in a tenure-track position, or a non-tenure track faculty member at a research university, this means producing academic journal articles that often sit behind gated, expensive, paywalls, and writing books that speak back to larger academic theories, discourse, and questions.

As scholars we must acknowledge that we also like being inside the academy. It is fun to ask big questions that do not always have answers easily translatable to practice. Scholars like approaches that allow them to ask big questions and connect back to larger theories about power, economics, society, and politics. Conducting exacting, methodologically rigorous research is fulfilling to us as scholars and also important to generating insights that help us know more about the world. As scholars we are also incentivized to do so. Sometimes scholarly questions are narrow, sometimes overbroad. That is the privilege of not having to produce outcomes that result in higher quarterly earnings or audience growth.

Often, the questions and findings from research lack an immediate use case, and indeed, are not intended to. This is an advantage of the academy: the space to ask questions and to answer them. The paycheck comes from the teaching, research, and service, not from a for-profit corporation that has profit incentives and benchmarks to assess quarterly job performance. Yet the demands of the academy around tenure, promotion, and scholarly legitimacy make it harder for journalism researchers to ask the applied questions journalists would like us to, even if we see the importance of studying them. However, when journalists and news organizations dismiss work as egg-headed and detached, it becomes harder for researchers to develop trusted collaboration efforts, creating additional barriers to doing journalism research that matters. That said, the last section of this volume includes contributions from journalists who share their ideas for reconciling this dilemma.

One area of concern among journalists and academics has been the deepening division between journalists and audiences. News organizations have routinely ignored or negatively profiled some communities. More generally, there is a disconnect between stories journalists cover and the way they cover them, and what the public says it wants from their news. Journalism research that matters addresses these problems, using research to draw attention to these problematic practices and to show how journalists can benefit by engaging with diverse audiences. Yet as this book shows, journalists are not always willing to acknowledge empirical findings of racial bias and inequity in their newsrooms or in their coverage. There is a process of translation that must occur for research to influence practice, and it depends on scholars and stakeholders being open to new ideas and, sometimes, to painful critique.

Signs of Success and Ways Forward

There are signs that journalism research can make a difference. Take the example of the policy group Free Press, which secured a $5 million state subsidy for local news in New Jersey. While not an enormous amount of cash given the news industry as a whole, this is more than a symbolic victory. Free Press grabbed the headlines, which spurred the legislative action, but in order to advocate for policy change from a position of strength, it took years of painstaking and expensive research conducted by scholars to empirically demonstrate what New Jersey's news deserts looked like. The research conducted by the then-Rutgers University professor Philip Napoli and his team made it clear that the haves in New Jersey were getting more than their fair share of news coverage, while the poorer a New Jersey resident was, the less likely it was that any news organization bothered to help that resident learn about her community.[5] This was a clear-cut case of how journalism is not incentivized by the commercial market to provide news and information to the "have nots." Free Press was able to use the research to support its goals of a policy intervention.

Journalism scholars can push the boundaries of many taken-for-granted assumptions held in the news industry. As scholars, we can provide solutions that are then integrated in journalism schools' curriculum, or that journalists can use in their everyday work. This is particularly the case when it comes to thorny problems such as race and diversity, ethics, and labor issues, in which scholars can use their research findings to hold journalism institutions accountable. Consider the work of Sue Robinson, a full professor at University of Wisconsin-Madison, who spent six years looking at information networks in five American cities.[6] Robinson found that while digital technologies can open doors to anyone who wants to participate, mainstream journalism practices remain highly racialized. She also observed that in communities that have been consistently marginalized by mainstream journalism, distrust runs deep and is hard to correct. Importantly, Robinson's work helped spearhead an honest discussion about the limitations of local mainstream media. A headline in her local paper in Madison, Wisconsin, summed up the kind of conversation the scholar was able to start: "Sue Robinson Wants White Reporters to Change the Way They Report."[7]

Other efforts are also showing how scholars can collaborate with journalists, so long as journalists are willing to listen. As part of an initiative between the Department of Communication at Namibia University of Science and Technology (NUST) and the Social Science Research Council's African Peacebuilding Network grant program, NUST senior lecturer Admire Mare brought scholars and media practitioners together to discuss best practices on how to report on conflict and peacebuilding in southern Africa. The project's participants also learned new approaches to writing, and to lessen the risk of those involved in conflict reporting.[8] These forms of initiatives have had an impact on African media practice and policies, changing the ways journalists do their work.

In other contexts, critiques have changed journalism practice precisely because scholars have remained outside the industry, using their methodological skills to generate robust empirical findings. When the research findings substantiate what journalists have observed but have not been able to conclusively demonstrate, scholarship can serve as a rallying cry. For example, volume editor Nikki Usher's research, along with that of another volume contributor Jesse Holcomb, found that US-based male political journalists dominate Twitter to the expense of female political journalists. This research helped raise awareness of implicit and explicit sexism on the social media platform, prompting discussions about how journalists could do better. Male journalists tweeted about their promises to do better and wrote commentary for news outlets vowing to pay more attention to their gendered social media practices.[9]

Academic institutions are also working to bridge the research–practice divide through dedicated centers that relieve scholars of some of the pressures of traditional scholarly journal article production, and infrastructure for raising funding to support journalism research. There are also numerous efforts from centers such as the Trusting News Project, Center for Media Engagement, the Knight Lab at Northwestern University, the Reynolds Journalism Institute, the Minnesota Journalism Center at the University of Minnesota-Twin Cities, the Columbia Tow Center for Digital Journalism, and the Reuters Journalism Institute for the Study of Journalism at Oxford University that are bridging the research–practice gaps in other ways, from community partnerships to supporting interventions aimed at improving civic engagement.

Other efforts include *The Conversation*, a nonprofit site dedicated to amplifying academic research. Conceived of in Australia in response to the Australian university system's emphasis on publicly facing scholarship, *The Conversation* expanded to Canada thanks to efforts by Journalism Studies scholars Alfred Hermida and Mary Lynn Young at the University of British Columbia, and in the United States, *The Conversation* is supported through funding provided by universities and foundations. Nieman Journalism Lab at Harvard has similarly included academic work in their reporting and critique of the profession. Professional associations have recognized such work such as the International Communication Association's Journalism Studies Division engagement award to academics (both editors of this volume have served on the committee). This book is not arguing that all researchers and journalists should be mirroring these efforts, but these are examples of how journalism research can inspire change.

Overview

This book is divided into four parts. Part I looks at "The Research–Practice Gap." Research-to-practice gaps have been part of the academy since its inception. Factors contributing to this problem include lack of funding or institutional support for translating scholarly research into actionable insights, and a lack of awareness or lapses in communication between researchers and practitioners. The chapters in this section address research–practice gaps and propose solutions for bridging them. In Chapter 1 the University of Illinois' Jane Yeah-In Pyo, along with volume co-editor Nikki Usher, show how journalism research has historically had a strong tradition of applied research that has faded as mass communication research has become a more traditional academic field. Through the case of the Illinois' Institute of Communications Research, Pyo and Usher argue for the recovery of an academic tradition that facilitates the coexistence of humanistic, social science, and industry approaches to research. In Chapter 2, Calvin College's Jesse Holcomb looks at public-facing research centers such as the New America Foundation and the Tow Center for Digital Journalism at Columbia University, as well as funding bodies such as the Knight Foundation. Making a call for transparency about the lack of peer-reviewed research at these centers, Holcomb argues that scholarly and peer-reviewed research need to be understood for their respective merits. Scholarly research goes through peer review, but applied, center-based research offers speedy publishing, a wide distribution platform, and takes advantage of access to proprietary and commercial data that scholars often lack.

In Chapter 3, Minnesota's Matthew S. Weber urges Journalism Studies researchers and practitioners to learn from other fields.[10] In particular, he shows how "knowledge brokers" perform specific, designated roles in health care facilities and hospitals to facilitate information exchange between researchers, policymakers, and health practitioners. Health researchers know that "knowledge brokers" play an important role in translating scholarship to practice, and as a result, researchers now intentionally write in plain language that knowledge brokers can understand and share with others. While research that connects with practice is often framed as almost entirely positive for all involved, the scholarly community has not fully defined or evaluated the efficacy of the many ways such dynamics work. Many journalism academics, in fact, take pride that their work is reaching outside of the academy but lack any real benchmarks aside from anecdotal evidence to suggest their work is actually reaching beyond the Ivory Tower. For better or worse, in Chapter 4, Minnesota's Benjamin Toff examines whether, in fact, academic research manages to cut through our crowded information environment. Through an analysis of the performance of Facebook posts by the news industry trade press, Toff finds that posts about academic research receive far less attention than posts about other industry-specific developments.

While the attention economy may make it harder to draw public attention to scholarly research, another problem facing efforts to bridge the research–practice gap has nothing to do with digital information. Instead, there are institutional barriers in higher education and deep social inequalities that make it harder to study the concerns of marginalized populations. In Journalism

Studies, these problems can reify inequities for our research participants, too. In Chapter 5, building from her work on foreign correspondents and stringers, Wisconsin's Lindsay Palmer talks about how qualitative researchers using interview and observation methods can avoid taking advantage of research participants to bolster their own academic reputation. Drawing from the rich tradition of qualitative methods,[11] Palmer notes the challenges of changing the minds of those in power.

Part II, "Answering the Crisis in Journalism: Key Areas of Research," showcases some of the most exciting new research developments and unanswered questions that scholars are pursuing to provide insight for journalists and the public at large. Topics include news and data literacy, the psychology of news consumption, and new business models for journalism. In surveying these key areas of research, the chapters show how academic research offers insights that are wider ranging than simply maximizing industry profits and can help us understand how to think about our fast-moving news and information environment. Similarly, these chapters show how academics have the benefit of being able to look across an entire industry rather than focusing on specific issues to help an individual news organization fix a discrete problem.

Journalism research that matters also pays close attention to how audiences are dealing with the challenges of our complicated news and information environment. In Chapter 6, Iowa's Melissa Tully shows how news literacy research, education, and practice can adapt and evolve to address 21st-century challenges. In Chapter 7, Northwestern's Stephanie Edgerly unpacks the underlying psychology of news consumption, including the obstacles and challenges that prevent news consumption and hinder audience engagement. Edgerly argues for the need to think of audiences in more specific ways that consider their relative news exposure and underlying inequities in education and political engagement. In Chapter 8, Margaret Ng of Illinois presents contemporary examples of successful collaborations across newsrooms that expand understandings of how journalists can work together rather than compete in a time of limited resources but ever-proliferating sources of data to analyze. Her scholarship addresses the potential of open-source repositories such as GitHub and strategies for under-resourced news organizations to maximize their impact, even on an international scale. In Chapter 9, Damon Kiesow a digital media pioneer who worked at *The Boston Globe* and McClatchy, among others, and is now Knight Chair in Digital Editing and Producing at the University of Missouri School of Journalism, talks about using human-centered design to consider the interplay between the needs and roles required for successful and sustainable digital journalism. And in

Chapter 10, Nikki Usher, University of Illinois, and Mark Poepsel, Southern Illinois University, call for scholars to be engaged with the economics of media beyond newspapers and digital-first outlets. They also ask scholars to be more intellectually honest and for universities who serve as innovation "bubbles" to consider the strengths and limitations in their experimentations and insulations from commercial pressures. Hopefully, the scholars do, however, show how such research can help journalism thrive.

Part III, "Research's Hidden Challenges," looks at the explicit and hidden challenges of practice-oriented research. In Chapter 11, Michigan State's Rachel R. Mourão and Soo Young Shin detail the development of a public affairs reporting course for journalism schools in resource-limited communities. In doing so, Mourão and Young show how journalism education and communities surrounding land-grant institutions can connect, such as by training students to engage with local communities that are underserved by the local news media. In Chapter 12, Iowa State's Jan Lauren Boyles highlights how the academy can play a role in improving data literacy and data accessibility. She discusses journalism training experiments in the Midwest, digital learning platforms, and K–12 journalism education. In Chapter 13, Iowa's Brian Ekdale critiques ethno-nationalism in Journalism Studies research and suggests that academia and the media are complicit in knowledge production that is oriented toward the Global North rather than the South. Though academics and practitioners tend to reproduce their own inequities, Ekdale points to possible solutions to tackle these structural problems, including developing support networks and making changes through academic curriculum development.

Scholars, particularly those who are people of color, face many barriers to entry and to access to studying newsrooms, including racial discrimination. These obstacles can lead to fatigue or even burnout, especially for junior scholars. In Chapter 14, Minnesota's Danielle Kilgo, a race and journalism scholar, discusses these challenges, and through her content analysis, shows that news organizations reify negative portrayals of racial struggle, using violent images, especially about race and crime, to garner public attention. Kilgo details the consequences she has faced after pointing out these racialized frames to journalists, who were not willing to acknowledge her data. Faced with this critique, these journalists ended her research access in their newsroom. Kilgo's work shows that scholars have the power to prompt journalists to face uncomfortable realities of their profession, including implicit and explicit racial bias, but her work also shows that change is not always welcome.

The calls from practitioners in Part IV "Practice Using Journalism Research Matters" push back against what they see as overly academic approaches to journalism research and provide suggestions for better working relationships between academics and journalists. In Chapter 15, Chase Davis, Senior Digital Editor for the *Star Tribune* (and formerly of *The New York Times*), points out that there is a storied legacy of journalists working with academics, but all too often a lack of shared understanding about the goals of the collaboration can cause these partnerships to implode. In Chapter 16, University of Minnesota-Duluth's Jennifer Moore explains what journalism education can do to equip young journalists with an understanding of how academic research can help their work. In Chapter 17, Derek Willis, a data journalist and news applications developer at ProPublica and a well-known Twitter critic of academic research, charts a set of research questions journalists want to know about the news industry and about news audiences, and how academics can help journalists answer them.

Finally, Matt Carlson, of the University Minnesota, provides an overview of the key themes of the book in a concluding chapter. Centering his analysis on the murky definition of the term "engagement," he argues that Journalism Studies should not think of engagement with the public or with journalists in absolute terms. Rather, Journalism Studies should evaluate whether journalism research matters by considering its impact on a complex ecosystem of actors, macro- and micro-structures, and their interactions, actions, and inactions. The ecosystem works recursively: practice shapes Journalism Studies scholarship and scholarship, at its best, can shape practice.

Regardless of whether you are an optimist or a pessimist about the future of journalism (or somewhere in the middle), journalism matters, especially right now in this messy, wonderful, and sometimes scary contemporary moment of institutional re-composition and sweeping technological and social change. Journalism research matters, too, especially if it can help make sense of what is happening and chart a path forward.

Notes

1. Meg Brenan, "Americans' Trust in Mass Media Edges Down to 41%," Gallup, September 26, 2019, https://news.gallup.com/poll/267047/americans-trust-mass-media-edges-down.aspx

2. Derek Barker, "The Scholarship of Engagement: A Taxonomy of Five Emerging Practices," *Journal of Higher Education Outreach and Engagement* 9, no. 2 (2004): 123–137.
3. Kevin J. Barge and Pamela Shockley-Zalabak, "Engaged Scholarship and the Creation of Useful Organizational Knowledge," *Journal of Applied Communication Research* 36, no. 3 (2008): 250–251.
4. Barbie Zelizer, "Journalism and the Academy," in *The Handbook of Journalism Studies*, eds. Karin Wahl-Jorgensen and Folker Hanusch (London, New York: Routledge, 2006), 29–41.
5. Philip M. Napoli et al., "Local Journalism and the Information Needs of Local Communities," *Journalism Practice* 11, no. 4, (2017): 373–395.
6. Sue Robinson, *Networked News, Racial Divides: How Power and Privilege Shape Public Discourse in Progressive Communities* (Cambridge: Cambridge University Press, 2018).
7. Pat Schneider, "Q&A: Sue Robinson Wants White Reporters to Change the Way They Report," *Madison.com*, January 28, 2018, https://madison.com/news/local/education/university/q-a-sue-robinson-wants-white-reporters-to-change-the/article_345954f7-996f-5c75-9fde-10c32f72cf66.html.
8. Mare, A. (ed.), Conflict Sensitive Journalism: A Practical Handbook for Journalists in Southern Africa (2018), https://www.nust.na/sites/default/files/documents/Final%20Handbook%2015%20Oct%202019%20.pdf.
9. Nikki Usher, Jesse Holcomb, and Justin Littman, "Twitter Makes it Worse: Political Journalists, Gendered Echo Chambers, and the Amplification of Gender Bias," *The International Journal of Press/Politics* 23, no. 3 (2018): 324–344.
10. At the time of publication, Weber had moved positions to Rutgers University in New Jersey, another land-grant Big 10 university.
11. James W. Chesebro and Deborah J. Borisoff, "What Makes Qualitative Research Qualitative," *Qualitative Research Reports in Communication* 8, no. 1 (2007): 3–14.

PART I

THE RESEARCH–PRACTICE GAP

1

Recovering the Midwestern Ethos
of Journalism Research

Jane Yeahin Pyo and Nikki Usher

Introduction

Every person who enters through either of the main entrances to Gregory
Hall at the University of Illinois' flagship campus in central Illinois will be
confronted with one of two signs: the first declaring the very ground the vis-
itor stands on as the birthplace of the idea of national public broadcasting
in the United States in 1949, and the second announcing the university's
postwar commitment to a free press. Across the quad, there are the Morrow
Plots, the oldest continually kept experimental research field in the United
States, where in 1867 scientists realized what now seems to be elemental
knowledge: soil quality matters. The juxtaposition of this historic agricul-
tural field to the signs proclaiming the birth of public broadcasting and the
post-WWII commitment to a free press seems at once quite jarring. After
all, what might public broadcasting and high-flying ideals about free speech
have to do with farming?

Upon closer inspection, these two diverse fields, communication and ag-
ricultural sciences, are joined by the very mission of the Morrill Act of 1862
that founded land-grant universities across the United States, wherein:

> . . . the leading object shall be, without excluding other scientific and clas-
> sical studies, and including military tactics to teach such branches of
> learning as are related to the mechanic arts . . . in order to promote the lib-
> eral and practical education of the industrial classes in the several pursuits
> and professions of life.[1]

As explained in an address at the University of Illinois' inauguration by educator and close friend of Abraham Lincoln, Newton Bateman, the land-grant

Jane Yeahin Pyo and Nikki Usher, *Recovering the Midwestern Ethos of Journalism Research* In: *Journalism Research
That Matters*. Edited by: Valérie Bélair-Gagnon and Nikki Usher, Oxford University Press. © Oxford University Press 2021.
DOI: 10.1093/oso/9780197538470.003.0002

university was never meant to be all practical, but was meant to facilitate a practice-oriented approach to "abstract laws and principles."[2] The birth of public broadcasting, the commitment to free speech, and the discovery of life-changing scientific knowledge are part and parcel of this ethos of education, application, and the pursuit of "higher" knowledge.[3]

Without romancing the vision of practical and forthright Midwesterners too much, it is at least fair to say that journalism research in the United States has its beginnings in the Midwest.[4] This research was also based on a deep engagement with practice, from understanding the role a newspaper could play in establishing a sense of community belonging to understanding how new technology like the radio might link Americans together over vast distances. These Midwestern connections and this land-grant ethos matters, especially given today's conundrum: we need more journalism research that can help us figure out how to address issues raised by declines in news sustainability, a rise in hyper-partisanship and misinformation, the omnipresence of big tech, and heightened social division and inequality more generally. Right now, journalism researchers are not doing enough of this research, or if they are, this research is living inside the academy and failing to translate to the public outside it—perhaps because either explicitly or implicitly, scholars are paying redress to the ill-fitting match of an applied field trying to justify its existence within the culture of the academy.

There has been considerable thought about what journalism education should be, but less attention to creating journalism research that matters (or attention to what "mattering" should even mean). de Burgh suggested that journalism education ought to enable journalists to think more deeply about the implications of their work:

> ... to put themselves and their society in perspective; find out anything and question everything. Motor skills yes, but also the intellectual confidence which comes from knowledge.[5]

This same can be said for the reorientation of journalism research around the vision expressed in the Morrill Act for scholarship more generally: as higher-order abstract knowledge whose immediate application is not necessarily obvious but nonetheless deeply tied to the understanding and improvement of social life.

In the post-WWII era, the Midwest emerged as a central place where battles played out in the academy amid applied work, humanistic scholarship, and social science research around journalism and mass communication. One particular case of this is at the Institute of Communication Research (ICR) at the University of Illinois, which at its outset aimed to serve a mix of stakeholders, from aspiring journalists and filmmakers to the US Central Intelligence Agency. A look at the ICR, its history, and its shifts in leadership and orientation helps ground a broader story about why the constraints on journalism research can often feel like checking boxes to please the doubters rather than doing work that answers meaningful questions in ways that lead to better social understanding.

Vestiges of Practical Communication Research

There is a joke (or snark) among social scientists about the large number of experiments and surveys whose sample is described as "undergraduate students at a large Midwestern university." But there's some truth to this little dig: the Midwest is home to most Big-10 and many Big-12 universities, and depending on how you count based on NCAA league alignments, the vast majority includes public universities created through the original Morrill Act of 1862 or universities with similar, if not longer, histories of research and education. Some of these Midwestern universities would lead the way in the formalization of research into journalism, mass communication, and journalism education.

The birth of journalism and mass communications research and educa-tion in the academy came as part of the larger turn in the progressive era toward professionalization, credentialing, and datafication.[6] There are a few key indicators of the importance of the Midwest to that early history. The University of Missouri School of Journalism, founded in 1908, bears the distinction of being the first journalism school in the country, if not the world.[7] The present-day Association for Education in Journalism and Mass Communication began in 1912, and its first president was Willard G. Bleyer, who also helped get Wisconsin's first journalism department up and run-ning.[8] In 1921, Northwestern University's journalism school was founded in honor of Joseph Medill, a Canadian-American newspaper editor and publisher whose stewardship of *The Chicago Tribune* raised its profile and national prominence. Wisconsin's journalism school opened shortly after in 1927, which is also the year that the first American public radio station was born, housed at the university. It is now honored by a landmark outside

Vilas Hall, which is the current home to the station as well as the School of Journalism and Mass Communication. Notably, at Wisconsin, journalism research was in the DNA of the creation of the school; the journalism minor doctoral program was approved the same year the school opened.[9] Graduate students could teach journalism at the university and minor in journalism while getting a PhD in political science, sociology, or history, by taking doctoral seminars on public opinion and propaganda.[10]

The Midwestern connection to the professionalization of journalism can also be found in efforts to create codes of ethics. The American Society of Newspaper Editors, founded in 1923, has its origins in a Bleyer-organized camping trip to Glacier National Park with ten Midwestern newspaper publishers.[11] However, as James W. Carey reminds us, even at Columbia (whose journalism school was founded in 1912), and certainly at state universities, journalism education was a vulgar cast-off from English and the humanities, dedicated to trade-based training with little room for anything else, and, as some argue, was designed as a form of social control over journalists who might otherwise be agitators.[12]

There were other ways in which the Midwest was becoming a home to early scholarly research in journalism and mass communication. Historically, the Midwest was a frontier of adopting the great European social science theories, especially through the University of Chicago and its eponymous "Chicago School," which pioneered social science research. The University of Chicago was founded in 1892 with a bequest from John D. Rockefeller Sr. and support from the Carnegie Corporation, and from roughly 1918 to 1932, the university would serve as a center for the development and professionalization of social science research.[13] The Chicago School realized the significance of the boom of immigrants coming into the city and saw immigrant communities as fertile places for research and "pro-social" Progressive Era interventions, including research on immigrant use of news media.[14] As Carey writes, the result was "distinguished scholarship devoted to the urban world of Chicago, virtually all of which had sections on the mass media."[15] Newspapers and the mass media more generally were a central preoccupation of the Chicago School and were even considered as a way to spread insights from scholarly research. In fact, John Dewey, George Herbert Mead, and Robert Park tried to publish a daily newspaper for social science, reflecting a practical orientation where scholarly knowledge was to be communicated to a wider public.[16]

While the University of Chicago has never offered formal journalism classes, Social Science 1, taught by Everett Hughes, was a close corollary. Students were assigned census tracts of the city, and their research assignments prompted extensive familiarity with the city's formal and informal institutions. Here, too, even in the city, the connection to the rural Midwest served as inspiration. Wahl-Jorgensen recalls Park's "romantic self-understanding" as an ordinary, practical Midwesterner, and requotes his proclamation of love of "the common things, earth, air—the song of the robin and the great herds of common people, simple and natural as cows."[17] While overwrought and possibly even patronizing, this sentiment nonetheless reflects a research orientation rooted in empiricism, inspired by ordinary people for whom social science would both generate and inspire insights into their lived realities.

As many have chronicled, communication itself grew as a central field during World War II and in the postwar era. The energy for communication research during World War II was centralized in Washington and to a lesser extent in New York, with scholars working for the Office of War Information who were initially lured there by a CBS News Radio commentator and Rhodes Scholar, Elmer Davis.[18] While it is difficult to confirm exactly why scholars like Paul Lazarsfeld, Howard Laswell, Kurt Lewin, Theodore Adorno, and Wilbur Schramm floc345ked to Washington, maybe a sense of wartime exigency (especially for European refugee scholars) but perhaps also the chance to do meaningful work, these scholars were able to conduct applied research under the purview of a director who had a strong respect for scholarship.

After the war, many of these scholars who had worked in Washington were intimately involved in the maturation of communication research as an academic discipline, with many heading to the Midwest to start schools that bridged practice and scholarship. Scholars Everette Dennis and Ellen Wartella explain that in the 1940s, a number of universities began to create "Schools of Journalism and Mass Communication," and "among these were pacesetters such as Minnesota and Wisconsin."[19] These changes mattered, in part because it meant that the field was looking at journalism more broadly with an eye toward new technology as well as part of the larger scholarly enterprise of communication. "Adding the name Journalism to Communication had a deeper significance . . . communication was a social science name rather than a vocational one."[20] They also note that Illinois "went further" by creating a School of Communication, placing journalism and other communication subfields under the leadership of a dean.

While there is some debate as to whether Wisconsin or the University of Iowa had the first PhD program in journalism or communication, Wilbur

Schramm, a Harvard and University of Iowa–educated former journalist and English professor, had something to do with both. At Iowa, Schramm became the director of the School of Journalism—a fortuitous link between a scholar trying to establish a formal academic program in communication and taking journalism more seriously as a scholarly discipline (though increasingly associated with sciences)—and began the first communication PhD program in a journalism school in 1943 at Iowa.

Schramm helped continue this postwar expansion in communication through the founding of the ICR at the University of Illinois in 1948, after leaving Iowa the previous year. A close look at Schramm's vision for the ICR shows how the land-grant ethos was baked into the formal study of communication and journalism: practical, applied training with an open-minded and interdisciplinary approach intended to sweep in humanistic and social scientific traditions. This support for interdisciplinarity, and a belief that practice and scholarly research could coexist at the same time, may have been the result of dealing with the University of Iowa's rejection of Schramm as a social scientist because of his humanist background, and the simultaneous snobbery of the humanities at the university who thought journalism, as training and research, was overly vocational. A look at the history of the ICR, then, tracks some of the ways in which journalism research is often uncomfortably positioned as a form of scholarly inquiry. The history detailed here is drawn from interviews with longtime professors in the ICR, primary source material, and accompanying accounts of the ICR in more general histories of communication research.

The Institute of Communications Research

Schramm's vision of the ICR can be summarized in two ways: first, to provide knowledge of mass media and its effect on society; and second, to prepare students for the application of their knowledge to professional fields. According to the original brochure for the ICR from 1948, the mission of the institute was "to apply the methods and disciplines of the social sciences to the basic problems of press, radio, and pictures; to supply verifiable information in those areas of communications."[21] The ICR also aimed to train graduate students so that they could contribute scientific research to newspapers, radio stations, magazines, and advertising agencies. Schramm saw communication studies as being empirical, quantitative, practical, and applied, and as such, the ICR would be an institute that would conduct research funded through both outside agencies and the university.

Situated in the Midwest and with a train station conveniently located in the city to connect the campus to Chicago, the University of Illinois also offered a favorable environment for such an enterprise. First, the University of Illinois was fully equipped with infrastructure where research could flourish: state-of-the-art IBM machines were available as a unique resource for quantitative and empirical research. Second, in addition to technological facilities, the university had a radio station, a school of journalism, and the University of Illinois Printing Press to provide many different kinds of communication media that students could test and apply their knowledge.[22] Notably, Schramm would go on to also manage the university's press and broadcasting stations; his biography itself was a manifestation of the link between the land-grant aspiration of practice blended with scholarship. The public land-grant university mission also played an important role in establishing the ICR's longevity. Illinois, like Iowa and Wisconsin, is a public school, and the ICR had a stable (though varying) level of budgetary support from the university budget, which gave a sense of permanency and stability, such that the pressure to craft research questions just for the sake of retaining corporate and federal dollars was at least muted.

While Schramm took the initiative in launching the ICR, the need to create a program with an interdisciplinary approach in order to understand the complexities of communications predated him and was set into motion by faculty members in journalism and advertising.[23] Indeed, at the outset journalism was part of this scholarly and applied conversation. Acknowledging that questions regarding communications were ones "which often refuse to be confined by one branch of social science or one medium of communication," the ICR's original faculty covered wide-ranging fields from advertising, journalism, sociology, and economics. Fred Siebert, director of the School of Journalism from 1941, had interests in history and philosophy and would later go on to coauthor the seminal communication text *The Four Theories of the Press* in 1956 (Schramm and Theodore Peterson, a journalism professor in the ICR, were coauthors).[24] Charles Sandage, head of advertising, had an academic background in economics and was interested in a theory-based approach to advertising. Sociologist J.W. Albig established a tradition of public opinion research. Dallas Smythe, appointed to the ICR in 1950 by Schramm, held a joint appointment in the Department of Economics and also worked for the Federal Communications Commission while at the ICR, formalizing the study of the political economy analysis of media institutions as a domain of communications research. The ICR of the 1950s brought together psychologists, political scientists, economists, sociologists, and journalism professors to conduct research funded by the US government, the Ford Foundation, and the Social Science Research Council.

When Schramm left Illinois, the ICR went through a shift that would bridge its social science orientation with more humanistic concerns. In 1957, Charles Osgood took over to become the director of the ICR. Using his expertise in psycholinguistics and the interdisciplinary character of the ICR, he expanded it to become the center of psycholinguistic research on campus at a time when psycholinguistics as a discipline was not well accepted across the university.[25] The University of Illinois did not have a separate linguistic department prior to Osgood's arrival, and rooting this inquiry into the ICR helped establish the more humanistic orientations in its scholarly reputation. This humanistic approach would continue under James W. Carey's leadership of the ICR.

The Humanistic Turn in Journalism Research

In 1969, James Carey was appointed as the director of the ICR, and his presence in the 1970s and 1980s created a major shift in the mission of communication studies. While most of the attention in communication studies was still highly related to measuring and understanding the effects of mass media, Carey brought the "interpretive turn"[26] to the field, arguing that communication, as social practice and symbolic practice, was embedded in culture and community and thus produced, maintained, and transformed reality.[27] Methodologically and epistemologically Carey had a view of the world and of the field of communication different from Schramm and Osgood. Nonetheless, as Willard D. Rowland Jr., the former dean of School of Journalism and Mass Communication at the University of Colorado, Boulder, recounts, Carey was "always to some extent at odds with Smythe, Gerbner, Schiller, and Gubackian tradition. But he valued it and wanted it there as a goad."[28]

Carey drew inspiration for the ICR from the Midwestern geography and its intellectual tradition. He sought to recover the tradition of the Chicago School, especially its highly interdisciplinary approach in its early years before scholars became overly obsessed with the quantification of their research across the social sciences. This meant thinking about communication as "an active process of community creation and maintenance."[29] In the guise of ICR director, Carey made the case for journalism scholarship as *Journalism Studies* rather than as vocational training or as one dimension of inquiry for social science approaches to communication. Doing this type of journalism scholarship at Illinois was particularly symbolic; the Illinois gravitas of serious theoretical contributions as well as applied research could coexist with a humanistic, cultural investigation of journalism. More significantly, the ICR served in part as a historical correction for the slight Schramm once felt as a rejected humanist at Iowa. Carey made the case that scholarly research on journalism could, in fact, be rigorously and carefully conducted with a humanistic tradition at the center.

There is no need to recite Carey's tremendous contributions to Journalism Studies, but it is worth noting that his critiques were historically grounded, centered on questions about journalism as social practice through which reality is represented and meaning is made. Nowhere, though, is his claim for the legitimation of journalism scholarship as a serious humanistic undertaking more visible than his call for a new approach to journalism history as cultural history. He despaired of what he referred to as a "whig" version of journalism history, which implied a continuous and forward march toward progress. And while acknowledging that this type of history was not necessarily wrong, it was nonetheless boring. This "whig" history reflected a narrow set of questions that kept journalism research in the disparaged box of a "vocation" and not a field of serious scholarly inquiry. Much of this scholarship, according to Carey, focused on histories of newspapers, overly chronological and detached from larger historiographic concerns and "needlessly focused on the overproduction of biographies of editors and publishers."[30]

On the other hand, to understand journalism as the production of social reality meant engaging in the cultural history of journalism. Carey explained it this way, a paragraph worth quoting in full:

When we grasp the history of journalism, we grasp one form of human imagination, one form—shared by writer and reader—in which reality has entered consciousness in an aesthetically satisfying way. When we study changes in journalism over time, we are grasping a significant portion of the changes that have taken place in modern consciousness since the enlightenment. But to do this we must temporarily put aside our received views of what journalism is and examine it afresh as a cultural form, a literary act, parallel to the movie, the essay, and the scientific report. Like these other works, journalism is a creative and imaginative work, a symbolic strategy: journalism sizes up situations, names their elements and names them in a way that contains an attitude toward them.[31]

Journalism scholarship, if understood as cultural history, was indeed another project of the humanities designed to give a better understanding of human consciousness and thought. In fact, the techniques to examine journalism could be akin to examining a novel or a work of art.

From his perch at Illinois, and then later at Columbia's School of Journalism, where Carey founded the PhD program, he used the structure of the academy to provide critiques of contemporary journalism. Much like he had issues with over-deterministic social science, he also found much to critique amid the presumptively scientific and objective reporting style of journalists.[32] He also tied this critique to questions about repair, becoming a leading intellectual voice of the public journalism movement, which sought to bring journalists in more active and direct conversation with the public.[33] We see new shades of this idea in today's engaged journalism research.

There is no doubt that Carey, as part of the ICR, played a significant role in recovering journalism research in its own right as a study of culture rather than as a study of an effect. However, the success he had in cementing the legitimacy of the field as a humanistic enterprise may have helped its standing in the academy but began the slow unraveling of journalism research's previous grounding within social science and its ties to applied research. Carey, in trying to establish a cultural approach to journalism scholarship, may have gone too far or been *too* good at setting in motion this approach to research. The ICR, as a micro-case of larger trends in communication and journalism scholarship, shows how journalism research might have lost its way. Journalism research's defensive posture further embedded it in a quest for continued legitimization by the academy, leaving behind research that might be viewed as vocational.

What Repair Looks Like, as Inspired by the ICR

In the eponymously named Peterson Room at the University of Illinois, the ICR's main seminar suite, there are six cartoons hanging on the walls, drawn by Theodore Peterson himself. The scope of these cartoons reflects the history and potential of the ICR at its inception and crystalizes the ICR as a case of a Midwestern center of thought leadership that blended research and practice. The cartoons, then, serve as a visual and graphic summary of the history outlined above, and taken together provide inspiration to think about what journalism research can learn from this rich tradition.

The ICR's beginnings, as Peterson attests in one cartoon, emerged out of uncertainty. He drew a dark foreboding cloud over the head of Schramm, dressed in a black raincoat. Schramm was leaving Iowa behind after starting its PhD program in journalism and communication but was still plagued by his rejection among Iowa's humanists and social scientists. Would the ICR be able to avoid this fate? It turns out that under Schramm, the ICR's future would be conceived as bold and robust. In a second cartoon, Peterson draws ban impossible trident, a classic U-shaped optical illusion, and underneath it notes:

> Wilbur allowed himself a flicker of rare pomposity when he wrote the aims of the Institute for the Board of Trustees. What he really meant, I think, was that the ICR would tackle some of the great mysteries that have always bedeviled the human race.

The impossible trident itself violates the laws of Euclidean geometry, because it cannot have one end with two prongs and the other with three simultaneously.[34] While tongue in cheek, the image and the caption represent some critical lessons for journalism research: be bold, ask big questions, and don't diminish the possibility of making great inroads through one's research. Perhaps, even, do the impossible, even if it seems this way. Thus, the first suggestion from this Midwestern legacy:

> *Journalism research needs to ask big questions and try to solve them, and even if seemingly impossible, try nonetheless.*

The second cartoon about this early history, where Schramm is depicted as holding two babies, one the ICR and the other the PhD program. Peterson captioned it, "The Institute and the PhD program, in my mind, are clearly intertwined, both were the babies of Wilbur Schramm, and were in their infancy when I first arrived here." The PhD program—the doctoral-level study concomitant with the demands and expectations of the academy, would also be part and parcel of the applied and theoretical approach. For journalism, it begs the charge that the doctoral-level study of journalism must be part and parcel of a broader interdisciplinary conversation that takes into account social science, humanistic approaches, and applied research questions.

A third cartoon shows a series of four stacked boxes or desks, a man crouched underneath each one, as if crushed by the weight of the one above. Petersen's caption here, "When the institute was born, the school of journalism was suffering a shortage of space" might be taken to mean physical space—that the school of journalism was growing and the ICR was crammed into a building. The "shortage of space" might also be thought of as intellectual space—that journalism in the academy was somehow crushed under its own vocational history, squeezed into the academy for purposes of professional training and little more. Thus, there is an important reminder:

> Journalism research must be academically rigorous but also part of an inclusive, interdisciplinary academic culture that provides institutional support and rewards for applied research.

The fourth cartoon about ICR's founding depicts Schramm, hunched over with a magnifying glass, watching another man draw a tally on a board. The caption: "Does research give us truth? Schramm thought working on that was at least as important as counting the angels who dance on the head of a pin." This cartoon pokes fun at the idea of positivism—and points out the importance of reflective social science. Is finding the ultimate truth possible? Of course not, or at least is as much folly as the old adage that serves as a touchstone to St. Thomas Aquinas's pondering about the number of angels that can exist in the same space at once.[35] In short, this kind of question—about truth—is like this question of angels; folly, perhaps even a waste of time to ask, and one considered only by zealots. Even in the tale of the social science direction associated with the ICR's embedding in major sponsored research, this focus on trying to "prove" with some sort of finality truths about human communication was considered over-deterministic.

The cartoon is a reminder that seeking some sort of normative vision of what the "truth" ought to be can sometimes stand in the way of critical social scientific and humanistic research. An obsession with some idealized form of journalism can lead to a lack of questioning both presumed knowledge and values of journalism, a dangerous case of nostalgia, and a push for reform and intervention guided by premises of what journalism ought to be without questioning these very premises. After Lazarfield's discussion of "administrative research," Daniel Kreiss calls this "administrative journalism." This form of journalism serves the purpose of considering how journalism can make better election predictions, overseeing bureaucracy, and understanding social processes.[36] But journalism research can do better, as Kreiss points out: the values undergirding much of journalism scholarship need to be questioned; what information is legitimated as civically important reflects a set of assumptions about the world, who counts as powerful, and what questions are of social interest. Thus, a third lesson is:

Journalism research needs to question fundamental normative orientations within the practice of doing journalism and journalism research.

A fifth cartoon shows Charles Osgood, the third director of the ICR, depicted as teaching in a classroom about semantic differentials and then depicted as suspended in air carrying a briefcase with the concept on it. The caption, "Charles Osgood was always flying off somewhere," also reflects an important lesson that can be taken from the ICR and applied to journalism scholarship more generally. While it is unclear whether this was with other academic institutions or with foundations and government agencies, the spirit of spreading knowledge outside the ICR is very much part and parcel of the public mission of the land-grant university itself. Significantly, he was probably not just jetting around on the ICR's budget, especially in this early era of commercial air travel when only a quarter of Americans had ever been on a plane.[37]

The sixth cartoon shows Charles Sandage, the advertising scholar, sending disciples into the world carrying suitcases filled with knowledge. This too, speaks to the scholarly training of applied researchers, who bring with them their solid research background, wherever they may be headed and whatever reason for their journey. It also speaks to the widespread propagation of a school of thinking so influential that it functions as an applied discipleship. Taken together, these cartoons suggest values of public engagement and the importance of legitimizing the subfield of journalism as part of the overall project of a social scientific approach to communication by bringing together research and scholarship. Thus, a final call emerges for journalism research:

Journalism scholarship should be publicly engaged and worthy of respect from key stakeholders inside and outside the academy.

There is much to dislike about the way in which journalism research has failed. For the sake of suitability within the academy, journalism research, when poorly set up as quantitative inquiry, becomes squeezed into the narrow framework and scholarly conventions of other social science. Carey made clear later in his career, at Columbia School of Journalism, that journalism research had missed the chance to be a "science of the complex relations among humans struggling to create a common life within conflict and division, a science deeply democratic, pluralistic, humanistic, and imaginative in its impulses."[38] If the ICR had failed to do this, and if Columbia University's new PhD program had not yet produced repair even under his reign, what hope was there for journalism research?

Carey, especially from his perch in New York at Columbia, could claim to be engaged with journalists. He *had* to be, in part because he worked with them at a hotbed of activity for the very best and most influential journalists in the English-speaking world. Would he have been able to claim this kind of engagement if he had remained in the Midwest at the ICR? It is hard to say. Years later, with the project of cultural history in journalism well established, much of Carey's call to think about a cultural, humanistic approach that sees journalism as a social practice now seems so scholarly that the words and concepts begin to lack meaning, even for academics familiar with them.

The long-standing tension is that journalism is indeed vocational, and that journalism schools offer vocational training that is suffocating; scholars are gasping to fit into scholarly conventions, and the industry needs applied work, not scholarship that aims to legitimize the subfield within the academy. Notably, this is a story rooted in the United States, and the intellectual legacies of mass communication research and Journalism Studies, not to mention social science writ large, have different origins and points of fracture. Now, applied research has never seemed more important; but applied research in the current academy, across most US institutions, is done as an add-on rather than an end on its own. There are few academic research institutions that would view administrative and applied journalism research as sufficient for tenure and promotion.

Carey's vision of journalism research is one that is "deeply democratic, pluralistic, humanistic, and imaginative in its impulses," a vision that returns us to the Midwest and to the Chicago School, and to the vision of the Chicago School that Carey so sought to recover for the ICR. Researchers ought to care about pluralism, humanism, and inclusivity, and researchers are engaging in work that has application to a polity as well as to questions of the imagination that ask us to push beyond. It is a charge to think about how to do journalism research that matters.

Notes

1. Richard A. Hatch, *Some Founding Papers of the University of Illinois* (Urbana: University of Illinois Press, 1967): 15, https://archive.org/details/somefoundingpape00hatc.

2. Hatch, *Some Founding Papers of the University of Illinois*, 20.

3. The Hartford Gunn Institute, "Educational Telecommunications: An Electronic Land Grant for the 21st Century," *Current*, October 22, 1995, https://current.org/1995/10/educational-telecommunications-an-electronic-land-grant-for-the-21st-century/.

4. Steve Weinberg, *A Journalism of Humanity: A Candid History of the World's First Journalism School* (Columbia: University of Missouri Press, 2008).

5. Hugo de Burgh, "Skills Are Not Enough: The Case for Journalism as an Academic Discipline," *Journalism* 4, no. 1 (February 2003): 110.

6. Michael Schudson, *Discovering the News* (New York: Basic Books, 1981).

7. "The J-School Legacy," University of Missouri, (n.d.), https://journalism.missouri.edu/the-j-school/the-j-school-legacy/.

8. "AEJMC History," Association for Education in Journalism and Mass Communication, http://www.aejmc.org/home/about/aejmc-history/.

9. This minor was the first PhD associated with journalism; thus there is some debate between Wisconsin or Iowa as to who had the first PhD program in communication in the United States.

10. Everett M. Rogers, "The Department of Communication at Michigan State University as a Seed Institution for Communication Study," *Communication Studies* 52, no. 3 (2001): 234–248.

11. "ASNE History," American Society of News Editors, https://www.asne.org/asne-history.

12. James W. Carey, "Some Personal Notes on US Journalism Education," *Journalism* 1, no. 1 (April 2000): 12–23.

13. Thomas F. Gieryn, "City as Truth-Spot: Laboratories and Field-Sites in Urban Studies," *Social Studies of Science* 36, no. 1 (February 2006): 5–38.

14. Gieryn, "City as Truth-Spot: Laboratories and Field-Sites in Urban Studies."

15. Carey, "Some Personal Notes on US Journalism Education," 18.

16. Carey, "Some Personal Notes on US Journalism Education."

17. Karin Wahl-Jorgensen, "The Chicago School and Ecology: A Reappraisal for the Digital Era," *American Behavioral Scientist* 60, no. 1 (2016): 11.

18. Rogers, "The Department of Communication at Michigan State University as a Seed Institution for Communication Study."

19. Everette E. Dennis and Ellen Ann Wartella, *American Communication Research: The Remembered History* (New York: Routledge, 1996).

20. Dennis and Wartella, *American Communication Research: The Remembered History*.

21. Brochure, "Institute of Communications Research," 1948, 3, https://www.slideshare.net/NikkiUsher1/icr-original-brochure-1948.

22. Everett M. Rogers, *A History of Communication Study: A Biographical Approach* (New York, Toronto: The Free Press, Maxwell Macmillan Canada, Maxwell Macmillan International, 1994).

23. Rogers, *A History of Communication Study: A Biographical Approach.*

24. Fred S. Siebert, Theodore Peterson, and Wilbur Schramm, *Four Theories of the Press: The Authoritarian, Libertarian, Social Responsibility and Soviet Communist Concepts of What the Press Should Be and Do* (University of Illinois Press, 1984).

25. Ellen Wartella, *A History of the Institute of Communications Research* (1987).

26. Eve Stryker Munson and Catherine A. Warren, "Introduction," in *James Carey: A Critical Reader*, eds. Eve Stryker Munson and Catherine A. Warren (Minneapolis, MN: University of Minnesota Press, 1996): 5.

27. James Carey, *Communication as Culture: Essays on Media and Society* (New York: Routledge, 1992).

28. Munson and Warren, "Introduction," 14.

29. James Carey, "The Chicago School and the History of Mass Communication Research," in *Communication as Culture: Essays on Media and Society.* (New York: Routledge, 1992), 26.

30. James Carey, "The Problem of Journalism History," *Journalism History* 1, no. 1 (1974): 3.

31. Carey, "The Problem of Journalism History," 3.

32. James Carey, "Afterword: The Culture in Question," in *James Carey: A Critical Reader*, eds. Eve Stryker Munson and Catherine A. Warren (University of Minnesota Press, 1996): 308–340.

33. Carey, "Afterword: The Culture in Question."

34. J. Donaldson, "Impossible Trident," The Illusions Index, July 2017, https://www.illusionsindex.org/i/impossible-trident.

35. Kevin Knight, "Question 52. The Angels in Relation to Place," *New Advent*, 2017 http://www.newadvent.org/summa/1052.htm#article3. [Original Source: *The Summa Theologiæ of St. Thomas Aquinas* (Second and Revised Edition, 1920)].

36. Daniel Kreiss, "Beyond Administrative Journalism: Civic Skepticism and the Crisis in Journalism," in *The Crisis of Journalism Reconsidered: Democratic Culture, Professional Codes, Digital Future*, eds. Jeffrey C. Alexander, Elizabeth Butler Breese, and María Luengo (Cambridge, UK: Cambridge University Press, 2016): 59.

37. Robert Poole, "If You Can Afford a Plane Ticket, Thank Deregulation," *Reason*, June 2018, https://reason.com/2018/05/26/if-you-can-afford-a-plane-tick/.

38. Carey, "Some Personal Notes on US Journalism Education," 18.

2

Groundwork for the Public

How Grey Literature Is Shaping What We Know about Local News

Jesse Holcomb

Introduction

America's local news crisis didn't start with the Great Recession, but for those looking back, 2008 was a watershed moment after which the local newspaper industry's problems accelerated. For much of the 20th century, newspapers had monopolized advertising revenue and claimed a big chunk of audience attention. While those advantages began to erode with the emergence first of cable news and then the internet, things took a nosedive after the financial crisis of 2007 and 2008. Newspapers, historically the standard bearers for public service and investigative journalism, were shedding staff in an effort to stay afloat by cutting costs. Indeed, the severe economic challenges brought on by the 2020 Covid-19 pandemic represented not just an inflection point for local news media, but an acceleration of a crisis that had been going on for many years.

Policymakers began to imagine a frightening scenario in which accountability journalism would recede, and waste, fraud, and abuse would flourish. Testifying on Capitol Hill during a 2009 hearing on the newspaper crisis, then–executive director of the Project for Excellence in Journalism Tom Rosenstiel said, "[m]ore of American life now occurs in shadow. And we cannot know what we do not know."[1] That same year, a U.S. Senator introduced a bill that would allow newspapers to operate as nonprofits.[2]

The urgency of the moment compelled more than policymaker action; it also prompted a wave of research initiatives, even giving rise to a new class of knowledge about the health of local news. Coming from institutions that sit outside or at the edges of conventional academic publishing, this research is embodied in think tanks, philanthropies, and institutes including the Pew

Jesse Holcomb, *Groundwork for the Public* In: *Journalism Research That Matters*. Edited by: Valérie Bélair-Gagnon and Nikki Usher, Oxford University Press. © Oxford University Press 2021. DOI: 10.1093/oso/9780197538470.003.0003

Research Center, the John S. and James L. Knight Foundation, and Columbia University's Tow Center for Digital Journalism. The research produced by this cohort of think tanks, foundations, university centers, and at least one government agency falls into three different buckets: the news ecology tradition, news desert studies, and a more pragmatic approach I would describe as inventory groundwork. The term "grey literature" describes this research genre as a whole, borrowing from the definition provided at the Twelfth International Conference on Grey Literature in Prague.[3] This grey literature has emerged, often in real time, to provide practical, empirical information targeted at practitioners and the general public. Unlike "gated" academic publications that are double-blind peer-reviewed and often sit behind a paywall, grey literature is freely accessible.

The stakes today are high: for scholars who study journalism, the object of inquiry is a moving target. The shape of the news industry itself is anything but static, as technology platforms and publishers increasingly serve similar functions. Meanwhile, the collapse of the newspaper business has accelerated the need for rapid-response solutions, which require timely and reliable data to help inform decision makers such as media owners, legislators, or investors.

Think tanks and university centers seem ideally primed for this moment, with their ability to produce data-rich, quantitative research about the local news environment, amplified by a communications apparatus that disseminates this research to a wide range of audiences in a timely fashion. Yet the dominance of these institutions has profound implications for how policymakers, industry leaders, and even the general public think about and ultimately understand the state of local news today.

This chapter traces the origins and expansion of public-facing research about the local news environment to its present role in the broader scholarly environment. I offer a taxonomy to help classify the three main genres that this work inhabits: the news ecology tradition, news desert studies, and inventory groundwork. Next, I offer a critique of this genre of public scholarship and argue that its heavy emphasis on description coupled with limited engagement of the broader scholarly literature, including theory, creates limitations. Finally, I offer several recommendations for ways that traditional scholarship and public-facing literature can speak to each other and ultimately benefit the actors most in need of actionable information: journalists and the communities they serve. In any emerging scholarly subfield, it becomes important to clarify boundaries, terms, and genres in order to help make sense of things. I will attempt to do so here, to give some further shape to the sprawling efforts that arose over the last decade to answer the question: Where does local news come from?

The News Ecology Tradition

In an essay that speaks directly to the various taxonomies, C.W. Anderson defines the news ecosystem as "the entire ensemble of individuals, organizations, and technologies within a particular geographic community or around a particular issue, engaged in journalistic production and, indeed, in journalistic consumption."[4] The ecological metaphor traces its origins to several prominent communication scholars including Neil Postman, Marshall McLuhan, and Jay Rosen—prominent, but also public-facing (McLuhan somewhat famously had a cameo appearance in a Woody Allen film).

In the same essay, Anderson offers a classification of ecological paradigms, suggesting research falls either into the "environmental" or "rhizomatic" camp, noting that much of the former emerges from outside of higher education. Some of the more widely cited studies of local news ecosystems are those commissioned by foundations and think tanks. For example, in 2010, the Pew Research Center published its study of the news ecosystem in Baltimore (*How News Happens*) and followed it with a tri-city study in 2015. Around this time, the Knight Foundation sponsored a series of reports detailing the information needs of American communities.

Other foundations commissioned similar work as well. The New America Foundation published a series of local news ecosystem maps around 2010, which identified the local news producers in communities such as the North Carolina Triangle area and the Scranton–Wilkes-Barre metropolitan area in Pennsylvania. Later the Democracy Fund would continue this work by commissioning white papers taking stock of the statewide news ecosystem in places such as North Carolina and New Mexico.[5] The Chicago Community Trust produced a series of studies in 2010 and 2011, including a network analysis, of the local news providers in Chicago.[6] Other foundations may not be as closely associated with this kind of local news groundwork as those mentioned above, but to varying degrees, the McArthur, McCormick, Ford, and Hewlett Foundations have all lent their support to underlying questions surrounding the contours of the local news environment in the United States.

These reports would fall into the environmental category of news ec-osystem analysis, though some, such as the 2010 Pew study, could also be described as rhizomatic by focusing on the networked nature of local news actors.

Empirical scholarly contributions to the study of local news ecosystems provide essential insight and depth to the broader understanding not just about where news comes from but also how it travels. Sue Robinson's work on information ecosystems surrounding race and education is canonical.[7] Anderson's Francisville Four study of the news ecosystem in Philadelphia also would find its place here.[8] Yet in some ways these studies are exceptions that prove the rule. Much of the empirical data on local news ecosystems today has emerged disproportionately from outside traditional gated, peer-reviewed scholarly venues. Even the theoretical roots of the tradition seem to have come from unusually visible communication scholars.

News Desert Studies

Nested within the news ecology tradition, the news desert concept emerged as a metaphorical framework to help interpret the arrangement of local jour-nalism actors and participants in American communities. It refers to the no-tion that some communities lack information resources to the extent that they are parched. The explicit study of news deserts did not appear until after the beginning of the local newspaper disruption. The expression can be tracked to a 2009 *Columbia Journalism Review* article about a community in Northern Iowa.[9] The "desert" framing was used and championed in 2010 and 2011 by Laura Washington (writing for *In These Times*) and Tom Stites, director of the nonprofit Banyan Project, aimed at strengthening democ-racy.[10] In a 2011 Nieman Journalism Lab article about news deserts, Stites was trying to describe a civic malnourishment problem, and was especially concerned with affluence as a dividing point between information haves and have-nots.[11]

Michelle Ferrier, then on faculty at Ohio University, was also an early stakeholder in this research, launching a publicly visible project in 2010 using "media desert" terminology, which Ferrier defines as a "geographic area lacking fresh news and information." Ferrier's work is especially signif-icant because it is attuned to questions around diversity and opportunity, while also being descriptive—mapping such deserts at the state level.

University centers and institutes have played a significant role in the production of empirical data on news deserts. But even here, much of the scholarship published has been released in the form of ungated white papers, outside of conventionally scholarly publishing practices. Key stakeholders in public-facing studies of news deserts include UNC–Chapel Hill's Center for Innovation and Sustainability in Local Media, Columbia University's Tow Center for Digital Journalism, Montclair State University's Center for Cooperative Media, Duke University's News Measures Project, and American University's J-LAB.

Out of Duke University's News Measures Project, Phil Napoli and colleagues conducted a 2015 study evaluating local news offerings in three different New Jersey cities.[12] They found that the poorest of them, Newark, suffered from a notable lack of local news (as of 2019, this work was being scaled beyond case studies and to 100 American communities).

Another ambitious news desert research initiative is being run by Penny Abernathy out of the University of North Carolina's Center for Innovation and Sustainability in Local Media. The Center's database identifies news deserts that lack original reporting in the form of a local newspaper or online publication and links this erosion to ownership consolidation. Abernathy's project is especially notable because it is one of the few projects attempting to scale news desert research to a national level, allowing us to see broad patterns rather than isolated cases.

Together, these studies demonstrated that access and exposure to local news, regardless of medium, are uneven and depend on socio-economic characteristics and geography. More importantly, these studies oriented their findings to a public audience and, in bypassing the peer review system, saw the light of day more quickly than they otherwise might.

Other projects studying news deserts suffered from significant flaws. *Columbia Journalism Review* launched a news deserts map in 2017, relying only on Alliance for Audited Media (AAM) data tracking daily newspapers, resulting in a notably incomplete picture.[13] Another study that suffered from similar flaws was published by *Politico* in 2018, which defined news deserts as "places with minimal newspaper subscriptions, print or online." The *Politico* study found itself in the unenviable position of being subject to a withering critique by Nieman Journalism Lab's Joshua Benton, who lambasted its dataset and questionable inferences.[14] The *Politico* piece claimed to show that Trump outperformed the previous Republican nominee, Mitt Romney, in counties with the lowest numbers of news subscribers, but didn't do nearly as well in areas with heavier circulation. This ignored obvious and important confounding variables, such as relative wealth and socio-economic differences, average educational attainment, overall shifts in partisanship, and beyond.

Inventory Groundwork

There is a third form of local news research that differs from the study of news deserts and the news ecology tradition because it is divorced from connections to physical geography. Inventory groundwork is research that offers empirical data on the presence and quantity of local news sources (chiefly professional news publishers) in the United States. In this way, it performs a role similar to that of the U.S. Census in offering baseline data on the institutions that form the vast and highly localized American news media system.

As with a fair amount of the news ecology and news deserts work, this strain of research emerges from public-facing institutions. The Pew Research Center's State of the News Media reports, as well as its studies of nonprofit journalism, low-power FM radio, Washington correspondents, and more, provide quantitative estimates of the number of news providers in each category. Pew's State of the News Media Report, created in 2004 and released in some form every year since, chronicled the industry's troubles in great detail by estimating the reach, economic value, and journalistic output across print, digital, and broadcast sectors.

In 2011 the Federal Communications Commission, under the guidance of media entrepreneur and journalist Steve Waldman, produced a nearly 500-page report on the information needs of communities, which, among other things, took inventory of the range of local news providers serving Americans.[15] And in a rare move, the FCC commissioned a follow-up data collection project assessing sources of local news in a series of media markets as well as the public's usage of those sources. The project was tabled after conservative media commentators cast the initiative as government meddling in the editorial affairs of local news outlets.[16] Likewise, Democracy Fund has produced research of its own documenting the state of Native American media and other ethnic media providers, with a similar approach used by Pew Research.[17]

Without these studies, it is likely we would have a much blurrier sense of the facts on the ground, in terms of the state and decline of local news in America. They answer foundational questions on the ground: How many local newspapers, broadcasters, and digital startups are there? Where are they clustered? How have these numbers changed in recent years? What functions do these news outlets perform in the local media environment? The highly descriptive nature of this work is a great asset to scholars, policymakers, and decision makers. At the same time, this by-the-numbers approach has its own limitations.

A Tendency toward Descriptivism

Much of the public-facing research and empirical data addressing the question of where local news comes from offers highly valuable contributions to public knowledge about civic spaces and informed communities. Many of the studies cited here serve as building blocks for further exploration and understanding. Yet at the same time, this line of work is at times somewhat divorced from theory, explanation, and normative reasoning. Why is this so? I suggest two key reasons—a reluctance outside of academic environs to make these kinds of claims; and the tendency for data, especially quantitative, to travel farther through elite news environments and gain wider reach.

First, foundation-driven research can be allergic at times to editorializing, and scrupulously avoids even the appearance of offering a point of view or recommending certain outcomes. The Pew Research Center, for instance, in its mission statement says, "we generate a foundation of facts that enriches the public dialogue and supports sound decision-making" and describes itself as "nonpartisan and nonadvocacy," a "fact tank" rather than a "think tank." This philosophy, adopted by Pew Research, the Knight Foundation, and others, can be highly effective in building trust among audiences. Yet it can result in research that hesitates to evaluate, interpret, or make judgments about its own data.

In addition, public-facing research institutions are incentivized to generate traction for their work, either through media hits, social media discussion, or by engaging the attention of elite audiences in government or others in the civic or private sector. This is how think tanks and foundations often measure their impact, an increasingly quantified art. Data points (often

quantitative ones) extracted at times from context and theory, for better or
worse, gain more mileage in the marketplace of ideas. There is a great deal
of value here—public conversations about local journalism or anything else
need trusted facts to anchor them. But the danger, if taken to its extreme, is
that this approach can lead to facts without understanding.

This model—descriptive, quantitative research on the local news
environment—holds implications for journalism studies, because the
public scholarship enterprise represented by think tanks, university centers,
foundations, and policymakers has the ability to set the agenda for the rest
of the scholarly community and commands an outsized audience for the research they produce. To suggest we need fewer facts and less empirical data
about local news would be the wrong conclusion. Rather, we need more conversation between these data and the rich theoretical contributions of the
scholarly community.

For example, practitioners in the grey literature arena could benefit from
Fuller's critique of Neil Postman's ecosystem model as overly anthropocen-
tric, a view that was expanded by Anderson with his discussion of environmental and rhizomatic media ecosystems.[18] Take Nadler's argument that the
"news ecosystem" terminology itself is ideologically oriented, suggesting a
model in which the news environment reaches a point of natural order and
balance when it is uninterrupted by outside interventions such as those by
the state. Nadler argues that the construct implies a kind of neoliberalism
at work.[19] Perhaps most promising for future research, especially mixed-
methods data collection, is Robinson's effort to bring field theory into the
news ecology framework, adding analysis of power and identity.[20]

To be clear, research emerging outside of traditional scholarly venues
offers an invaluable service to the field; the highly descriptive nature of this
work provides accessible and actionable data for those who need it most.
However, divorced from theory and wider scholarly traditions, this work
can lack nuance and is limited in its ability to diagnose problems and offer
solutions. There are ways to mitigate this that involve more collaboration
across scholarly and para-scholarly worlds.

De-Siloing Public Scholarship on Local News Sources

To summarize, there is a long and rich history of local news groundwork that
has emerged in uniquely public formats, thanks in part due to interest by

policymakers, foundations, think tanks, and university centers whose mission it is to engage the public debate. When we typically think about public scholarship, it is often of faculty members who translate their work beyond journal articles, books, and conference papers, and bring it to bear upon the pressing problems facing their respective fields. The grey literature emerging out of public-facing institutions is arguably more effective than traditional, gated scholarship at connecting with citizens, journalists, and others in this space. Yet, they can sometimes be hamstrung in their ability to equip those audiences to understand what the data mean.

I'd like to suggest a few ways to remove some of the siloing that has occurred in this subgenre of Journalism Studies so that public-facing institutions and theory-driven academic work can complement each other. Ultimately, a healthier research environment is one that is more collaborative and where groundwork is driven by good questions, and less by strictly inductive approaches to data collection.

These recommendations can be summarized as follows:

1. More intentional use of scholarly advisory boards,
2. utilization (and reinvention) of literature review and meta-analysis,
3. better archival practices,
4. adoption of a "traffic cop," and
5. an embrace of causal claims.

First, public and scholarly-adjacent research on local news would do well to invite and cultivate robust advisory boards made up of scholars immersed in the theoretical traditions in the Journalism Studies field. This practice has been adopted already to some extent. A noteworthy example is the American Press Institute's practice of convening networks of leading academic scholars to advise its original research, and in some cases commissioning research by those same academics. Ideally this practice would be embraced not simply to bring smart people into the room or to create a sense of buy-in, but also to help researchers understand the scholarly context of the work at hand, including qualitative groundwork, which can at times be a blind spot.[21]

Second, public scholarship around local news groundwork should more consciously reference scholarly literature on the subject. Here too is an opportunity to recast the literature review in the same way that public scholarship has restructured the data and findings components of traditional scholarship.

Third, public scholarship on local news should adopt more permanent archival practices. While gated scholarly work has its own set of problems, including inaccessibility by the general public, research institutions that publish their own work in the form of white papers suffer from the same link-rot issues that news publishers are dealing with. Studies representing substantial expenditures of grant money and labor become difficult to surface over time, and in some cases are all but vanished.

Fourth, the institutions producing groundwork would benefit from a traffic cop—some person, team, or organization whose job it is to facilitate communication between institutions. Large sums of grant money are poured into many of these studies. The crisis in local news is acute. Simply put, the field cannot afford to inadvertently produce duplicative or replicative studies.

Finally, after rampant productivity in groundwork over the past decade, we will begin to exhaust some of the major "what" questions and in time turn to the "why" and "what next." We know much more now than we did in 2009 about where local news comes from. As a scholarly community, we have a fairly strong grasp of the many different institutions that produce journalism, including digital outlets, which at the time were scattered and disparate and, prior to becoming institutions in their own right, hard to count and measure. Those days are over in a sense, so it may now be time for the field to turn its energies away from understanding the shape of the ecosystem and toward the task of understanding its influence. We need a causal turn in empirical work on local news. And understanding the forces that shape and evolve these ecosystems will likely require more investment in field-based qualitative work, as controlled experiments maintain limited capacity to fully illuminate these complex ecosystems. It remains to be seen whether the para-scholarly institutions discussed in this chapter have the appetite for this kind of work, given the strategic incentive structure in which these institutions operate.

That is not to say we should abandon entirely the work of taking inventory of our media systems, but rather consider how that work must evolve to adapt to our changing forms of journalism, news, and information distribution. As news in some ways is being formed by new forces, and less so by the institutions of the past, it will be increasingly irrelevant and perhaps even impossible to take inventory in these ways in the future. This raises the question: How does one measure or count objects in an ecosystem where every business, agency, organization, government, association, and in fact, individual contributes to the public information in any given community?

Turning our attention to these new questions will require researchers and scholars, from both public-facing institutions and scholarly traditions, to work together. The good news is that there is a surplus of goodwill, spurred on by a continued sense of urgency about the threatened role of local journalism in civic life.

Notes

1. Tom Rosenstiel, "Where the News Comes from—and Why it Matters," *Pew Research Center*, September 25, 2009, https://www.pewresearch.org/2009/09/25/where-the-news-comes-from-and-why-it-matters/.
2. Benjamin Cardin, "Senator Cardin Introduced Bill that Would Allow American Newspapers to Operate as Non-Profits," Press release, March 24, 2009, https://www.cardin.senate.gov/newsroom/press/release/senator-cardin-introduces-bill-that-would-allow-american-newspapers-to-operate-as-non-profits. After this point, it wouldn't be until 2018 and 2019 that news and journalism became the focus of congressional attention, with the rise of big technology companies such as Google and Facebook, and questions over subsidizing the news industry; see Robert Picard, Valérie Bélair-Gagnon, and Sofia Ranchordás, "The Impact of Charity and Tax Law/Regulation on Not-for-Profit News Organizations," The Reuters Institute for the Study of Journalism and University of Oxford Information Society Project, Yale Law School, March, 2016, https://reutersinstitute.politics.ox.ac.uk/sites/default/files/2017-11/The%20impact%20of%20charity%20and%20tax%20law%20regulation%20on%20not%20for%20profit%20news%20organisations.pdf.
3. From the 12th International Conference on Grey Literature, Prague, 2010, "Grey literature stands for manifold document types produced on all levels of government, academics, business and industry in print and electronic formats that are protected by intellectual property rights, of sufficient quality to be collected and preserved by libraries and institutional repositories, but not controlled by commercial publishers; i.e. where publishing is not the primary activity of the producing body."
4. C.W. Anderson, "News Ecosystems," in The SAGE Handbook of Digital Journalism, eds. C.W. Anderson et al. (London, New York: SAGE Publications, 2016).
5. Jessica Durkin and Tom Glaisyer, "An Information Community Case Study: Scranton," New America Foundation, May 2010, https://ecfsapi.fcc.gov/file/7020450503.pdf.
6. Rich Gordon and Zachary Johnson, "Linking Audiences to News: A Network Analysis of Chicago News Websites," The Chicago Community Trust, 2011.
7. Robinson, *Networked News, Racial Divides: How Power and Privilege Shape Public Discourse in Progressive Communities* (Cambridge, UK: Cambridge University Press).
8. C.W. Anderson, "Journalistic Networks and the Diffusion of Local News: The Brief, Happy News Life of the 'Francisville Four,'" *Political Communication 27*, no. 3 (2010): 289–309.

9. Nathaniel Popper, "Good Morning, Postville! An Unlikely Thorn in Agriprocessors' Side," *Columbia Journalism Review*, March/April 2009, https://archives.cjr.org/feature/good_morning_postville_1.php.

10. Laura Washington, "The Paradox of Our Media Age and What to Do about It," *In These Times*, April 5, 2011, http://inthesetimes.com/article/7151/the_paradox_of_our_media_ageand_what_to_do_about_it.

11. In a June 2018 Poynter Institute article, Stites extended his metaphor to note that deserts attract harmful things; misinformation and fake news fill a void where nutritious information is lacking.

12. Philip Napoli, Sarah Stonbely, Kathleen McCollough, and Bryce Renninger, "Assessing the Health of Local Journalism Ecosystems," prepared for the Democracy Fund, the Geraldine R. Dodge Foundation, and the John S. and James L. Knight Foundation, June, 2015, http://mpii.rutgers.edu/wp-content/uploads/sites/129/2015/06/Assessing-Local-Journalism_Final-Draft-6.23.15.pdf.

13. Yemile Bucay, Vittoria Elliott, Jennie Kamin, and Andrea Park, "America's Growing News Deserts," *Columbia Journalism Review*, Spring, 2017, https://www.cjr.org/local_news/american-news-deserts-donuts-local.php.

14. Joshua Benton, "That Politico Article on 'News Deserts' Doesn't Really Show What It Claims to Show," Nieman Journalism Lab, April 9, 2018, https://www.niemanlab.org/2018/04/that-politico-article-on-news-deserts-doesnt-really-show-what-it-claims-to-show/.

15. Steve Waldman and the working group on information needs of communities, "The Information Needs of Communities: The Changing Media Landscape in a Broadband Age," July, 2011, https://transition.fcc.gov/osp/inc-report/The_Information_Needs_of_Communities.pdf.

16. One of the researchers on the team, Phil Napoli, later recalled the experience of being subject to anonymous threats as a result of being involved in the project. Also see Corey Hutchins, "FCC Revamps Controversial Study of TV Newsrooms," *Columbia Journalism Review*, February 17, 2014, https://archives.cjr.org/united_states_project/fcc_revamps_controversial_study_of_tv_newsrooms.php.

17. Jodi Rave, "American Indian Media Today," Democracy Fund, November, 2018, https://www.democracyfund.org/publications/american-indian-media-today.

18. Anderson, Rebuilding the News (Philadelphia: Temple University Press, 2016).

19. Anthony Nadler, "Nature's Economy and News Ecology," *Journalism Studies 20*, no. 6 (2018): 1–17.

20. Robinson, *Networked News, Racial Divides: How Power and Privilege Shape Public Discourse in Progressive Communities.*

21. This chapter is focused on the American context, but it is worth looking to the Reuters Institute for the Study of Journalism at Oxford University as a model for how scholars from both quantitative and qualitative methodological traditions work together to produce applied research about the journalism field.

3

Advocating for Journalism Studies' Impact on Policymaking

Matthew S. Weber

Introduction

As a field, Journalism Studies has struggled to find a footing in larger discussions and debates pertaining to core issues of media policy. In the context of current debates in the United States about the role of media as a check on polarization and divisiveness in society,[1] scholars and scholarship within Journalism Studies have the opportunity to take a more mature, substantive role in policymaking pertaining to the state of modern news media. To that end, this chapter examines the role of Journalism Studies as a mechanism for influencing and shaping policy and policymaking processes.

Within the academy, scholars recognize the need for a shift in thinking about the role of journalism research. University of Pennsylvania's Barbie Zelizer argued that journalism, as a field of research, "has favored proven routes of academic investigation that stay close to familiar topics of inquiry rather than accommodate the changing landscapes in which journalism finds itself."[2] More recently, University of Texas scholar Stephen D. Reese observes that in the midst of the modern complex media environment, journalism research has struggled to map connections outside the immediate focus of the academy.[3] Given the salience of current themes within the discipline to the public writ large, a clear opportunity is emerging for journalism scholars to have a voice in policymaking. The time has come to develop a research agenda that builds toward policy recommendations regarding economics, competition, and information provision, as well as the production of news.

First, I argue that Journalism Studies scholars are uniquely positioned with policy domains to connect disparate areas of knowledge and to forge connections that advance policymaking. "Policymaking" refers to activities that create policies and guidelines impacting the structure and production

Matthew S. Weber, *Advocating for Journalism Studies' Impact on Policymaking* In: *Journalism Research That Matters*. Edited by: Valérie Bélair-Gagnon and Nikki Usher, Oxford University Press. © Oxford University Press 2021. DOI: 10.1093/oso/9780197538470.003.0004 of news media. More narrowly, public policymaking refers to activities pertaining to local, state, and federal legislative policymaking processes. Within those contexts, this chapter begins by exploring the various ways in which Journalism Studies have focused on policy issues. Second, I advocate for the role of journalism researchers in policymaking, building on research focused on the brokerage of knowledge. Finally, in this chapter, I make connections to broader epistemological conversations about the use of research evidence as a policymaking mechanism.

Journalism Studies and Policymaking

The maturation of Journalism Studies has taken place in tandem with an evolving academy. In recent years, additive pressures, including an acceleration in publication cycles, public criticism and questioning of research within the academy, and declines in research funding have given rise to a push for accountability in research. In turn, scholarship across domains has shifted to focus on understanding the ways in which research is utilized in practice.[4] One key avenue toward impact from Journalism Studies to the field of journalism is the use of research evidence in policy and policymaking processes. For instance, recent scholarship in political science has focused on examining and explaining the impact of misinformation on election cycles;[5] in public health, an emerging body of work focused on implementation science examines how research impacts medical policy and procedure;[6] and in education (and health), a domain of study examining the use of research evidence has arisen, looking at how policymakers access and utilize academic studies.[7] Each of these streams of research has situated the respective field at a crossroads between academy and practice or between academy and policymaking.

Journalism Studies is unique in that the object of study is also a key avenue for public engagement. The nature of journalism emphasizes production of information and knowledge that often is directly related to policy; for instance, policymakers in Congress often turn to media coverage as an indicator of future policy priorities. Moreover, Journalism Studies examines both the production of news media and the changing consumption of news media. Thus, researchers within this space have not only a unique perspective on the way in which an industry is evolving but also have an obligation to take a stand in recommending future directions based on prior research.

The extant body of Journalism Studies research focused on policy issues has tended toward two poles of commentary: the first approach examines the role of policies within the practice of journalism, and the second approach advocates for the need for broader policy oriented toward protecting the diversity and democracy of news media. Yet there is clearly a space for broader policy discussions that take the shape of advocacy for specific propositions, policy proposals, or newsroom policies. This requires researchers to step outside the traditional mold of academic publishing and to engage in public forums through editorials, commentaries, and white papers. In part, this requires researchers to think about making clear the connections between public policy debates and the explicit findings that emerge from ongoing research. In the midst of calls for a greater emphasis on research impact and accountability, Journalism Studies should step outside its niche and establish a clear voice in ongoing discussions about the shape of modern media industries.

Policy and the Practice of Journalism

he first pole of policy-related research in Journalism Studies pertains to development of appropriate policy within newsrooms and policies related to the practice of journalism. The examples presented here are not meant to be comprehensive; the breadth of Journalism Studies covers a significant terrain of research. Rather, these examples are meant to highlight some of the key ways in which Journalism Studies approaches policymaking.

Recent scholarship within the domain of Journalism Studies has made important contributions to our understanding of the media industry today and to our understanding of how audiences engage with news. In doing so, a relatively wide body of work has looked at how technology is used in newsrooms and how technology is impacting the evolution of the newsroom. This role of Journalism Studies in policymaking moves beyond extant work that connects journalism to policy concepts. For instance, work on agenda setting, which focuses on how journalists mobilize research and coalesce narratives around a particular issue, is focused internally on the practice of journalism without emphasizing the broader impact on policy related to journalism.[8]

There are, however, a number of instances in which journalism research extends to advocate for policy impacting financial sustainability within the journalism industry. In recent years, the ongoing acceleration of technological change and the inherent intersection of journalism with other domains of research have given some scholars a foothold to argue for policy-oriented perspectives. This work is relatively limited yet increasingly important. For instance, scholarship has shown the potential negative impact of changing business models on the shape of modern democracy,[9] suggesting the need for broader federal policy to protect the health of news media in the United States. Economic research has pursued this line of inquiry more directly, examining the competitive impact of new technologies and establishing policy recommendations based on economic models. For instance, research looking at news aggregators found that an increased presence of news aggregators has mixed effects on news distribution, and while the presence of aggregators can push newspapers to improve the overall quality of coverage, their presence has a general negative impact on the financial health of commercial news.[10]

A multitude of scholars have examined the role of technology in the newsroom and pushed forth research that advocates for—or could advocate for—policies in the newsroom regarding the use of technology. Some have looked at policies within the newsroom focusing, for instance, on the role of internal newsroom policy on managing or mitigating the way technology is utilized in the day-to-day work of journalists.[11] Napoli took up the issue of social media and automation in news media to argue for policy that regulates the production and distribution of social media from the perspective of news as a public good.[12] Others, such as Tandoc and Thomas, examined metrics in modern newsrooms and argue that using web analytics to segment audiences and thus presume audience preference presents problematic ethical considerations.[13] While this last example does not explicitly put forth policy solutions, there are clear connections between examinations of technology in the newsroom and future policies pertaining to technology.

The focus of this line of scholarship is on the newsroom or the reporter as the unit of analysis, with policy emerging as a byproduct of the research. To that end, this line of work generally places the researcher in a position to serve as an advocate for particular technological policies within the newsroom or across the industry, although researchers often fall short of taking a particular stance or advocating for a particular point of view.

Policy, the Audience, and Democracy

The second pole of policy-oriented research within Journalism Studies has looked broadly at issues related to media diversity, media production, and audience consumption. This work often focuses on specific issues, such as the impact of industry consolidation on the production of local news, but as with the first pole, often falls short of explicitly engaging in public policy discussions.

Focusing on the impact of news media on democracy, Barnett and Townend use a case study of a hyperlocal journalism effort to argue that hyperlocal journalism has the potential to inform local democracy.[14] Framed in the context of a policy analysis, the authors argue that there is a need for policy focused on the local level to combat trends sparked by consolidation and deregulation. Related work focuses on the role of conflict of interest policies within newsrooms outside the United States and looks at how the establishment of such policies helps to create a degree of professionalism when interacting with public audiences.[15] This broad area of Journalism Studies emphasizes the external effects of the production of journalism and the interaction of news products with external stakeholders.

One byproduct is research focusing on how news work impacts policy processes. Work in this space often looks at the ways in which the media take a role in shaping policy. Recently, Nisbet focused on the critical role of journalists in providing evidence-based research to public audiences in science-based debates.[16] Ettema's examination of advocacy for death penalty reform focused on the processes by which newspapers engage in policymaking through reason giving and framing.[17] In recent work Sjovaag and Krumsvik argued for policy directions that could help to foster innovation and growth in the Norwegian news industry.[18] Their study was grounded in a mixed-method approach of interviews and policy document analysis and analyzed the broad domain of policies related to news work. While this arena of research focuses on policy, the emphasis of studies in this space is on the connection between media and policy rather than on crafting policy related to media.

Journalism Studies Researchers as Policy Advocates and Knowledge Brokers

Often, Journalism Studies research that pertains to policy tends to have no explicit focus on the formulation of a policy perspective or advocacy for a particular agenda. And yet, Journalism Studies scholars are well positioned as experts in the production of media, the crafting of news, and the interrelationship between audiences, news work, and technology, among other factors. But Journalism Studies researchers are uniquely positioned to serve as knowledge brokers, translating research findings into policy and serving as key connectors who can bridge the gap between academic research and industry practice—and should take on this role more directly.[19]

Why are Journalism Studies researchers well positioned as knowledge brokers? Looking broadly at policymaking and policy processes, research evidence—empirical findings derived from systematic research methods and analyses—is a critical component in crafting, implementing, and evaluating effective policies and practices.[20] The field of Journalism Studies occupies a central role in producing research evidence about the production of news media, along with the impact of technology on news media production, the nature of competition, the role of social media in distribution, the flow of misinformation, and a host of other issues central to society today. Thus, journalism scholars produce the central ingredients for successful policy advocacy. As such, researchers in this space have unique connections both to other sources of research and to industry partners; by advocating for policy and bridging connections between these groups, researchers have the capacity to broker and advance policy solutions.

Why is it the case, then, that scholars of Journalism Studies still struggle to translate research evidence into policymaking contexts? Nielsen effectively argues that a central problem is a lack of engaged scholarship, and that academics as a whole have an obligation to engage more meaningfully with public audiences.[21] Yet, the challenges of translating research into policymaking contexts are not unique to Journalism Studies; this is an issue that presents challenges for scholars across the academy. That said, there are still lessons to learn.

Advocating for Policy through Research

Evidence-based decision making has long been the gold standard of sound policy and practice, but critical gaps remain regarding the use of research evidence to inform policy decisions and actions.[22] There has been significant social investment in scientific research, which in turn has yielded massive pools of knowledge and evidence relevant to many policy domains. Nevertheless, the utilization of such knowledge by policymakers has been relatively infrequent and inconsistent—and, at times, misinformed.[23]

Transferring the knowledge developed in a research capacity—scientific knowledge—from research domains into policy domains often requires significant labor beyond the practice of research. It is in this capacity that knowledge brokers occupy a key role, serving as skilled intermediaries and taking a central role in moving research from academia into policymaking contexts.[24] Journalists have often been cast as intermediaries or brokers based on their role in translating events and information for audiences; the media are cast, in this way, as central to the flow and exchange of information in society.[25]

The reality is that "research use unfolds within a social ecology of relationships, organizational settings, and political and policy contexts";[26] it is difficult to prescribe a single path to engaging in the dissemination of research evidence. Scholarship on the science of communication has used a metaphor of "two communities" to prioritize and explicate the inherent challenges academics face in communicating and translating research from academia into policy. Work in that field is generally concerned with developing strategies for effective dissemination of research evidence and understanding the barriers policymakers face to access and use research evidence.[27]

Knowledge brokers navigate this domain, and their work can occupy a number of different roles in translating research to policymaking contexts. Yanovitzky and myself identify five key roles core to the process of knowledge brokering in policymaking: awareness, accessibility, engagement, linkage, and mobilization.[28]

Through awareness, researchers can help to make key stakeholders aware of timely and relevant knowledge. Awareness refers to the way in which researchers communicate with journalists and policymakers and act to make them aware of relevant knowledge. For example, this type of activity would include efforts by researchers to proactively share key research with university public relations offices or to directly reach out to journalists to share information on forthcoming publications.

Through accessibility, researchers can help others to access diverse information and knowledge. The accessibility function or role refers to the process by which researchers make research accessible to others. This type of activity includes publishing key research findings, data, and research summaries in locations where others are able to locate and access the information. This could include publishing findings and data on accessible hubs such as Academia.edu or publishing to one's own personal website. Alternatively, some universities maintain public-facing research repositories that also make research searchable and accessible by keyword or by researcher name.

Through engagement, researchers are able to help stakeholders to understand and translate research evidence. Engagement can be challenging for researchers; this role involves making research available in a way that allows others, such as policymakers and journalists, to easily comprehend and utilize research findings. For instance, FirstDraftNews.org recently published a report on the 2019 UK elections and incorporated images of Tweets and videos highlighting findings to help translate the implications of the report.[29] Admittedly, engagement is time consuming, but it is clearly an important step to communicating research to policymakers.

Next, through linkage, researchers are able to bridge gaps and forge connections between disparate groups of stakeholders and other researchers. In part, when researchers undertake engaged scholarship and work actively with community members, they are inherently engaging in the linkage role by connecting partners with one another. Education researchers have performed this role for years through what are called Research Practice Partnerships whereby researchers and community partners establish long-term community relationships to advance research and educational practices (i.e., http://nnerpp.rice.edu). The Center for Media Engagement at The University of Texas at Austin is an example of a research center that aims to create a deeper level of engagement between community partners and researchers within the university.

Finally, through mobilization, researchers are able to advocate for specific policy solutions based on the findings from their work. When researchers engage in mobilization, they engage in action to propose potential solutions to challenges they have studied. For instance, researchers may choose to write op-ed articles for their local newspapers or to advocate for industry solutions through platforms such as The Conversation (TheConversation.com). Viewing the functions of knowledge brokerage as a spectrum, it is clear that mobilizing research requires a higher level of engagement and places added responsibility on the researcher. In sum, these examples highlight the diversity of means by which a researcher may engage in the policymaking process.

Successful Implementation of Research as Policymaking

While the barriers to translating research evidence into policy are notable, the situation presents a key opportunity for Journalism Studies to translate journalism research into policy-relevant language in a politically fraught environment. To that end, I have spent the better part of a decade looking at processes of information flow, including work examining the way in which research moves from academic environments through to policymaking contexts. Broadly, I have focused on the role of journalists as brokers,[30] but have also sought to better understand how research moves through policymaking networks.[31] In a review of 4,647 newspaper articles covering news related to the federal process of policymaking pertaining to childhood obesity, along with co-authors, I found that there were 803 articles that specifically mentioned an academic research study. Media coverage tended to cite research evidence more frequently than legislative activity,[32] but there is clearly still a gap between the domain of research on a given topic and the information that translates through to policymaking.

Related, in one attempt to contextualize journalism as policy, a recent study examined 757 articles resulting from investigative journalism and found a clear connection between the articles published and policy outcomes.[33] The work points to the importance of sourcing, as well as the importance of the relationship between journalists and policymakers, in impacting policy outcomes. In a similar vein, Ali's recent work shows that local media occupy a central role as a tool for policymakers. He then advocates for policy reform to protect the health and diversity of local news endeavors, an argument that appeals to policymakers' self-interest.[34] Some have directly argued for the future of journalism, making the case that the news is a public good, or advocating for public funding for journalism.[35] Each of these studies provides examples of research that advocated for specific perspectives or specific policies, but they also raise the question of what successful public policymaking looks like in Journalism Studies.

The Barriers to Use of Research Evidence

Where, then, do barriers exist that prevent journalism scholarship from moving into a more public and policy-oriented space? In recent work focusing on the specific barriers to translation, a number of specific restrictions were identified, including: (1) limited access by policymakers to research evidence (journal paywalls, databases, etc.); (2) a scarcity of systematic reviews that synthesize the state of the field; (3) challenges in identifying research directly relevant and responsive to policymaker needs; and (4) the absence of tools and metrics for assessing the quality of research evidence.[36]

For journalists to take on a more active role as knowledge brokers, it is important to recognize the variety of ways in which brokerage may occur. Returning to Gesualdo, myself, and Yanoviztky, it is clear that brokerage can happen across a variety of different activities. Indeed, for academics it can be challenging to act as a policy advocate, especially early in one's career.[37] And yet advocacy through generating awareness or improving accessibility is also brokering that can lead to policy outcomes. In short, there are myriad ways in which researchers can take small steps to advocate for specific outcomes. Indeed, within Journalism Studies there are many public avenues for research dissemination and many scholars who engage in public debate of issues related to journalism. Nieman Lab, *The Columbia Journalism Review*, the Poynter Institute, and the Reuters Institute for the Study of Journalism, among others, serve as critical outlets for public debate of current topics within the media industry. These domains are important trading zones but often focus on industry rather than policy. More engaged participation across Journalism Studies will help to improve these spaces of translation and to improve the knowledge brokering capacity of scholars in this domain.

In sum, while Journalism Studies has a storied history of examining and analyzing the nature of the industry, there are clear opportunities to move toward a stronger policy orientation. Indeed, Journalism Studies as a field of research has its roots across domains of the academy, dating back well beyond the recent wave of renewed scholarly interest.[38] As a field of research, the domain has seen a number of different incarnations, having evolved from a normative emphasis to an empirical phase, through a sociological turn, to an emphasis on global comparison, and most recently to an emphasis on a sociotechnical perspective.[39] To many, this period of evolution represents a natural maturation of the field as it has developed to its current state. Looking at Journalism Studies today, Carlson and colleagues state that Journalism Studies, as a field of research, "examines the realm of informative, public texts involving news and the people, organizations, professions, institutions, and material artifacts and technologies that produce those texts as well as the individuals and multivariate forces shaping their circulation and consumption."[40] Despite the increasing stature of the field and its relevance to a wide range of societal issues, the connection between Journalism Studies and policymaking processes remains minimal. Moving forward with a knowledge brokering mindset will help journalism scholars take a more active role in advocating for policy and having a clear voice with regard to the future of news.

Notes

1. Pablo J. Boczkowski and Zizi Papacharissi, *Trump and the Media* (MIT Press, 2018).
2. Barbie Zelizer, "Introduction: On Finding New Ways of Thinking About Journalism," *Political Communication* 24 (2007): 111–114.
3. Stephen D. Reese, "The New Geography of Journalism Research: Levels and Spaces," *Digital Journalism* 4, no. 7 (2016): 816–826.
4. J. Lavis et al., "Developing and Refining the Methods for a 'One-Stop Shop' for Research Evidence About Health Systems," *Health Research Policy and Systems* 13 (2015): 1–10; L.A. Palinkas et al., "Measuring Use of Research Evidence: The Structured Interview for Evidence Use," *Research on Social Work Practice* 26 (2016): 550–564.
5. Nir Grinberg et al., "Fake News on Twitter During the 2016 Us Presidential Election," *Science* 363, no. 6425 (2019): 374–378.
6. Ross C. Brownson, Graham A. Colditz, and Enola K. Proctor, *Dissemination and Implementation Research in Health: Translating Science to Practice* (Oxford University Press, 2018).
7. Richard Paquin Morel and Cynthia Coburn, "Access, Activation, and Influence: How Brokers Mediate Social Capital among Professional Development Providers," *American Educational Research Journal* 56, no. 2 (2019): 247–288.
8. Thomas Hanitzsch, "Deconstructing Journalism Culture: Toward a Universal Theory," *Communication Theory* 17, no. 4 (2007): 367–385.
9. Rasmus Kleis Nielsen, Frank Esser, and David Levy, "Comparative Perspectives on the Changing Business of Journalism and Its Implications for Democracy," *The International Journal of Press/Politics* 18, no. 4 (2013): 383–391.
10. Doh-Shin Jeon and Nikrooz Nasr, "News Aggregators and Competition among Newspapers on the Internet," *American Economic Journal: Microeconomics* 8, no. 4 (2016): 91–114.
11. Nicholas Bloom et al., "The Distinct Effects of Information Technology and Communication Technology on Firm Organization," *Management Science* 60, no. 12 (2014): 2859–2885.
12. Philip M. Napoli, "Social Media and the Public Interest: Governance of News Platforms in the Realm of Individual and Algorithmic Gatekeepers," *Telecommunications Policy* 39, no. 9 (2015): 751–760.
13. Edson C. Tandoc and Ryan J. Thomas, "The Ethics of Web Analytics," *Digital Journalism* 3, no. 2 (2015): 243–258.
14. Steven Barnett and Judith Townend, "Plurality, Policy and the Local," *Journalism Practice* 9, no. 3 (2015): 332–349.
15. Cherian George, Yuan Zeng, and Suruchi Mazumdar, "Navigating Conflicts of Interest: Ethical Policies of 12 Exemplary Asian Media Organisations," *Journalism* (2019): 1–17.
16. Matthew C. Nisbet and Declan Fahy, "The Need for Knowledge-Based Journalism in Politicized Science Debates," *The ANNALS of the American Academy of Political and Social Science* 658, no. 1 (2015): 223–234.

17. James S. Ettema, "Journalism as Reason-Giving: Deliberative Democracy, Institutional Accountability, and the News Media's Mission," *Political Communication* 24, no. 2 (2007): 143–160.

18. Helle Sjovaag and Elrik Stavelin, "Web Media and the Quantitative Content Analysis: Methodological Challenges in Measuring Online News Content," *Convergence* 18, no. 2 (2012): 215–229.

19. Nicole Gesualdo, Matthew S. Weber, and Itzhak Yanovitzky, "Journalists as Knowledge Brokers," *Journalism Studies* (2019); Itzhak Yanovitzky and Matthew S. Weber, "News Media as Knowledge Brokers in Public Policymaking Processes," *Communication Theory* 29, no. 2 (2018): 191–212.

20. Steven L. Gortmaker et al., "Changing the Future of Obesity: Science, Policy, and Action," *The Lancet* 378, no. 9793 (2011); Peter Davis and Philippa Howden-Chapman, "Translating Research Findings into Health Policy," *Social Science & Medicine* 43, no. 5 (1996): 865–872.

21. Rasmus Kleis Nielsen, "No One Cares What We Know: Three Responses to the Irrelevance of Political Communication Research," *Political Communication* 35, no. 1 (2018): 145–149.

22. Sandra M. Nutley, Isabel Walter, and Huw T.O. Davies, *Using Evidence: How Research Can Inform Public Services* (Policy press, 2007); Vivian Tseng, *The Uses of Research in Policy and Practice* (Society for Research in Child Development Washington, DC, 2012); National Research Council, "Using Science as Evidence in Public Policy," eds. Kenneth Prewitt, Thomas A. Schwandt, and Miron L. Straf (Washington, DC: The National Academies Press, 2012).

23. Pete Lunn and Frances Ruane, *Using Evidence to Inform Policy* (Gill & Macmillan, 2013); Christopher Deeming, "Addressing the Social Determinants of Subjective Wellbeing: The Latest Challenge for Social Policy," *Journal of Social Policy* 42, no. 3 (2013): 541–565; National Research Council, "Using Science as Evidence in Public Policy"; L. Orton et al., "The Use of Research Evidence in Public Health Decision Making Processes: Systematic Review," *PLoS One* 6 (2011): 1–10.

24. Vicky Ward, Allan House, and Susan Hamer, "Knowledge Brokering: The Missing Link in the Evidence to Action Chain?" *Evidence & Policy* 5, no. 3 (2009): 267–279.

25. Elizabeth A. Shanahan et al., "Conduit or Contributor? The Role of Media in Policy Change Theory," *Policy Sciences* 41, no. 2 (2008): 115–138; Peter Van Aelst and Stefaan Walgrave, "Information and Arena: The Dual Function of the News Media for Political Elites," *Journal of Communication* 66, no. 3 (2016): 496–518.

26. Tseng, *The Uses of Research in Policy and Practice.*

27. L. Orton et al., "The Use of Research Evidence in Public Health Decision Making Processes: Systematic Review," *PLoS ONE* 6 (2011): 1–10; Karen Bogenschneider and Thomas J. Corbett, "Family Policy: Becoming a Field of Inquiry and Subfield of Social Policy," *Journal of Marriage and Family* 72, no. 3 (2010): 783–803; Charles Moseley et al., "Using Research Evidence to Inform Public Policy Decisions," *Intellectual and Developmental Disabilities* 51, no. 5 (2013): 412–422; Lunn and Ruane, *Using Evidence to Inform Policy.*

28. Yanovitzky and Weber, "News Media as Knowledge Brokers in Public Policymaking Processes."

29. Ali Abbas Ahmadi, Bethan John, and Alastair Reid, "UK General Election 2019: CCHQ's Fact-Check Stunt, Fake Newspapers and a Squirrel Hoax Dominate the Third Week," FirstDraftNews.org, November 22, 2019, https://firstdraftnews.org/latest/uk-general-election-weekly-roundup-cchq-swinson-fake-newspapers/.

30. Gesualdo, Weber, and Yanovitzky, "Journalists as Knowledge Brokers."

31. Yanovitzky and Weber, "News Media as Knowledge Brokers in Public Policymaking Processes"; Itzhak Yanovitzky and Matthew Weber, "Analysing Use of Evidence in Public Policymaking Processes: A Theory-Grounded Content Analysis Methodology," *Evidence & Policy: A Journal of Research, Debate and Practice* (2019): 65–82.

32. Gesualdo, Weber, and Yanovitzky, "Journalists as Knowledge Brokers."

33. Gerry Lanosga and Jason Martin, "Journalists, Sources, and Policy Outcomes: Insights from Three-Plus Decades of Investigative Reporting Contest Entries," *Journalism* 19, no. 12 (2018): 1676–1693.

34. Christopher Ali, *Media Localism: The Policies of Place* (University of Illinois Press, 2017).

35. Sigurd Allern and Ester Pollack, "Journalism as a Public Good: A Scandinavian Perspective," *Journalism* (2017): 1423–1439; Geoffrey Cowan and David Westphal, "Public Policy and Funding the News," *USC Annenberg School for Communication & Journalism Center on Communication Leadership & Policy* 3 (2010).

36. Kathryn Oliver et al., "A Systematic Review of Barriers to and Facilitators of the Use of Evidence by Policymakers," *BMC Health Services Research* 14 (2014): 1–12; Christopher J. Jewell and Lisa A. Bero, "Developing Good Taste in Evidence: Facilitators of and Hindrances to Evidence-Informed Health Policymaking in State Government," *The Milbank Quarterly* 86, no. 2 (2008): 177–208.

37. Gesualdo, Weber, and Yanovitzky, "Journalists as Knowledge Brokers."

38. Barbie Zelizer, *Taking Journalism Seriously: News and the Academy* (Thousand Oaks, CA: Sage Publications, 2004).

39. Matt Carlson et al., "Journalism Studies and Its Core Commitments: The Making of a Communication Field," *Journal of Communication* 68, no. 1 (2018): 6–25.

40. Carlson, "Journalism Studies and Its Core Commitments: The Making of a Communication Field".

4

Sharing Research Amidst the Cat Videos and Clickbait

You'll Never Believe What Happens Next

Benjamin Toff

Introduction

Academics are often criticized for focusing too narrowly on scholarly debates unfolding in the pages of journals almost nobody reads, rather than the urgent matters occupying the public sphere. For those who study journalism, this critique is particularly sensitive as it strikes at the very core of our subject matter expertise. We know more than most what it means for something to be notable and newsworthy, and we know the strategies for communicating complex subjects. Like all researchers, we may sometimes be guilty of navel-gazing and using too much impenetrable jargon, but the challenge of engaged research does not end merely with more effective translation. In the contemporary media landscape, even well-packaged research on highly topical subjects can have an abbreviated shelf life and limited reach.

In this chapter, I argue that our saturated and competitive attention economy makes the task of engagement far more challenging than is typically appreciated. While there is no doubt that scholars can improve how they produce and package research to better communicate the relevance of their findings, the insularity of academia or the institutional incentives that constrain academics are only part of the puzzle. Distribution is too often overlooked. In our contemporary media landscape, where publishers routinely struggle to differentiate their content from all the shiny objects littering consumers' social media feeds, well-crafted and even provocative research findings must compete for the attention of highly distracted audiences. Digital media has led to the emergence of several important new outlets for

Benjamin Toff, *Sharing Research Amidst the Cat Videos and Clickbait* In: *Journalism Research That Matters.*
Edited by: Valérie Bélair-Gagnon and Nikki Usher, Oxford University Press. © Oxford University Press 2021.
DOI: 10.1093/oso/9780197538470.003.0005

publishing academic findings for non-academics, but does such work count as "engagement" if no one is reading it?

What Does Engaged Research Mean Today?

In 2018, Rasmus Kleis Nielsen wrote a provocative essay for *Political Communication* entitled, "No one cares what we know" in which he asserted that even as public discussion of topics relevant to the scholarly field of political communication had proliferated in recent years— "Brexit" in the United Kingdom, the rise of Donald Trump in the United States, concern over viral misinformation and stealth advertising on social media, and so on—the scholarly community conducting research on these subjects had largely remained on the margins of public conversation and deliberation about such matters.[1] Nielsen noted that a lack of engaged scholarship, whatever the engrained structural reasons for it, has resulted in "substantially important public (and policy) discussions of issues at the core of our field [that] are dumber than they could have been."[2]

The same complaint could very well be leveled—and often is—about the contemporary relationship between journalism research and current crises in journalism.[3] For decades, news organizations have flailed about in their efforts to adapt to an intensely competitive digital media environment. The Pew Research Center estimated that even amidst the pre-Coronavirus economic expansion, newspaper industry advertising revenue continued to decline precipitously, falling 10% in the United States between 2016 and 2017 alone.[4] Circulation has steadily dwindled as well, reaching levels not seen since the 1940s when the population of the country was two and a half times smaller.[5] Business model chaos—and associated disruptions caused by mergers and consolidation—has also contributed to the rapid decimation of the practice of professional journalism.[6] The number of newsroom employees at American newspapers fell by 45% between 2008 and 2017.[7] In one particularly shocking example, the *Plain Dealer* of Cleveland, Ohio, announced in April 2019 it would be slashing its staff by a third, thereby reducing the size of its unionized newsroom to 33, as compared to the 340 serving in that capacity two decades ago.[8]

Even as audiences for news have changed, and the economics of newsgathering has proven increasingly tenuous, parallel questions of diversity, representation, fairness, and accuracy have only grown in urgency. Conventional rituals of objectivity[9] have given way to new practices of interpretive journalism,[10] emotionality in news content,[11] and ideologically separate spheres of information dissemination,[12] which makes the task of understanding the impact of news in society that much more complex. In the era of #MeToo and #BlackLivesMatter, media organizations are understandably more sensitive to accusations of bias and blind spots in the way they perform their roles as information gatekeepers and moderators of public discourse.

Assessing these changes and analyzing their implications has become the focus of a wide-ranging, interdisciplinary set of scholars who consider themselves journalism researchers. As Karin Wahl-Jorgensen and Thomas Hanitzsch note in their handbook on the field of Journalism Studies, such scholarship is increasingly oriented toward "tracing the consequences of profound transformations in journalism organizations, production practices, content and audiences that have come about as a result of globalization and political, economic, social, and technological change."[13] The vast quantities of research such scholarship has produced has only multiplied over the last decade. And yet, many practitioners—and more than a few scholars—protest that too often relevant academic research remains hidden away in obscure journals or inaccessibly dense tomes. As Seth C. Lewis argued in his end-of-the-year Nieman Lab reflection,[14] there remains a persistent disconnect between the research topics examined by scholars on the one hand, which sometimes fail to align with industry priorities, and engagement on the other hand with the reams of existing research which do in fact speak to broad industry concerns about filter bubbles, bots, and people's willingness to pay for news. Too often, Lewis noted, a "culture of indifference and defensiveness" gets in the way of ideas and findings being shared and considered across the boundaries separating university campuses, technology companies, and newsrooms.[15]

I agree with much of this critique. But perpetual handwringing about such divides misses other dimensions of the problem. Our 24/7 media-saturated environment compounds the problem of translation. It is not simply that relevant research is too often disseminated in clunky, ineffective ways; it is also the case that discovering and engaging with research involves tremendous obstacles which are often obscured by simplistic folk theories about the openness of information platforms. Anyone can publish anything these days, but very few are ever read. As Matthew Hindman notes in his book *The Internet Trap*,[16] the unprecedented availability of information online has not democratized the media landscape but instead concentrated power among a small number of technology companies who determine how likely any given snippet of information will be seen and read. In other words, no matter how engaged journalism researchers may be with communities of practice, scholars must contend with a media environment in which their findings compete for attention with all the other content that fills the social media feeds of their intended audiences.

In the remaining sections of this chapter, I describe a small study that I conducted using a unique dataset of social media engagement with posts made by the Columbia Journalism Review (CJR), Nieman Journalism Lab, and the Poynter Institute—three organizations that seek to bridge the divide between academia and professional communities of practice. By examining what posts do—and do not—receive attention on Facebook, I show that although some scholarly research garners engagement, it largely pales in comparison to other posts circulated. The findings suggest that translating research in the contemporary media environment requires more innovative and active outreach strategies.

Collecting and Analyzing Relevant Social Media Engagement Data

To investigate the reach of engaged journalism research online, I conducted a small empirical study using data collected from the Crowdtangle platform. Crowdtangle is an analytics tool owned by Facebook which allows publishers to monitor levels of engagement with their posts in real time, along with those of other public pages on the social media platform, at any given moment. Crowdtangle collects information on the number of shares and comments on each post as well as "Likes" and other emoji reactions. I focused on Facebook rather than other social media platforms because it is the most widely used social media platform in the United States by a wide margin; seven in ten Americans say they use it compared to 27% who say they use LinkedIn and 22% who say they use Twitter.[17]

I gathered historical data from Crowdtangle tracking engagement with posts by three organizations during the calendar year of 2018. The three organizations' pages tracked were Columbia Journalism Review, Nieman Journalism Lab, and the Poynter Institute. All three organizations explicitly claim as part of their missions an objective to propagate cutting-edge information and best practices relevant to the future of professional journalism.

Nieman Journalism Lab, an offshoot of the Nieman Foundation at Harvard University, aims to "find good ideas for others to steal" by highlighting "attempts at innovation and figur[ing] out what makes them succeed or fail."[18] Poynter describes itself as "the world's most influential school for journalists," with a mission more tailored to journalistic practice, providing tools and training for journalists to "sharpen skills and elevate storytelling throughout their careers." At the same time, Poynter defines itself as a "thought leader"—an "instructor, innovator, convener and resource for anyone who aspires to engage and inform citizens."[19]

CJR, the oldest of the three organizations and based out of Columbia University's prestigious journalism school, describes itself as "the intellectual leader in the rapidly changing world of journalism." Their objective, as captured in CJR's mission statement, explicitly refers to academic audiences as well as a practical industry focus. They seek to serve as "an essential venue not just for journalists, but also for the thousands of professionals in communications, technology, academia, and other fields reliant on solid media industry knowledge."[20] More so than any other institutions, these three organizations seek to bridge the divide between professional communities of practice and academic networks where research on journalism and news has flourished. If media scholars are to engage and make an impact beyond the academy, it would be here, at a bare minimum, that we would expect to find attention paid to research findings and efforts made at translating empirical results.

The three organizations have relatively modest followings on Facebook. Each was followed by around 70,000 users in 2018, a modest sum compared to most media organizations. The *Minneapolis Star Tribune*, for comparison, is followed by more than 180,000 users on Facebook, and the *New York Times* by more than 16 million.[21] Each of the three organizations' pages posted less frequently than once a day on average but more often than every other day. In Table 4.1, I provide summaries of basic social media engagement information about the public pages of each organization.

As is typically the case for social media engagement data, levels of interaction with social media posts are highly skewed, with a small number of posts receiving the vast majority of attention and engagement. This results in a highly lopsided distribution when all posts are plotted in Figure 4.1 according to how many "Likes" and other reactions (e.g., "Love," "Angry," "Haha," or other emojis) each received. Most posts are clustered at the low end, with very few attracting more than 100 reactions on the platform.

Table 4.1 Descriptive information about the three organizations' public
Facebook pages in 2018

	Columbia Journalism Review	Nieman Journalism Lab	Poynter Institute
Followers (average at time of posts)	69,405	70,963	66,829
Number of posts over 2018	201	212	308
Median number of "Likes" per post	44	19	45
Median number of other "Reactions" per post	11	2	8
Median number of shares per post	26	10	27

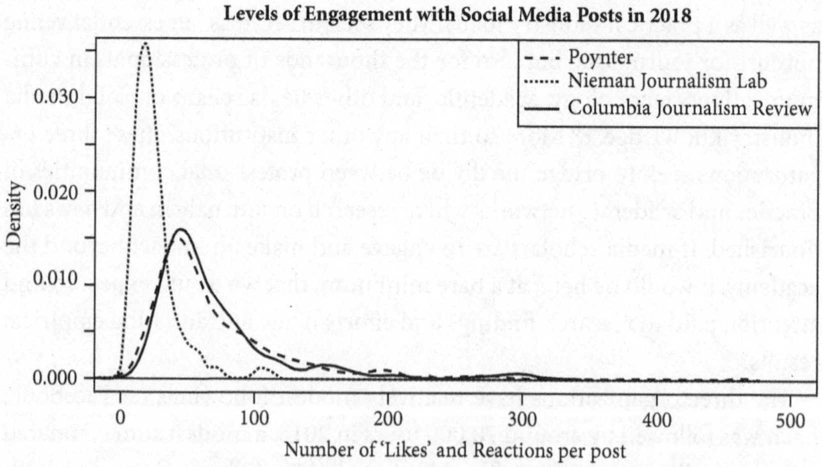

Figure 4.1 Distribution of engagement with social media posts by the three
organizations.

I limited the analysis to the posts that received the most engagement overall
in order to focus only on those posts that realistically had a chance of being
seen by the audiences following each page, selecting the top-performing 200
posts across the three organizations as measured by relative engagement for
each page according to a metric provided by Crowdtangle.[22] These posts with
above-average rates of interactions amounted to approximately 25% of all
posts made by the organizations in 2018. In excluding posts with minimal
engagement, the findings below are arguably a more conservative estimate of
the challenges associated with disseminating research broadly.

For each of the 200 social media posts that I examined, I coded whether the messages and/or pages reached when clicking through the accompanying links referenced research outputs (e.g., peer-reviewed articles, think tank studies, or other reports). I also classified posts according to what type of media content best described it (e.g., opinion articles, feature stories, profiles, spot news) and what substantive topic area it addressed (e.g., posts about newspaper closures, award winners, or labor and employment issues). Given the relatively small sample of posts involved, I coded the content inductively, which meant working in a recursive manner as new categories were created. To be clear, the analysis that follows is exploratory in nature; as the sole coder, my efforts to describe this content cannot be characterized as exhaustive nor free from subjective interpretation. I offer no inter-coder reliability statistics. Instead, my purpose here is mainly to bring some basic descriptive data to bear on the question of how academic research on journalism and communication fares on social media. What I find is confirmatory evidence that scholarship examining journalism remains largely on the margins of public discussion of contemporary issues in journalism.

The Struggle to Communicate Communication Research

My exploratory analysis of social media engagement with the three organizations' pages offers few reasons for optimism about the prospects for scholarly research to attract much attention. Peer-reviewed studies were almost entirely absent from the 200 top-performing posts. Just three posts referenced academic research published in scholarly journals: two posts by Poynter, one by Nieman Lab, and not a single post from CJR. The two Poynter posts featured research on misinformation and "fake news." One summarized findings from a recently published article online in *Mass Communication and Society* on an experiment testing the effects of elite discourse about fake news on the public's evaluation of news media.[23] The other profiled six scholars across political science, psychology, computer science, and other fields engaged in the study of information processing and exposure to misinformation online, linking to published research and other scholarly activities each had produced.[24] The third post, from Nieman Lab, was a cross-posted article from Journalist's Resource, a project of Harvard's Shorenstein Center on Media, Politics, and Public Policy, which catalogued five recent papers published by scholars in the "digital media and journalism space."[25]

Since peer-reviewed academic work hardly constitutes the entire universe
of research, I took a broader approach to categorizing posts that referenced
research and included any and all posts that referred to scholarship more
generally, including foundation- or industry-funded reports. I still found
only a small share of the posts—less than 14% ($N = 27$)—referenced research
of any kind. Instead, most of the content circulated by the three organizations
were feature stories (23%), opinion essays (19.5%), or industry news (15%).
These content areas are plotted in Figure 4.2.

As research posts sometimes linked to articles that referenced multiple
studies, to further investigate what research gets circulated I separately
tracked the types of research referenced in these 27 posts. Doing so produced
a somewhat higher estimate for the number of peer-reviewed journal articles
in the organizations' coverage ($N = 10$, out of a total of 33 studies) as well as
a small number of working or conference papers ($N = 3$) or summaries of
other in-progress work ($N = 2$). The remaining research referenced consisted
of reports funded by foundations ($N = 9$), think tanks ($N = 6$), or news organizations ($N =1$). A small number of research posts featured descriptions of
new technological tools aimed at improving media literacy ($N = 2$).

Despite the limited attention paid to research in the social media pages
of the three organizations, more encouraging data can be found in examining the relative levels of engagement received across the 200 posts. While
few messages posted included a specific reference to research, those that
did actually performed somewhat better overall in terms of social media

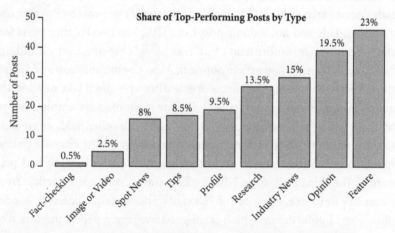

Figure 4.2 Posts across the three pages categorized by type of content.

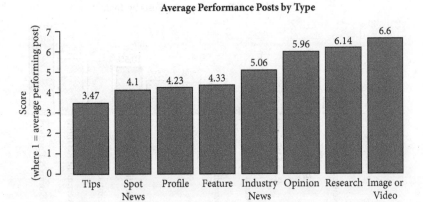

Figure 4.3 Average levels of relative engagement for posts by content area.

engagement compared to other forms of content (Figure 4.3). Among the top-performing posts examined, I found that posts categorized as focusing on research performed approximately six times better than an average message posted by each page, slightly better than opinion essays, and second only to images or video in terms of relative numbers of interactions. It is worth emphasizing, however, that the sample of posts examined excludes the lowest performing posts, which may include many more references to research findings. In other words, the research posts with high engagement may be exceptional cases.

Lastly, in addition to overall engagement, I examined the substantive content of posts made by the three organizations (Figure 4.4) as well as the subject of the research studies referenced in the posts (Figure 4.5) to determine whether a disconnect between the priorities of industry professionals and academic researchers might be contributing to the minimal attention paid to scholarly findings. I do find some evidence in support of this hypothesis. For example, three content areas were responsible for nearly 40% of all the top-performing posts made by the pages: professional norms and practices (17.5%), press–government relations (12.5%), and labor and employment issues (12%). Only four of the 33 research studies featured across the posts examined any of these topics, and none examined labor and employment issues.

Instead, the most common substantive research topic referenced by the three organizations concerned issues of media literacy and misinformation, which accounted for more than half of all studies mentioned ($N = 17$). It is

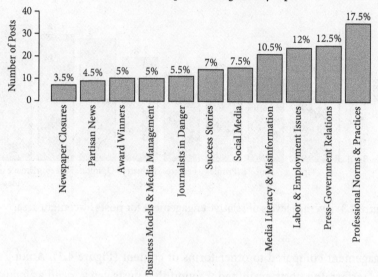

Figure 4.4 Substantive topics of top-performing posts.

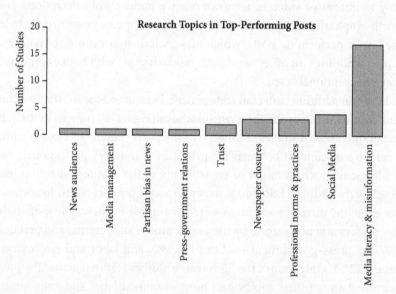

Figure 4.5 Substantive topic areas of research studies referenced in top-performing posts.

likely no coincidence that this particular area of research is dominated by scholars outside of Journalism Studies, including political science, computer science, and psychology—more established disciplines whose scholarship may be perceived as more rigorous or at least higher on the social hierarchy of the sciences.[26] Just six of the 17 studies referenced in this area were authored by researchers who could plausibly be categorized as primarily communication researchers.

Do Not Underestimate What It Takes to Be Seen and Heard

The findings detailed above concerning the top-performing posts by CJR, Poynter, and the Nieman Lab present a pessimistic view of the reach of journalism and communication research on social media. I found only minimal engagement with research even among those organizations most likely to feature studies and findings—groups who define as part of their missions the objective of disseminating and translating cutting-edge information relevant to professional communities of journalistic practice. While some might look at these numbers and conclude, as Nielsen warns, that "no one cares what we know,"[27] the data do not actually reveal what people care about so much as the types of content that get seen and heard in our information-saturated media environment. What these findings underscore is the exceptionally high barriers engaged scholars are up against when they seek to reach audiences beyond those ordinarily circumscribed by conventional academic practices. Simplistic folk theories about the openness of information platforms obscures persistent challenges related to cutting through the steady stream of distracting information confronting audiences online.

The type of engagement observed in the social media data collected from Crowdtangle is limited. It does not include engagement on other platforms like Twitter, where journalists are particularly active, nor does it include engagement resulting from other media coverage or by the authors themselves sharing their work publicly or directly with relevant decision makers. That said, the interactions tracked by Crowdtangle are not particularly indicative of depth or meaningfulness. Liking or sharing posts is almost by definition a minimal level of engagement; it hardly qualifies as measurable impact, and yet even using such modest metrics, the results do not inspire much confidence.

Why aren't audiences engaging more with our research? It is difficult to say. Is it the content itself? Are our findings described in ways that are too dense and opaque or too disconnected from the concerns of working journalists and those responsible for making media management decisions? Or does the problem lie with the reputation of journalism and media research more generally, with its lack of consensus around core methods and theories? The fact that the study of journalism and media has long embraced approaches to knowledge production that span the social (and increasingly computational) sciences as well as more humanistic critical and cultural studies approaches to inquiry is sometimes held up as a strength of our field,[28] but it may also contribute to misunderstandings about the value proposition of our research, its legitimacy, and its practical utility.

Whether or not professional communities of practice care about our research, the more immediate concern may be similar to the one many news organizations currently struggle with: getting in front of the right audiences. The exceptions to the rule identified in the social media data offer some guidance about what it takes to attract attention for research findings. Very few of the posts referred to published peer-reviewed articles. Instead, more often than not, where research findings were featured, it was often industry- or foundation-funded reports—documents crafted with the express purpose of being read more widely beyond academic circles. The findings underline the important role played by strategic communication professionals at these organizations (including at outlets such as the Pew Research Center), which devote considerable resources to packaging research and purposefully disseminating findings. Few individual scholars at universities have access to similar public relations operations.

It is also worth noting that amidst all the competition online for attention, very few of the studies referenced in the top-performing posts were published in conventional scholarly journals. Such outlets, however, remain the compulsory destination for most of the scholarship conducted by university faculty, especially those on the tenure track. As long as our academic institutions continue to privilege forms of scholarly publishing, which are unlikely to be read widely outside the academy and are often hidden behind expensive paywalls, and as long as hiring and tenure and promotion practices continue to incentivize such work over other forms of public engagement, it is likely that highly engaged scholarship will remain primarily the domain of a small contingent of well-funded senior scholars who can afford to orient their research toward audiences beyond their narrow peer groups.

These gloomy findings notwithstanding, the relatively high levels of social media engagement found for research-related posts does provide some reason for optimism. What these results suggest is that well-designed and rigorous research can, under some circumstances, pierce through the vast and cluttered digital landscape of people's social media newsfeeds. There may even be, in fact, many who *do* care about what we know about our changing media systems but perhaps not enough to specifically seek it out amidst everything else they consume in their bloated media diets. Translation is not only about making research more understandable; it is also about presenting research in digestible, clickable formats that are likely to stand out. In all likelihood, the audience of people who care about our research is far larger than the small circles our research currently reaches, but just as news organizations have been slow to adapt to the digital arena for distributing their content, academic scholars have been even slower.

If we want people to care about what we know, we must first remind them that our scholarship exists. Engaged journalism researchers must make more active efforts to condense and translate our findings in ways that take into consideration the fact that many of the audiences we wish to reach are *dis*engaged, passively encountering our findings (if at all) in newsfeeds populated with posts about a wide range of other, more seductive topics. The challenges associated with disseminating research in these conditions should be not understated; extensive, coordinated efforts are likely needed to package and organize research findings for distracted digital audiences. But of all academic departments and disciplines, one would surely hope that schools and departments of journalism and communication research would be uniquely positioned to take up such a challenge. A continued failure to attract attention for our research could be taken as compelling evidence that perhaps we know far less about the way digital media systems work than we think we do.

Notes

1. Rasmus Kleis Nielsen, "No One Cares What We Know: Three Responses to the Irrelevance of Political Communication Research," *Political Communication* 35, no. 1 (2018): 145–149.
2. Nielsen, "No One Cares," 146.

3. See also Nikki Usher, "Does Anyone Care about Journalism Research? (No, Really)," *Poynter*, April 5, 2017, https://www.poynter.org/newsletters/2017/does-anyone-care-about-journalism-research-no-really/.

4. Pew Research Center, "Newspapers Fact Sheet," 2018, https://www.journalism.org/fact-sheet/newspapers/.

5. Pew Research Center, "Newspapers Fact Sheet," 2018.

6. Ken Doctor, "Newsonomics: The Newspaper Industry Is Thirsty for Liquidity as It Tries to Merge Its Way Out of Trouble," *Nieman Journalism Lab*, April 18, 2019, https://www.niemanlab.org/2019/04/newsonomics-the-newspaper-industry-is-thirsty-for-liquidity-as-it-tries-to-merge-its-way-out-of-trouble/.

7. Elizabeth Grieco, "Newsroom Employment Dropped Nearly a Quarter in Less Than 10 Years, With Greatest Decline at Newspapers," *Pew Research Center*, July 30, 2018, https://www.pewresearch.org/fact-tank/2018/07/30/newsroom-employment-dropped-nearly-a-quarter-in-less-than-10-years-with-greatest-decline-at-newspapers/.

8. Tom Feran, "Plain Dealer Lays off a Third of Unionized Newsroom Staff," *Plain Dealer*, April 1, 2019, https://www.cleveland.com/news/2019/04/plain-dealer-lays-off-a-third-of-unionized-newsroom-staff.html.

9. Michael Schudson, "The Objectivity Norm in American Journalism," *Journalism*, no. 2 (2001): 149–170.

10. See, for example, Katherine Fink and Michael Schudson, "The Rise of Contextual Journalism, 1950s–2000s," *Journalism* 15, no. 1 (2014): 3–20, and Matthew Pressman, *On Press: The Liberal Values That Shaped the News* (Cambridge, MA: Harvard University Press, 2018).

11. Karin Wahl-Jorgensen, "The Strategic Ritual of Emotionality: A Case Study of Pulitzer Prize-Winning Articles," *Journalism* 14, no. 1 (2013): 129–145.

12. See, for example, Kevin Arceneaux and Martin Johnson, *Changing Minds or Changing Channels? Partisan News in an Age of Choice* (Chicago: University of Chicago Press, 2013), Matthew Levendusky, *How Partisan Media Polarize America* (Chicago: University of Chicago Press, 2013), and Natalia J. Stroud, *Niche News: The Politics of News Choice* (Oxford, UK: Oxford University Press, 2011).

13. Karin Wahl-Jorgensen and Thomas Hanitzsch, eds., *The Handbook of Journalism Studies* (London: Routledge, 2009), 9.

14. Seth Lewis, "The Gap between Journalism and Research Is Too Wide," *Nieman Journalism Lab*, December 2018, https://www.niemanlab.org/2018/12/the-gap-between-journalism-and-research-is-too-wide/.

15. Lewis, "The Gap Between," para. 7.

16. Matthew Hindman, *The Internet Trap: How the Digital Economy Builds Monopolies and Undermines Democracy* (Princeton, NJ: Princeton University Press, 2018).

17. Andrew Perrin and Monica Anderson, "Share of U.S. adults using social media, including Facebook, is mostly unchanged since 2018," Pew Research Center, April 10, 2019, https://www.pewresearch.org/fact-tank/2019/04/10/share-of-u-s-adults-using-social-media-including-facebook-is-mostly-unchanged-since-2018/.

18. See Nieman Journalism Lab, "About Nieman Lab," accessed April 1, 2020, https://www.niemanlab.org/about/.

19. See Poynter, "Mission & Vision," accessed April 1, 2020, https://www.poynter.org/mission-vision/, and Poynter, "Poynter is a Thought Leader," accessed April 1, 2020, https://www.poynter.org/poynter-thought-leader/.

20. See Columbia Journalism Review, "Mission Statement," accessed April 1, 2020, https://www.cjr.org/about_us/mission_statement.php.

21. The organizations each have two to three times as many followers on Twitter, although so too do the media organizations referenced for comparison here.

22. Crowdtangle measures relative engagement by taking the sum of all reactions to a post (including shares, comments, "Likes" and other reactions) and divided by the average received for a given page's previous 100 posts. More information about this measure is provided at https://help.crowdtangle.com/faqs-and-troubleshooting/metrics/how-is-overperforming-calculated as well as https://help.crowdtangle.com/faqs-and-troubleshooting/how-do-you-calculate-overperforming-scores. None of the sampled posts were marked by Crowdtangle as sponsored or branded content, which suggests engagement information reflects organic reach on the platform. Crowdtangle excludes any posts by pages that are targeted at specific segmented audiences, which it deems non-public.

23. Emily Van Duyn and Jessica Collier, "Priming and Fake News: The Effects of Elite Discourse on Evaluations of News Media," *Mass Communication and Society* 22, no. 1 (2019): 29–48.

24. Only one of the six scholars profiled, Leticia Bode, is on faculty in a media or communications department.

25. Denise-Marie Ordway, "Polarizing the Network: The Most Interesting New Digital and Social Media Research," *Nieman Journalism Lab*, November 20, 2018, https://www.niemanlab.org/2018/11/polarizing-the-network-the-most-interesting-new-digital-and-social-media-research.

26. Social sciences generally are often perceived to be at the bottom of these hierarchies. See Stephen Cole, "The Hierarchy of the Sciences?" *American Journal of Sociology* 89, no. 1 (1983): 111–139.

27. Nielsen, "No One Cares," 145.

28. See Barbie Zelizer, "Communication in the Fan of Disciplines," *Communication Theory* 26, no. 3 (2016): 213–235.

5

Critiquing Ethnocentrism and Hierarchy in International Journalism

Critical Research for More Equitable Practice

Lindsay Palmer

Introduction

The gap between academics and practitioners is especially problematic in the context of international news work. Scholarly research on international journalism helps us better understand how journalists are currently grappling with massive changes in their profession, as well as understanding how they could do things better in the future. This research can be even more helpful when it takes care to consider the vast differences among journalists from disparate socio-cultural backgrounds.[1]

Despite the seeming ubiquity of Western representations of international events, there are of course numerous other news industries and employees scattered around the world, and they draw upon a variety of competing routines and values in an effort at constructing their own representations. Even those news organizations based firmly within the geographical and cultural borders of the United States or Britain engage in international reporting practices that routinely bring their employees into contact with journalists and other media workers from disparate cultural contexts. The reality of these cross-cultural encounters has long served to complicate the discussion of what journalistic norms even are (or should be), as scholars in the field of global journalism ethics have particularly shown.[2] Although new digital practices have the potential to better illuminate these different values and routines, the labor of international reporting is still profoundly hierarchical in the digital era.[3]

For instance, international freelance journalists operate at much greater peril in the field than staff correspondents who receive from their

Lindsay Palmer, *Critiquing Ethnocentrism and Hierarchy in International Journalism* In: *Journalism Research That Matters*. Edited by: Valérie Bélair-Gagnon and Nikki Usher, Oxford University Press. © Oxford University Press 2021. DOI: 10.1093/oso/9780197538470.003.0006 organizations insurance, hazardous environment training, and other protections, while the local stringers and fixers hired by big news outlets to assist their staff correspondents with translation and logistics receive the least protection of all.[4] And although the Internet has allowed local stringers and fixers to take some control of their own careers—advertising their services on websites like World Fixer and using social media to network with each other—for the moment, these inegalitarian hierarchies remain intact.

The mainstream news outlets based in the Anglophone West are certainly dominant voices in the global media sphere,[5] and they are often accused of engaging in ethnocentric representations of "other" people and places—most especially those in postcolonial or so-called "developing" nations.[6] The explosion of digital practices in the past few decades has not necessarily brought a systematic end to this problem. As some of my own previous research has shown, the celebrated notion of international "connectedness" has a darker side.[7] The very technologies so often thought to bridge the divide between disparate cultures sometimes deepen those divides instead, making radical differences more visible but offering no way of finding common ground.[8] In this vexed digital milieu, ethnocentrism continues to haunt the work of international reporting, a phenomenon that can make certain international correspondents' stories highly unpopular in particular regions of the world.[9]

Even so, it is crucial that scholars perpetually ask the tough questions, questions that could ideally lead to a more egalitarian, culturally sensitive type of international news work. In this spirit, this chapter will make the following suggestions:

1) Scholarship on international journalism should be prepared to more directly and publicly critique the ethnocentrism that has long plagued international correspondence based in the English-speaking West, and that continues to be a problem in the digital age.

2) Scholars of international news work need to be prepared to interrogate the structural inequalities that inform journalistic labor on an international scale, inequalities that have not disappeared with the rise of digital technologies.

3) Scholars of international journalism need to more directly engage not only with big-brand correspondents, editors, and news executives, but also with the freelancers, stringers, and local fixers who hold these international news professions on their backs. We

should be building more bridges between journalism scholarship and journalism practice not only by sharing our research with industry practitioners, but also by asking for their feedback—especially from journalists who are positioned at a greater disadvantage in international news hierarchies.

In order to follow these suggestions, I argue that we as journalism scholars need to hang on to some of our most time-tested qualitative research methods, while also looking for innovative digital methods that can help us ask new questions in fresh ways. Qualitative methods should remain important to journalism researchers, even in the age of "big data," because journalists tend to be qualitative thinkers. Journalists are storytellers who are themselves grappling with constantly changing digital methods for bringing news events to life. If we want to connect with them in a way that really matters, then we need to be capable of speaking their language. What is more, this approach is best suited to asking the tough, critical questions that don't have "black and white" answers, but questions that we must be asking if we hope to gain a more nuanced understanding of the labor of international reporting in the 21st century.

Bringing Postcolonial Studies and Journalism Studies into Conversation

Scholarly analyses of international news work in the digital context would greatly benefit from engaging with the insights found in postcolonial studies and critical global studies—two fields of thought that drive the more specific questions pursued by global journalism ethicists. Almost twenty years ago, communication scholars Raka Shome and Radha Hegde asserted that postcolonial theory is of grave relevance to communication studies, because "the politics of communication are of central importance in the understanding of the contradictions and ambivalence in our deeply divided world."[10] Postcolonial theorists have long been interested in this "deeply divided world," interrogating the subjugation of some societies at the hands of others, as well as investigating the insidious ways in which cultural expressions like film, literature, and journalism might subject certain cultural groups to epistemic violence.[11] Similarly, scholars of critical global studies critique the unequal distribution of power and resources on a global scale,[12] in an effort at illuminating the forces that continue to dominate the world as well as the "contradictions and ambivalences" that work alongside these forces.

These "contradictions and ambivalences" continue to inform communication in the context of digitization, making the continued problem of ethnocentric news reporting even more dangerous than perhaps it was in the past.[13] While some journalism scholars and practitioners may continue to believe that journalists simply report the truths they encounter in the field, the more critical global journalism ethicists tend to be suspicious of the Enlightenment-era notion that any type of communication can ever be culturally or politically neutral.[14] Instead, they remind both journalists and scholars from the Global North that they are inheriting a historically entrenched socio-cultural privilege that can deeply shape their work. This privilege can lead to ethnocentric representations of cultural difference, both in journalism scholarship as well as in journalism itself.[15]

Significantly, global media ethicists often conduct empirical, qualitative studies of news work. When they do so, they ask questions that do not easily lend themselves to "black and white" answers, as well as attempting to discuss topics that might be uncomfortable for some of their interviewees. These are some of the same questions that might benefit scholars of international news work more broadly, because they can help us dig deeper into some of the less savory aspects of the international journalism profession. For example, we might ask foreign desk editors how they and their correspondents decide what angles they will take on international news stories, and how wedded they are to those specific angles ahead of the actual reporting process. As some of my own interviewees have suggested, foreign reporters tend to come into the field with predetermined "angles" that betray a great deal of cultural bias toward certain regions of the world.[16]

We might also ask foreign correspondents to describe their perceptions of the people on whom they have recently been reporting, asking them to then explain how they translate those perceptions into visual and text-based stories that will be distributed across different platforms. How does cultural difference get constructed at the level of the journalist's craft, in other words, and how do foreign correspondents and their editors rework these representations for distinct digital venues that might require different storytelling techniques? There is something to be learned by observing this process of digitally "translating" a news report from one story format to another, a skill that is expected of more and more journalists in the digital age.[17] Every time a journalist reworks a story about cultural difference for a new platform, a new set of ethical questions potentially arise: how have the visual elements of the story been changed, for example, and how might this in turn transform the representation of the cultural "Other?" Has any of the important context been lost in this process of translation, and if so, what could that do to the fair and accurate representation of the people being featured in the story?

The goal in asking these questions would not be to ascertain the actual news audience's reaction to cultural difference; rather, these questions would help researchers understand how international journalists believe that their own work functions. International reporters and news editors often reveal that they have an imagined audience in mind when they are pursuing certain angles or constructing their stories in particular ways.[18] Sometimes, foreign reporters will even use this imagined audience as an overt justification for why they need to pursue what they know very well is a culturally biased angle.[19] This is an important problem for journalism ethicists to investigate, because it raises questions about whether or not international journalists are going far enough to seek the "truth"—the messy, complex truth of cultural difference.

Yet, it is not enough for scholars of international news work to stop at an analysis of individual journalists' decisions. We also need to study the broader structural constraints within which these journalists and news editors work, constraints that decisively limit ethical, culturally sensitive decision making in the field.[20] In the digital era, international journalists and news editors are competing with citizen journalists, digital activists, documentarians, and numerous other professional and amateur media producers in order to get the attention of a highly diverse assortment of potential news audiences.[21] At the same time, international news budgets have been shrinking, at least in the West, leaving journalists with far less time and resources to pursue their stories in a nuanced fashion.

I reference these broader issues here because I want to clarify that I see ethnocentrism as a systemic problem rather than as an individual problem. There are myriad journalists and editors who care deeply about reporting as fairly and accurately as possible, and often these people produce amazing reports. But if we look only at individual practices, without situating them within the broader structures of power that are critiqued by postcolonial and critical global studies, then scholars of international news work will unfortunately miss some of the most important—and troubling—aspects of the international news profession. These deep structural constraints also inform the professional hierarchies that inform international reporting in the age of digitization.

The Importance of Interrogating Hierarchies

Scholars of international news work should constantly interrogate the hierarchies that riddle the profession of international reporting, hierarchies that are sometimes subtly organized through an ethnocentric lens.[22] Since the 1970s, journalism scholars have discussed the complex, hierarchical nature of news work,[23] and yet, the hierarchies still often seem to be taken for granted. Journalism scholars need to renew their focus on these hierarchies, especially in the international context. For example, "local" stringers, fixers, and translators working in postcolonial or so-called "developing" nations are often paid far less money than Western correspondents, despite the fact that these correspondents depend heavily on the local media workers' material knowledge of the conditions on the ground.[24] These "local" media workers also face a general sense of distrust from their Western colleagues, distrust that has a long history and that is sometimes explicitly ethnicized or racialized.[25] Finally, these "local" media workers are simply not protected in dangerous environments in the same way that white, Western "staff" correspondents are protected.

This matters, because international journalists are now expected to operate in the 24/7 news environment, competing with social media, citizen reporters, and digital activists to distribute their stories around the world. Within this context, news organizations may pay lip service to safety in the field, but they also subtly encourage and reward journalists for taking greater and greater risks to get the story.[26] For the highly visible (and usually white) staff correspondents working for Anglo news outlets, taking greater risks is actually less risky than it is for local journalists; the staff correspondents have medical insurance, the support of security advisors, the experience afforded by hazardous environment training for which they do not have to pay out of pocket, and the protection of safety equipment where needed. Freelance journalists only receive these perks in an uneven and undependable fashion, however, and "local" stringers and fixers rarely receive any of these things at all. This is an issue that needs more discussion in scholarship on international news work.

One way of questioning these hierarchies would be to gather data that addresses the issue, interviewing news editors, bureau chiefs, and staff correspondents about their relationships with local freelancers, stringers, and fixers. But in order to avoid replicating the very hierarchies we are trying to illuminate, journalism scholars should also seek more nuanced perspectives in our research design, which would lead us to gather more culturally complex data. If we follow feminist and postcolonial ethnographers in conceptualizing research methods such as interviewing and participant observation as the active collaboration with the people whose life worlds we are trying to understand,[27] then it becomes easier to see how a vigorous engagement with diverse industry practitioners can occur as early as the moment of recruiting interview subjects or choosing the sites where we conduct our participant observation. The goal in this case would be to ask: Whose viewpoints are ignored, submerged, or simply invisible in journalism research and education?

For example, rather than seeking to conduct interviews solely with well-known foreign correspondents who were born and raised in the United States, the United Kingdom, Canada, or Australia, qualitative scholars of international journalism might instead try to speak with some of the freelance journalists who work for Western news outlets but who were not born and raised in the West. Scholars might also more actively seek to interview news workers whose names do not appear in the bylines or whose faces do not appear on camera: news workers such as photographers, videographers, editors, producers, translators, and fixers.

These marginalized news employees often do the jobs that famous foreign correspondents simply cannot do on their own. They help these well-known journalists secure compelling interviews with sources, translate languages the correspondents do not understand, gather information in places where the correspondents cannot travel, and capture images that the correspondents and their news editors may not be able to capture themselves. Yet, all too often, journalism scholars fall into the trap of making it appear that "big name" correspondents are the only news workers in the field, and that they are solely responsible for the news reports attributed to them.[28]

This is something that might start changing, as news work continues to "digitize." Freelancers and news fixers have certainly begun to draw upon digital technologies to take more control of their own careers. For example, international freelancers now often align themselves with the Freelance Frontline Register, an online collective through which freelancers can organize themselves and issue statements about the safety and treatment of freelancers around the world. Similarly, news fixers can now advertise their services on websites like HackPack and World Fixer. These websites allow correspondents to search for fixers by region of the world and to identify people with the precise skill set that is needed. In this way, fixers can move past their traditional dependence on the informal recommendations of previous clients and make themselves much more visible to an array of potential media workers who might hire them.

Still, these digital tools only go so far in helping the more vulnerable international media workers to overcome the deeply entrenched hierarchies that are a foundational part of international reporting. Scholars need to spend more time talking with these news workers, in order to get a better sense of how they are becoming more empowered, as well as how they are still placed at a disadvantage. By seeking different perspectives at the data-gathering stage, international journalism researchers could develop a more complex picture of the labor of international reporting—labor that is difficult, confusing, and wholly dependent on local news workers whose names and faces are often hidden from the public eye.

Publicly Engaging International News Workers

International journalism scholars should renew their focus on public engagement, though they should do so without inadvertently bolstering the hierarchies mentioned above. In journalism scholarship, this could mean anything from organizing brainstorming sessions or conferences with members of the news industry, to publishing more accessible versions of our research online or in news industry trade journals, to conducting research in partnership with organizations that seek to improve news production, such as the Knight Foundation.

Each of these strategies is valuable. Yet, even in the national context, it is important to periodically evaluate whether we are publicly engaging with the people who are most affected by the research we conduct and the decisions that this research might help news executives to make. In the context of international news, it is essential that scholars push their research toward a "real world" impact, not only on the famous English-speaking correspondents and foreign desk editors who work for legacy news outlets, but also on the freelancers, stringers, and fixers scattered around the world.

Pursuing this goal might take journalism scholars into a rather uncomfortable space, especially where our most elite industry contacts are concerned. Since many freelancers, stringers, and fixers arguably comprise an underground economy on which the more visible international news workers heavily depend,[29] there is the potential for a great deal of tension to arise in the public conversations we might initiate on the topic—especially if we are directly or even indirectly criticizing the practices of news organizations and journalists who regularly associate with us through our J-schools or through other avenues. Yet, we cannot help to improve the international news professions in the English-speaking West without asking foreign desk editors why they don't protect news fixers and why they so often exploit the (necessarily) competitive drive of freelancers in dangerous environments. Therefore, international journalism scholars should actively target the Op-Ed sections of major Western newspapers as well as journalism trade publications serving the Western, English-language news industries, in order to successfully "translate" and share even our most uncomfortable data.

But alongside this type of public engagement, international journalism scholars could also partner with groups like the Freelance Frontline Register or with the creators of websites like HackPack and World Fixer. These partnerships could involve the more accessible distribution of our data on the labor of freelancing and fixing to the people who originally served as the subject of our research questions: the freelancers and fixers themselves. This might lead to future research collaborations with these undervalued news workers, collaborations that could be driven by the freelancers' and fixers' *own* most pressing questions. Such collaborations could also involve the development of public campaigns for funding that could be used to provide freelancers and local fixers with more training and protection. Finally, these partnerships could result in the planning of events where freelancers, fixers, and stringers from around the world could interact with the academics who research their labor and give feedback on the existing research.

The idea is that engagement should go both ways. We should be ready to learn from the journalism practitioners whose voices rarely get heard, at the same time that we work to share even our most critical insights with the practitioners whose voices dominate the field. In sharing these insights, journalism scholars should constantly be assessing whether their work is accessible to the people who might benefit from it the most, as well as to the people who helped us arrive at these insights in the first place. Will these people be able to read our studies without having to pay for them, for example, and are these studies written in a straightforward, jargon-free way? These may seem like small questions, but they are crucial to the "two-way street" of public engagement.

Conclusion

At this point in time, international journalism scholars face two major challenges: (1) conducting research that adequately addresses the hierarchies and misrepresentations that this chapter has outlined, and (2) closing the "research–practice" gap, so that journalists themselves can begin to address these problems as well. There are a few concrete solutions to these challenges.

First, in order to effectively build these rather precarious bridges between journalism scholars and professionals, it is crucial that journalism scholars hang on to some of their most time-tested research methods—methods that are both qualitative and empirical—at the same time that they also experiment with innovative ways of studying news work in the digital age. Retaining these more qualitative methods can help to close the research–practice gap. Though the digitization of news work has brought with it an array of new practices such as reporting with big data, artificial intelligence journalism, and more, there continues to be a focus in journalism on the need to (1) go into the field and talk to the people who live there, and (2) find compelling ways of narrativizing the events that journalists cover. Journalists are storytellers, and their stories are crafted through their material interactions with specific people and places. For this reason, it makes sense that scholars of international journalism should continue to draw upon methods like in-depth interviewing and participant observation—even when addressing the highly technical digital practices in which foreign correspondents increasingly engage.

Since these correspondents are famously ambivalent about the rise of digital technologies within their profession, studying the digitization of international reporting through a qualitative lens might be a fruitful way to foster better connections between international journalism scholars and industry practitioners. What impact might it have, in other words, if qualitative scholars could more directly and more often share their interview data with journalists who themselves conduct interviews for a living—especially interview data coming from a large volume of international news workers whose perspectives are rarely considered? And how might international journalism scholars gain more trust from suspicious industry practitioners, merely through the act of traveling to the places where these news employees work, and subjecting ourselves to some of the same challenges that these news workers face? This kind of trust still matters, even at a time when the digitization of news work makes it easier for international journalists—and international journalism scholars—to avoid traveling very much at all.

Yet, it is also rather paradoxically important that scholars stay abreast of the most cutting-edge methods being used, not only by their fellow academics but also by journalists themselves. Many international news reporters are venturing into digital, data-driven approaches to reporting the world's stories, and this means that news scholars should find innovative ways of doing the same. Crucially, in those cases where international journalism scholars do embrace digital approaches to studying 21st-century news reporting, it would be beneficial to continue to frame those studies through a critical, cultural lens. For instance, though international news scholars have long been engaging in social network analysis and textual analysis, they have much to gain from deploying the digital tools that would optimize these methods and allow for larger data samples. Indeed, some scholars are already using these tools for international journalism research, although not typically to analyze news work.[30]

A digital social network analysis of the interconnection between news organizations, correspondents, and news fixers would be fascinating. So, too, would an automated textual analysis of interview transcripts from much, much larger samples of freelancers and news fixers than most qualitative researchers could currently accommodate. The challenge is to carve out a space in what has come to be referred to as "computational methods" for qualitative research. How do we ask qualitative questions of network analyses of international news work, for example, and how do we use these sophisticated digital tools in a way that does not erase the cultural nuance from our analyses? These are only some of the questions that international journalism scholars should be asking in the 21st century, questions that can in turn have the promise to change journalism practice.

The concerns I have outlined point to the need for more critical, cultural investigation of international news work in the digital age, investigation that takes the direct engagement of journalism industry practitioners as one of its primary goals. This increased attention to public engagement would ideally help to close the "research–practice gap," allowing academics to learn more from journalists as well as to more effectively share their concerns with professional news workers. News industries need their own "watchdogs," and academic researchers are well positioned to contribute to this effort. Yet, we currently suffer (rather paradoxically) from being *both* too distant and too close to the news workers whose labor we wish to understand.

We are too distant in the sense that we do not always make the effort at seeking a dialogue with the most diverse journalists working in the world's various news industries, nor do we always talk about journalism using language that resonates for the people we are talking *about*. At the same time, we are often too close in the sense that we might work alongside professional journalists at our universities, or we might rely too heavily on the good will of our industrial contacts to maintain the access that allows us to conduct our research in the first place.

Notes

1. Shakuntala Rao and Seow Ting Lee, "Globalizing Media Ethics? An Assessment of Universal Ethics Among International Political Journalists," *Journal of Mass Media Ethics* 20, no. 2–3 (2005): 99–120; Herman Wasserman, "Towards a Global Journalism Ethics Via Local Narratives," *Journalism Studies* 12, no. 6 (2011): 791–803.
2. Nick Couldry, "Why Media Ethics Still Matters," in *Global Media Ethics: Problems and Perspectives*, ed. Stephen J.A. Ward (Chichester: Wiley-Blackwell, 2013), 13–29; Shakuntala Rao and Herman Wasserman, *Media Ethics and Justice in the Age of Globalization* (London: Palgrave Macmillan, 2015).
3. Lindsay Palmer, *Becoming the Story: War Correspondents since 9/11* (Urbana: University of Illinois, 2018); Lindsay Palmer, *The Fixers: Local News Workers and the Underground Labor of International Reporting* (New York: Oxford University Press, 2019).
4. Lindsay Palmer, "'Being the Bridge': News Fixers' Perspectives on Cultural Difference in Reporting the 'War on Terror,'" *Journalism* 19, no. 3 (2016): 314–332; Palmer, *The Fixers*.
5. Daya Kishan Thussu, "The 'Murdochization' of News? The Case of Star TV in India," *Media, Culture & Society*, 29, no. 4 (2007): 593–611; Chris Paterson, *The International Television News Agencies: The World from London* (New York: Peter Lang, 2011); Kaarle Nordenstreng and Daya Kishan Thussu, eds., *Mapping BRICS Media* (London; New York: Routledge, 2015).
6. Edward W. Said, *Orientalism* (New York: Pantheon Books, 1978); Bethami A. Dobkin, *Tales of Terror: Television News and the Construction of the Terrorist Threat* (New York: Praeger, 1992); Suzanne Franks, "Reporting Africa: Problems and Perspectives," *Westminster Papers in Communication and Culture* 2, no. 0 (2005): 129; Suzanne Franks, "The Neglect of Africa and the Power of Aid," *International Communication Gazette* 72, no. 1 (2010): 71–84; Wasserman, "Towards a Global Journalism Ethics"; Herman Wasserman, "Global Journalism Studies: Beyond Panoramas," *Communication* 37, no. 1 (April 1, 2011): 100–117; Des Freedman and Daya Kishan Thussu, eds., *Media and Terrorism: Global Perspectives* (Los Angeles: CA SAGE Publications, 2012); Deepa Kumar, *Islamophobia and the*

Politics of Empire (Chicago: Haymarket Books, 2012); Jairo Lugo-Ocando and An Nguyen, *Developing News: Global Journalism and the Coverage of "Third World" Development* (London, New York: Routledge, 2017); Palmer, *Becoming the Story.*

7. Palmer, *Becoming the Story.*
8. Couldry, "Why Media Ethics Still Matters."
9. Palmer, *Becoming the Story.*
10. Raka Shome and Radha S. Hegde, "Postcolonial Approaches to Communication: Charting the Terrain, Engaging the Intersections," *Communication Theory* 12, no. 3 (2002): 261.
11. Said, *Orientalism*; Gayatri Chakravorty Spivak, "Can the Subaltern Speak?" in *Marxism and the Interpretation of Culture*, eds. Cary Nelson and Lawrence Grossberg (Urbana: University of Illinois Press, 1988), 271–313; Gareth Griffiths, "The Myth of Authenticity," in *The Post-Colonial Studies Reader*, eds. Bill Ashcroft, Gareth Griffiths, and Helen Tiffin, 2nd ed. (London, New York: Routledge, 2006), 165–168.
12. William I. Robinson, "What Is a Critical Globalization Studies? Intellectual Labor and Global Society," in *Critical Globalization Studies*, eds. Richard P. Appelbaum and William I. Robinson (New York: Routledge, 2005), 11–18; Mark Juergensmeyer, ed., *Thinking Globally: A Global Studies Reader* (Berkeley: University of California Press, 2014).
13. Couldry, "Why Media Ethics Still Matters"; Palmer, *Becoming the Story.*
14. Wasserman, "Towards a Global Journalism Ethics Via Local Narratives"; Rao and Wasserman, *Media Ethics and Justice.*
15. Wasserman, "Towards a Global Journalism Ethics Via Local Narratives"; Shakuntala Rao, "The 'Local' in Global Media Ethics," *Journalism Studies* 12, no. 6 (2011): 780–790.
16. Palmer, *Becoming the Story*; Palmer, *The Fixers.*
17. Usher, *Making News at The New York Times* (Ann Arbor: Michigan University Press, 2014).
18. Palmer, *The Fixers.*
19. Palmer, *The Fixers.*
20. Couldry, "Why Media Ethics Still Matters."
21. Palmer, *Becoming the Story.*
22. Mark Pedelty, *War Stories: The Culture of Foreign Correspondents* (New York: Routledge, 1995); Mel Bunce, "'This Place Used to Be a White British Boys' Club': Reporting Dynamics and Cultural Clash at an International News Bureau in Nairobi," *The Round Table* 99, no. 410 (2010): 515–528; Mel Bunce, "The New Foreign Correspondent at Work: Local-National 'Stringers' and the Global News Coverage of Darfur" (Oxford: Reuters Institute for the Study of Journalism, 2011), http://openaccess.city.ac.uk/id/eprint/3600/1/The_new_foreign_correspondent_at_work.pdf; Soomin Seo, "Marginal Majority at The Postcolonial News Agency," *Journalism Studies* 17, no. 1 (2016): 39–56; Palmer, *Becoming the Story*; Palmer, *The Fixers.*
23. Gaye Tuchman, *Making News: A Study in the Construction of Reality* (New York: Free Press, 1978); Herbert J. Gans, *Deciding What's News: A Study of CBS Evening News, NBC Nightly News, Newsweek, and Time* (New York: Vintage Books, 1980).

24. Palmer, *The Fixers*.

25. Pedelty, *War Stories*; Jerry Palmer and Victoria Fontan, "'Our Ears and Our Eyes': Journalists and Fixers in Iraq," *Journalism: Theory, Practice & Criticism* 8, no. 1 (2007): 5–24; Colleen Murrell, *Foreign Correspondents and International Newsgathering: The Role of Fixers*, Routledge Research in Journalism 9 (New York, London: Routledge, 2015); Palmer, *Becoming the Story*.

26. Palmer, *Becoming the Story*.

27. Sharlene Nagy Hesse-Biber, *Feminist Research Practice: A Primer*, 2nd ed. (Thousand Oaks: SAGE Publications, 2013).

28. Palmer, *The Fixers*.

29. Palmer, *The Fixers*.

30. Tal Samuel-Azran and Tsahi Hayat, "Counter-Hegemonic Contra-Flow and the Al Jazeera America Fiasco: A Social Network Analysis of Al Jazeera America's Twitter Users," *Global Media and Communication* 13, no. 3 (2017): 267–282. Peter Verweij and Elvira van Noort, "Journalists' Twitter Networks, Public Debates and Relationships in South Africa," *Digital Journalism* 2, no. 1 (2014): 98–114; Elad Segev, *International News Flow Online: Global Views with Local Perspectives* (New York: Peter Lang, 2015); Harsh Taneja and James G. Webster, "How Do Global Audiences Take Shape? The Role of Institutions and Culture in Patterns of Web Use," *Journal of Communication* 66, no. 1 (2015): 161–182.

PART II
ANSWERING THE CRISIS IN JOURNALISM
Key Research Areas

6

Why News Literacy Matters

Melissa Tully

Introduction

As concerns about "fake news" and misinformation have proliferated in the
past few years, calls for more and better media literacy education have sur-
faced from media professionals, scholars, educators, and researchers.[1] These
calls often focus on developing the knowledge and skills necessary to navigate contemporary news environments where disinformation and misinformation circulate, and where many people get the bulk of their news
and information on social media.[2] At the same time, others such as danah
m. boyd have criticized media literacy education, describing "backfire"
effects and warning that it is not a panacea for what ails our democracy or
news environment.[3] Although media literacy is not a cure-all, it should be
part of a solution to developing a media system that provides audiences with
news and information that is relevant to their lives. This broader "solution"
should also include improved reporting and fact-checking, changes in how
news is funded, produced, and circulated online, and government oversight
and regulation of media and technology companies, among others.[4]

Although news literacy and related efforts could be an effective and important part of changing how audiences interact with news and information, particularly on social media, it is imperative that educational efforts
and initiatives are developed using theoretically sound and empirically rich
research. Well-intentioned interventions and programs could potentially
cause more harm than good if they are not supported by sound research.
Developing and promoting news literacy efforts will be best accomplished by
collaboration among scholars, educators, researchers, journalists, and other
media professionals who rely on research to make informed decisions about
how to best serve news audiences.

This chapter will explore the nuances of news literacy and the possibilities and challenges of developing a more engaged and critical citizenry. News

Melissa Tully, *Why News Literacy Matters* In: *Journalism Research That Matters*. Edited by: Valérie Bélair-Gagnon and
Nikki Usher, Oxford University Press. © Oxford University Press 2021. DOI: 10.1093/oso/9780197538470.003.0007

literacy efforts address news content, production, consumption, and contexts to holistically explore the role of news in society, with a particular focus on the importance of news for informing self-governing citizens.[5] First, I define news literacy and its core components and make the case for why it matters. The next section looks at how news literacy research can inform educational efforts and journalism practice. Finally, the chapter concludes with a discussion of how news literacy can address the pressing challenges facing news consumers and creators in the 21st century. Developing news literacy equips citizens to make informed choices about where to get their news and information and how to make sense of it in their lives.

What Is News Literacy?

News literacy is a type of media literacy, which is often defined as the ability to access, analyze, evaluate, and communicate mediated messages.[6] This broad definition seeks to cover the range of mediated content that we encounter, from advertising to video games, and therefore must be adaptable and applicable across media. Developing news literacy means building knowledge and skills related to accessing, analyzing, and evaluating news and understanding its importance in society. However, this definition does little to describe the core elements of media literacy, or in other words, what contributes to one's "ability." In a popular textbook on media literacy, Potter argues that knowledge structures, skills, and personal locus are the building blocks of media literacy, noting, "the combination of all three is necessary to build your wider set of perspectives on the media. Your skills are the tools you use to build knowledge structures. Your knowledge structures are the organizations of what you have learned. Your personal locus provides mental energy and direction."[7]

Taking a step back, however, and looking at the definition of literacy as "the ability to read and write," my colleagues and I argue that news (and other forms of media) literacy should remain focused on the knowledge and skills that contribute to one's ability, and that other factors, like personal locus and attitudes, are essential to applying knowledge and skills. Given this, we offer a definition of news literacy that seeks to distill and capture its core elements: *news literacy is **knowledge** of the personal and social processes by which news is produced, distributed, and consumed, and **skills** that allow users some control over these processes.*[8] This definition offers a clearer picture of what news literacy is and isn't, thus providing much-needed conceptual clarity for researchers, educators, and practitioners interested in developing curricula and interventions to improve news literacy.

To develop news literacy, then, requires building knowledge and skills in key areas that are relevant to the entire news process, starting with creators and ending with audiences. We propose and define five domains—context, creation, content, circulation, and consumption—that make up news literacy (see Table 6.1).[9] These domains address the role of news in society and build on existing work that argues that developing news literacy requires an understanding of both the content and contexts of news production and consumption.[10]

Distilling news literacy into five knowledge and skills domains (5 Cs) allows us to develop a set of questions to gauge knowledge and skills that can be measured, assessed, and taught in news literacy courses or reinforced in interventions. These domains are derived from existing news literacy and media effects research and media theory. For example, the context and creation domains rely on news sociology and gatekeeping theory to explain the various forces that influence news production.[11] Consumption draws on selective exposure and hostile media effects research to examine how personal factors like political partisanship affect news consumption.[12] By narrowing the scope of what "counts" as news literacy, we are able to develop measures to empirically test and evaluate news literacy efforts—such as classes, curricula, online interventions, efforts by news organizations, and advertisements—using a range of methods and approaches.[13] We can also measure individuals'

Table 6.1 Defining News Literacy: 5 Cs

Domain	Definition
Context	Social, legal, and economic environment in which news is produced
Creation	Process in which journalists and others engage in conceiving, reporting, and creating news stories and other journalistic content
Content	Characteristics of a news story or piece of news that distinguishes it from other types of media content
Circulation	Process through which news is distributed and spread to potential audiences
Consumption	Personal factors that contribute to news exposure, attention, and evaluation

Adapted from Vraga et al., 2021.

news literacy to see if and how it influences news choices, analysis, and evaluation, with the ultimate goal of working to improve the knowledge and skills that actually matter for critically engaging with news.[14]

Importantly, this definition of news literacy only addresses the core components of knowledge and skills that make up "literacy," but it does not determine how or if this literacy is put to use. If we consider the analogy of reading, literacy only describes the ability to read; it does not address if one actually reads or how well one does it. Therefore, to understand if and how news literacy is put to use, we must consider another set of factors, such as attitudes, norms, and perceived sense of control.[15] Putting news literacy to use would mean that audiences critically engage with news by making an effort to expose themselves to news, interpret that news using knowledge and skills (applying their news literacy), make meaning from that news, and ultimately make decisions based on the information garnered from the news.[16] These decisions—from who to vote for to what food to eat to how to stay healthy—are of major concern as audiences make important personal and social choices based on the news they see and believe.

Why Does News Literacy Matter?

Developing news literacy is one way that the public can exert some control over the news and information they receive, potentially empowering citizens to make informed news decisions and to hold others accountable for the quality of the news and information environment. Public opinion data suggests that the public is worried about the potential spread of false or misleading news and information, feels that it is difficult to recognize this content, and is not necessarily equipped to recognize or respond to it.[17] For example, 73% of respondents in Edelman's 2019 survey said they worry about false news and information "being used as a weapon." And, few Americans think the news and information they get on social media is trustworthy, despite relying on social media heavily as a source.[18] However, it is not all bad news; Edelman, the communications firm, reports that people consumed more news in 2018 than in the previous year and are recognizing the challenges to finding credible information online.[19] Taken together, this data suggests that the public is attuned to the need to consume trustworthy and credible news and information and is seeking ways to do so online, particularly on social media, but faces challenges to finding quality news in their day-to-day lives.

Developing and applying news literacy is one proactive step that we can take to navigate complex news and information environments. Although news literacy is not a panacea, it is something that is within our control and has the potential to change our relationship with the news and information we consume. For example, a more news-literate consumer is well positioned to correct false and misleading information that they encounter, to call on news organizations and social media companies to make changes that could improve the news ecosystem, or to support or challenge legislation regarding news.[20] In short, this news-literate public should be able to make more informed decisions on social, political, and personal matters.

How Can Research Inform News Literacy Efforts?

One strand of news and media literacy research focuses on evaluating courses, modules, interventions, or curricula to see how these efforts improve literacy, which is usually measured as a specific type of knowledge, attitude, or skill that is often directly related to the effort.[21] Another strand of research looks at the relationship between news and media literacy and a range of outcomes related to critical news consumption, such as perceptions of news and information accuracy, bias, credibility, and hostility.[22] For example, research suggests that news literacy efforts can improve credibility perceptions of news and can make people more skeptical of biased, false, or misleading information and conspiracy theories even when this content aligns with their worldviews.[23] And, a third strand extends beyond news consumption per se to examine the relationship between news and media literacy and a range of democratic outcomes, such as political efficacy and political engagement.[24] Overall, this research suggests that news and related media literacy efforts can be effective at improving knowledge and skills (literacy) and encouraging critical news consumption and outcomes relevant to civic life.

However, the effectiveness of these efforts often depends on a number of factors, including the content of the course, module, or online intervention; personal characteristics of the students or study participants; and the context of where the effort or intervention takes place.[25] Certain news literacy messages may resonate more or less with certain audiences and may be more or less effective depending on where they are viewed or read. For example, my colleagues and I have found that short news literacy tutorials and videos designed like public service advertisements are effective at reducing perceptions of bias and boosting credibility perceptions of news for certain groups of people in certain environments.[26] But when we took the content of these messages and attempted to distill them into tweets to serve as reminder messages on Twitter, we ran into additional challenges of conveying key information and prompting action in a crowded social media environment.[27] Testing multiple news literacy messages on Twitter, we found that some messages can promote skepticism toward misinformation, and others can boost one's confidence about their own news literacy, but that no single message was able to achieve all desired outcomes in our study. This research further suggests that news literacy efforts need to tackle key issues from multiple perspectives, and that audiences need to be exposed to these messages over time and in different contexts.

News literacy efforts should address the knowledge, skills, and other sets of key factors (e.g., attitudes, motivation, perceived norms) that contribute to applying news literacy in everyday life.[28] For example, an intervention can focus on conveying a key piece of information about how journalists and news organizations work, or how misinformation is often designed to look like news, or it can remind news consumers of a news literacy skill such as verifying the source of the information. This intervention can boost confidence in one's ability to apply this knowledge and skills to actual news consumption.[29] News literacy researchers are well positioned to test these efforts and to experiment with both form and content to develop messages and interventions that resonate with audiences, and to translate this research into teaching and practice for the classroom and beyond.

Much of my research has focused on developing news literacy messages and interventions for online and social media environments in an attempt to address two key shortcomings on traditional classroom media literacy efforts. First, classroom efforts are limited to students enrolled in formal education; and second, they are somewhat removed from actual news consumption. Of course, research should still be dedicated to developing, implementing, and evaluating news literacy curricula and classroom efforts, as this education is critical in the 21st century.[30] And, many researchers and educators are dedicated to this effort; in fact, the National Association of Media Literacy Education has seen dramatic growth in recent years and is a leader in supporting classroom-based media literacy efforts.[31] However, the focus of my work has been on messages and interventions that can be used outside of classrooms to extend the scholarship and practice in this under-researched area.

By developing and testing news literacy messages and interventions for digital and social media, we are targeting messages to adults, who are often neglected by traditional education, in the context where they consume news. These messages could act as reminders or reinforcement messages "in the moment" when someone might click or share a news story or more dubious content masquerading as news. Clayton and colleagues found that warning people about potentially misleading articles on Facebook affected perceptions of both misleading *and* accurate headlines, echoing my own work and suggesting a need to continue to develop and test messages for social media environments.[32] These kinds of mixed findings highlight the difficulty in promoting news literacy and healthy skepticism without making people less trusting of actual news or promoting cynicism.[33] By moving these efforts out of the class and onto the Internet, we must engage with the challenges of creating compelling content that is able to attract audiences' attention and deliver useful information that prompts action. This is a difficult task, but one that researchers can tackle to empower audiences and improve the information ecosystem.

Media professionals also have a role to play, as they can incorporate similar interventions or messages into their work. For example, using glossaries or other "explainers" to provide insight into how journalists do their job, or the decisions that went into a story, not only increase transparency and bolster credibility but also double as news literacy efforts, as audiences learn more about the news-making process.[34] If audiences become more familiar with how news is produced and what constitutes solid reporting, for example, they may be more equipped to recognize when a false story or opinion piece is masquerading as news. The Trusting News project, for example, works to train journalists and media professionals to be more transparent as a way to improve trust with audiences.[35] Their work is premised on the idea that if news creators understand why public trust is low, they can work on actively improving it rather than simply lamenting the problem. These efforts have resulted in changes in a number of newsrooms, and the creation of the kind of interventions that put news literacy in front of news consumers.[36] Scaling up this kind of work by making it standard practice in traditional and digital-only news organizations would be a tremendous step forward for news producers and audiences alike.

How Can News Literacy Address Challenges Facing
News Consumers?

For news literacy to be effective at promoting critical news consumption, news audiences need to develop their knowledge and skills and then regularly apply them when encountering news and information. To effectively apply the various news literacy "tips and tricks" that often circulate online requires knowledge, skill-building, and practice. It is unreasonable to expect that audiences are equipped to evaluate news and information if they have never been exposed to news literacy education or do not see the value of critically engaging with news.[37] We would not expect a person to be literate if they were never taught to read, nor would we expect them to read if reading had no value in their lives. In addition, most news consumers are adults who have long since finished K–12 or college education and who are attempting to navigate a digital and social media environment that is completely different than what they encountered a decade ago, and that continues to transform regularly (often on a seeming whim and at the discretion of a few major companies). Therefore, it is imperative that news literacy efforts extend beyond classroom environments to reach adult audiences in the places and spaces where they consume news.[38] In addition, these news literacy interventions should be developed and evaluated to determine if they are effectively conveying key concepts and encouraging relevant outcomes, like critical news consumption or political participation. Messages that don't "work" are useless, at best, and counterproductive at worst.[39]

Organizations like the News Literacy Project (NLP) have been working to develop small and large interventions for classroom and non-classroom settings.[40] Importantly, they rely on research to inform their work and conduct their own internal research to evaluate their efforts. The NLP has continued to evolve to address contemporary challenges and has been a leader in this field. Continuing to work with scholars and researchers, efforts like those developed by NLP have the potential to be long-lasting and effective tools in our news literacy toolbox.

To address the challenges facing news consumers now, news literacy efforts need to cut across dividing lines like political partisanship, and need to encourage audiences to be active news consumers who are willing and able to critically engage. These are difficult challenges to address as partisan divides continue to grow in the United States, journalism itself has become a politically charged topic, and motivation to consume news varies widely among groups in the United States and around the world. For example, using interviews with adults in the United States, we found that even people with basic news literacy were often cynical about the value of engaging with news or of applying news literacy. Others were simply not motivated to consume news or to critically evaluate it. In addition, many participants had a nuanced view of news bias and recognized how their worldviews and perspectives influence their news choices and evaluations in the abstract, but were quick to rely on source cues and shortcuts when evaluating actual news content, suggesting that overcoming entrenched views will continue to be a challenge.[41]

With this in mind, we as researchers, educators, practitioners, and professionals need to think about how to teach news literacy *and* encourage its application. This work cannot be relegated to research locked away in journal articles behind paywalls, or college classrooms that only reach a part of the population. News literacy efforts must be developed and tested for media environments and reevaluated to ensure they are a part of the solution and not contributing to the problem. In addition, simply telling news consumers to check the source of content, or to read carefully, or to correct misinformation when they see it, won't be enough to encourage critical engagement with news in the moment or in the long term. Audiences need to know how to do it (knowledge and skills), but also must feel that critical news consumption is valuable and doable. Efforts should strive to improve news literacy, increase confidence in individuals' abilities, and convince audiences that news literacy is applicable to their lives. News literacy matters if we want to help people become informed citizens who can contribute to a functioning democracy.

Notes

1. Monica Bulger and Patrick Davison, "The Promises, Challenges, and Futures of Media Literacy," Data & Society Research Institute (2018), https://datasociety.net/library/the-promises-challenges-and-futures-of-media-literacy/; Stephan Lewandowsky, Ullrich K.H. Ecker, and John Cook. "Beyond Misinformation: Understanding and Coping with the 'Post-Truth' Era," *Journal of Applied Research in Memory and Cognition* 6, no. 4 (2017): 353–369.
2. Bulger and Davison, "The Promises, Challenges, and Futures of Media Literacy"; Alice E. Marwick and Rebecca Lewis, "Media Manipulation and Disinformation Online," Data & Society Research Institute (2017), https://datasociety.net/library/

media-manipulation-and-disinfo-online/; Pew Research Center, "News Use Across Social Media Platforms 2018" (2018), https://www.journalism.org/2018/09/10/news-use-across-social-media-platforms-2018/.

3. danah m. boyd, "Did Media Literacy Backfire?" (2017), https://points.datasociety.net/did-media-literacy-backfire-7418c084d88d.

4. Alice E. Marwick, "Why Do People Share Fake News? A Sociotechnical Model of Media Effects," *Georgetown Law Technology Review* 474, no. 2 (2018): 474–512, https://georgetownlawtechreview.org/why-do-people-share-fake-news-a-sociotechnical-model-of-media-effects/GLTR-07-2018/.

5. Stephanie Craft, Seth Ashley, and Adam Maksl, "Elements of News Literacy: A Focus Group Study of How Teenagers Define News and Why They Consume It," *Electronic News* 10 no. 3 (2016): 143–160; Emily K. Vraga and Melissa Tully, "Effective Messaging to Communicate News Media Literacy Concepts to Diverse Publics," *Communication and the Public* 1 (2016): 305–322.

6. Patricia Aufderheide and Charles M. Firestone, Media Literacy: A Report of the National Leadership Conference on Media Literacy (Queenstown, MD: Aspen Institute, 1993), https://files.eric.ed.gov/fulltext/ED365294.pdf.

7. W. James Potter, *Media Literacy* (9th ed.) (Thousand Oaks, CA: Sage, 2019), 20.

8. Emily K. Vraga, Melissa Tully, Adam Maksl, Stephanie Craft, and Seth Ashley, "Theorizing News Literacy Behaviors," *Communication Theory* 31, no. 1 (2021): 1–21.

9. Melissa Tully, Adam Maksl, Stephanie Craft, Emily K. Vraga, and Seth Ashley, "Understanding Critical News Consumption: Theorizing and Measuring News Literacy," Paper presented at the Future of Journalism Conference, Cardiff, UK (September 2019); Vraga et al., "Theorizing News Literacy."

10. Seth Ashley, Adam Maksl, and Stephanie Craft, "News Media Literacy and Political Engagement: What's the Connection," *Journal of Media Literacy Education* 9, no. 1 (2017): 79–98; Melissa Tully and Emily K. Vraga, "Effectiveness of a News Media Literacy Advertisement in Partisan Versus Nonpartisan Online Media Contexts," *Journal of Broadcasting & Electronic Media* 61, no. 1 (2017): 144–162; Emily K. Vraga, and Melissa Tully, "Media Literacy Messages and Hostile Media Perceptions: Processing of Nonpartisan Versus Partisan Political Information," *Mass Communication and Society* 18, no. 4 (2015): 422–448.

11. Pamela J. Shoemaker and Timothy P. Vos, *Gatekeeping Theory* (New York: Routledge, 2009); Jane. B. Singer, "User-Generated Visibility: Secondary Gatekeeping in a Shared Media Space," *New Media & Society* 16, no. 1 (2014): 55–73.

12. Natalie Jomini Stroud, *Niche News: The Politics of News Choice* (Oxford: Oxford University Press, 2011); Tully and Vraga, "Effectiveness of a News Media Literacy Advertisement."

13. Adam Maksl, Stephanie Craft, Seth Ashley, and Dean Miller, "The Usefulness of a News Media Literacy Measure in Evaluating a News Literacy Curriculum," *Journalism and Mass Communication Educator* 72, no. 2 (2017): 228–241.; Vraga and Tully, "Effective Messaging to Communicate News Media Literacy Concepts to Diverse Publics."

14. Craft et al., "Elements of News Literacy"; Melissa Tully and Emily K. Vraga, "A Mixed-Methods Approach to Examining the Relationship Between News Media Literacy and Political Efficacy," *International Journal of Communication* 12, (2018): 766–787; Vraga et al., "Theorizing News Literacy."

15. Icek Ajzen, "Perceived Behavioral Control, Self-Efficacy, Locus of Control, and the Theory of Planned Behavior," *Journal of Applied Social Psychology* 32 no. 4 (2002): 665–683.

16. Vraga et al., "Theorizing News Literacy."

17. Edelman, "Trust Barometer" (2019), https://www.edelman.com/trust-barometer; Pew, "News Use."

18. Pew, "News Use."

19. Edelman, "Trust Barometer."

20. Marwick, "Why Do People Share Fake News?"

21. Andrea M. Bergstrom, Mark Flynn, and Clay Craig, "Deconstructing Media in the College Classroom: A Longitudinal Critical Media Literacy Intervention," *Journal of Media Literacy Education* 10, no. 3 (2018): 113–131, https://digitalcommons.uri.edu/jmle/vol10/iss3/7; Maksl et al., "The Usefulness of a News Media Literacy Measure."

22. Joseph Kahne and Benjamin Bowyer, "Educating for Democracy in a Partisan Age: Confronting the Challenges of Motivated Reasoning and Misinformation," *American Educational Research Journal* 54, no. 1 (2017): 3–34; Vraga and Tully, "Media Literacy Messages and Hostile Media Perceptions."

23. Katherine Clayton, Spencer Blair, Jonathan A. Busam, Samuel Forstner, John Glance, Guy Green. . . Brendan Nyhan, "Real Solutions for Fake News? Measuring the Effectiveness of General Warnings and Factcheck Tags in Reducing Belief in False Stories on Social Media," *Political Behavior* (2019): 1–23; Stephanie Craft, Seth Ashley, and Adam Maksl, "News Media Literacy and Conspiracy Theory Endorsement," *Communication and the Public* 2, no. 4 (2017): 388–401; Melissa Tully, Emily K. Vraga, and Leticia Bode, "Designing and Testing News Literacy Messages for Social Media," *Mass Communication and Society* 6, no. 1 (2020): 22–46.

24. Ashley et al., "News Media Literacy and Political Engagement"; Joseph Kahne, Nam-Jin Lee, and Jessica Feezell, "Digital Media Literacy Education and Online Civic and Political Participation," *International Journal of Communication* 6 (2012): 1–24; Tully and Vraga, "A Mixed-Methods Approach to Examining the Relationship Between News Media Literacy and Political Efficacy."

25. Kahne and Bowyer, "Educating for Democracy in a Partisan Age"; Tully and Vraga, "Effectiveness of a News Media Literacy Advertisement."

26. Emily K. Vraga, Melissa Tully, and Hernando Rojas, "Media Literacy Training Reduces Perception of Bias," *Newspaper Research Journal* 30, no. 4 (2009): 68–81; Tully and Vraga, "Effectiveness of a News Media Literacy Advertisement."

27. Tully et al., "Designing and Testing News Literacy Messages for Social Media."

28. Craft et al., "Elements of News Literacy"; Tully et al., "Understanding Critical News Consumption"; Vraga et al., "Media Literacy Training Reduces Perception of Bias"; Vraga et al., "Theorizing News Literacy."

29. Tully and Vraga, "A Mixed-Methods Approach to Examining the Relationship Between News Media Literacy and Political Efficacy"; Vraga and Tully, "Effective Messaging to Communicate News Media Literacy Concepts to Diverse Publics."

30. Paul Mihailidis and Benjamin Thevenin, "Media Literacy as a Core Competency for Engaged Citizenship in Participatory Democracy," *American Behavioral Scientists* 57, no. 11 (2013): 1611–1622.

31. https://namle.net/about/.

32. Clayton et al., "Real Solutions for Fake News?"

33. Melissa Tully, Emily K. Vraga, and Anne-Bennett Smithson, "News Media Literacy, Perceptions of Bias, and Interpretation of News," *Journalism* 21 no. 2 (2020): 209–226.

34. Alexander L. Curry and Natalie Jomini Stroud, "The Effects of Journalistic Transparency on Credibility Assessments and Engagement Intentions," *Journalism*. Online First. (2019). doi:10.1177/1464884919850387.

35. https://trustingnews.org/about-us/.

36. https://trustingnews.org/hownewsworks/news-literacy/.

37. Tully and Vraga, "A Mixed-Methods Approach to Examining the Relationship Between News Media Literacy and Political Efficacy"; Tully et al., "News Media Literacy, Perceptions of Bias."

38. Clayton et al., "Real Solutions for Fake News?"; Vraga and Tully, "Media Literacy Messages and Hostile Media Perceptions."

39. boyd, "Did Media Literacy Backfire?"; Clayton et al., "Real Solutions for Fake News?"

40. https://newslit.org/.

41. Tully et al., "News Media Literacy, Perceptions of Bias, and Interpretation of News."

7

News Consumers (and Non-Consumers)

A News Repertoire Approach to Understanding Audiences in a High-Choice Media Environment

Stephanie Edgerly

Introduction

The modern media environment is one of high choice. At any given moment there are a multitude of media options competing for the public's attention. If a person wants news, they can watch one of many 24-hour news channels, visit the homepages of many news organizations, or visit any number of social media and curation sites. While some of these options include news, many others include entertainment offerings. What impact does such an ample and diverse media environment have on journalism?

In this chapter, I discuss the underlying psychology of news consumption, including the obstacles and challenges that prevent news consumption and hinder news engagement, as well as the need to think of audiences in more specific ways. This understanding requires journalists to learn and develop a new skill set that marries news judgment with audience-based research. In other words, today's journalists need to know *who* consumes *what, how,* and *why*. Armed with this knowledge, journalists have the ability to tell important stories from a perspective that audiences care about and to create innovative distribution channels for their work. Such insight is necessary for combating the growing inequalities in how much people intentionally seek out news or incidentally consume it, or what researchers refer to as "news exposure."

For many people, the question is not just *if* they consume news, but rather *how* they consume news and *what* types of news they consume. As such, it is pertinent to no longer think of news audiences as a unitary, monolithic entity (*the* news audience), but rather to identify the different segments of news audiences that consume different types of news for different reasons. In

Stephanie Edgerly, *News Consumers (and Non-Consumers)* In: *Journalism Research That Matters.* Edited by: Valérie Bélair-Gagnon and Nikki Usher, Oxford University Press. © Oxford University Press 2021. DOI: 10.1093/oso/9780197538470.003.0008 short, increased media availability and choice allow people to consume news (and media generally) in more specifically tailored ways.

Research adopting a news repertoire approach seeks to identify different audience segments by the combination of news sources and genres they consume and avoid. The underlying logic is that the overall pattern of news that people choose to consume (or choose not to consume) is meaningful, particularly in a high-choice media environment.[1] Key to any study of news audiences and their repertoires is considering a wide range of opportunities for news exposure. This includes legacy news options as well as newer opportunities via digital native organizations, partisan media outlets, and even media that mix news and entertainment. The medium and devices that audiences use to consume news are also important. While it is impossible to account for all possible news options, I have generally used 20 to 30 news exposure items to uncover different news repertoires. This research provides researchers, the news industry, and the public with a more detailed picture of how different audience segments are engaging with different types of news, giving us a better grasp of how people consume news and information in a high-choice media environment.

Types of News Audiences: An Example From 2016

Taking a repertoire approach to news exposure provides a deeper insight into identifying audience types. In 2016, my co-authors and I identified five distinct audience segments among U.S. adults, based on their news repertoires.[2] The first segment, *"Digital News Mixers"* (16% of survey respondents), has individuals with a strong preference for getting news through Facebook, and also gravitate toward newer forms of news (e.g., online-only news sites, news satire) as well as the traditional (national newspapers, NPR). Digital News Mixers tend to be younger, from high socioeconomic backgrounds, identify as Democrats, and are politically interested.

The second segment, *"Network News Loyalists"* (24% of survey respondents), has the highest level of exposure to national network TV news and local TV news. They also consume above average levels of network morning TV news. These people are TV users. Network News Loyalists tend to be older, women, nonwhite, from low socioeconomic backgrounds, identify as Democrats, and are politically interested.

"Conservative News Loyalists" (6% of survey respondents) are the smallest and most narrow audience segment in terms of their news consumption.

Individuals with this repertoire have the highest levels of exposure to conservative talk radio and *Fox News*, and above average exposure to local TV news. Conservative News Loyalists tend to be older, men, identify as Republican, and are politically interested.

"*News Omnivores*" (9% of survey respondents), on the other hand, have the most diverse repertoire. They are above average in most of the news items and don't exhibit a clear preference, except in the variety of news they consume. For example, they consume both *Fox News* as well as *MSNBC*, local news (via TV and print) as well as news through Facebook. News Omnivores tend to be younger, men, nonwhite, and politically interested.

Lastly, "*News Avoiders*" (48% of survey respondents) make up the remaining audience segment. These people have very low consumption on all measured news items. When they do consume news, it is through local TV news and Facebook—though this is very infrequent. News Avoiders tend to be younger, white, from low socioeconomic backgrounds, Republican, and uninterested in politics.

Not all news audiences are the same. Different audience segments share distinct news consumption experiences, orienting their consumption practices around different formats, devices, and attributes. For example, several repertoires include the element of local television news; however, there are clear differences in what Network News Loyalists, Conservative News Loyalists, and News Omnivores pair with it. A mere measurement of only local news consumption would gloss over this important distinction.

"Audience insight" is a buzzword often tossed about by scholars and journalists, typically assessed by audience metrics that can include measuring who visits news websites, listens to news podcasts, or watches television news. Ironically, this approach to audience insight offers only limited insight. Meaningful assessments of audience insight help us understand what other types of news (and entertainment) content audiences are also consuming. Armed with this knowledge, we can then start identifying deeper insights about audience news consumption patterns. Why do Network News Loyalists, Conservative News Loyalists, and News Omnivores watch local television news? Is it out of habit? Is it a deliberate decision to take a break from the negativity of national news? To get practical information about weather and commute? Given what we know about the differences in who these people are and what they pair local news with, the answers likely differ among Network News Loyalists, Conservative News Loyalists, and News Omnivores. Moreover, the above example of audience segmentation is based on a national sample of U.S. adults; a similar segmentation can be done within certain populations of interest, such as specific age cohorts, geographic regions, or by focusing on certain genres of news.

Not only does the high-choice media environment result in a fracturing of the news audience, but it also produces a widening gap in the overall news consumption. People who want news have a variety of options to choose from (as seen by the difference between Digital News Mixers, Network News Loyalists, Conservative News Loyalists, and News Omnivores). Conversely, those who don't want to consume news can more easily avoid it (as seen by the large proportion of individuals that are considered News Avoiders). News repertoires tell us about more than just patterns of news consumption; they also point to different effects on public engagement and civic participation among different audience segments. People who are regular consumers of news—no matter the type or repertoire—engage in civic and political participation at a higher level compared to people who do not regularly consume news.[3] My research finds that News Avoiders exhibit the lowest levels of participation across a variety of election and community-based activities.[4] Their voices, their concerns, and their help are largely absent in these spaces of discussion and decision making. In case you are wondering, News Omnivores participate at the highest levels.

A second and perhaps most obvious effect of the widening gap in overall news consumption is the shrinking audience for news and the negative implications for news organizations. It is problematic if the number of News Avoiders is increasing. At the most fundamental level, news organizations need news audiences (news audiences also need news organizations). In a media environment where people are more in control of their media choices and can select media that best fulfill their preferences and tastes, news avoidance is a viable option for those that see little reason for consuming news.[5] I don't think it is too controversial to say that the news industry cannot afford the proportion of News Avoiders to significantly grow. A preferable outcome would be to convert News Avoiders into more regular consumers of news. As such, audience insight needs to include both understanding why people consume news *and* why people do not consume news.

Learning the Habit of News Exposure: It Starts Early

One way of understanding why some people consume news, while others do not, is through a socialization lens. Much research and journalism-related interventions are directed at adults, and yet many people develop their habits of news consumption (or lack thereof) well before adulthood. The period of adolescence, roughly defined as the time from 12 years of age to 17, is an important time of socialization when we learn and develop the attitudes, values, and behaviors that we carry into adulthood.[6] In other words, the seeds of news exposure (or avoidance) are sown during many people's formative teenage years.[7] As evidence of this, my co-authors and I studied news repertoires among U.S. youth (12 to 17 years of age) and found many of the same patterns discussed above already at work.[8] Even among teenagers there is a segment of News Avoiders (52% of youth survey respondents) who habitually consume lower levels of news (and also participate in civic and political activities at lower rates). We identified three different news exposure repertoires among youth: (1) News Omnivores (14%), (2) Traditional-news-only (19%), and (3) Curated-news-only (15%). Similar to adults, youth News Omnivores participate at a higher level compared to their peers. As such, the widening gap of overall news consumption (and its participatory implications) starts early; this pattern is *already* at play among youth. What, then, do we know about how youth develop the habit of news exposure in the first place?

Research points to three key "socialization agents" that have the power to shape the development of news patterns: parents, schools, and peers.[9] First, parents are a powerful force in modeling news behavior for their children. When parents consume news, this sends a powerful signal to youth that consuming news is something that they should also be doing. It signals the value and importance of developing a habit of regular news consumption. In a study exploring youth news consumption across a variety of devices, my co-authors and I found that parents' news repertoires were the strongest predictor of whether their children consumed news.[10] Specifically, we found evidence of device-specific modeling, such that the strongest predictor of youth consuming news via the television (or computer, or smartphone, or tablet) was a parent who also consumed news on that device. Even in an age where media consumption has become more individualized, parents' own news use is a powerful predictor of youth developing the habit of news consumption. It is worth noting that there is also evidence of parental modeling of news behavior even at the genre-specific level. I found the strongest predictor of youth consuming news satire (e.g., *The Daily Show*, *Last Week Tonight*) was a parent who similarly consumed news satire. This result stands even when accounting for other types of parental news exposure.[11]

While parents play an important role in socializing their children into news use, it does little to ameliorate the widening gap between those who consume news and those who do not. If anything, the role of parents is a factor contributing to this issue. There is, however, evidence that schools and peer groups also play a role in youth developing the habit of news consumption, above and beyond the strong role that parents play.[12] Peers groups who discuss current events result in increased youth news consumption, particularly via mobile devices. Additionally, schools are an important socialization agent for developing the habit of news consumption, especially when teenagers do not have this behavior modeled at home. My research consistently finds a news-based school curriculum (e.g., learning what makes good reporting, following a news topic for a class assignment, etc.) results in higher levels of youth news consumption across all devices (e.g., television, computer, phone, tablet).[13] As such, one avenue for converting News Avoiders into one of the news-related audience repertoire segments is to fund a news-based school curriculum.

These research findings raise the question of how these socialization agents—parental modeling, peer groups, school curriculums—encourage news consumption. One explanation is that they work to reduce the cognitive cost of consumption and/or increase the value of news consumption. Parental modeling provides an example of how youth should use their devices, and specifically, what sources (or genres) they can turn to. In a high-choice media age, an abundance of news options can lead to some youth not knowing which options to turn to.[14] By observing how a parent integrates news into his or her media routines, teenagers can start building similar types of routines. School curriculums that teach students how to navigate the new media environment can also reduce these costs. Additionally, news consumption takes on increased value when it relates to one's needs and interests.[15] Belonging to a peer group that regularly discusses current events places an increased value on consuming news content. The same is true for school assignments that require students to follow specific news topics or events. Similarly, the strong role that political interest plays in predicting a variety of adult news repertoires points to the increased value that news exposure has among those who are interested in politics, and the lack of value it has among those who are uninterested in politics.

Adopting a socialization lens provides a framework for understanding how the habit of news consumption is learned at an early age. One answer for why some individuals do not consume news is that they were never socialized—either by their parents, school, or peers—into the long-term practice of news exposure. Support and interventions directed at school curriculum, in particular, can be effective in securing the news audiences of the future. Audience insight, however, does not stop here. Efforts to reduce the gaps in the overall news consumption can also be informed by a closer look at how adults access the cost and value of news consumption, and what steps news organizations can take.

Audience Understanding of Journalism: Some Data

If news organizations want to get serious about news avoidance, they need to better understand which audience segments excel in the high-choice media environment and which audience segments struggle. They need to understand where there is an opportunity to better serve certain audience segments. One challenge in converting news avoiders into more regular consumers of news is that many people do not understand how news is produced. The professional norms and processes of journalism have largely been kept out of the view of audiences. The remaining section of this chapter is based on data from an online survey administered to 1,000 U.S. adults, in April of 2019, exploring perceptions of local and national news. The commercial sampling company, Dynata, was used to obtain a sample of U.S. adults that mirrors the population along major demographic categories. Data from the survey is used to explore which audiences perceive news in a more negative light and how this can inform what steps are taken by news organizations.

Survey participants were asked, "How often do you think reporters get paid by the sources in their stories?" Overall, 40% said reporters are paid "fairly often" or "very often." Moving beyond this overall distribution, a regression model was constructed predicting perceptions of increased frequency. Included in the regression model were the basic socio-demographic measures of age, gender, race, education, and political ideology. Who thinks that journalists are paid by their sources? Respondents with low levels of education and conservatives are more likely to think that reporters frequently pay their sources (see Table 7.1).

Survey respondents also indicated their level of agreement on six survey items (3 about local news, 3 about national news). A measure of *local news value* includes the average of two items ("Issues I care about are covered in my local news," "My local news covers topics that impact my life"; $m = 3.52$,

$sd = .88$, *Pearson's* $r = .62$). A measure of *national news value* includes the same two items for national news ($m = 3.4$, $sd = .95$, *Pearson's* $r = .62$). And lastly, the average of two items is used to measure general *news fatigue* ("I am worn out by the amount of local news there is these days," "I am worn out by the amount of national news there is these days;" $m = 2.83$, $sd = .85$, *Pearson's* $r = .49$). It should be noted that all three measures have a significant relationship with frequency of news exposure, such that more frequent consumers of news report *higher* levels of local news value, *higher* levels of national news value, and *lower* levels of news fatigue.

A closer look at how these audience attitudes relate to audience characteristics can provide additional insight as to why some people consume news, while other people do not. Separate regression models were constructed predicting each of the three attitude measures.

As indicated in Table 7.1, results from the model predicting local news value indicate that older respondents, women, and those with high levels of education correspond to higher levels of local news value. Or, to state the inverse, it is younger respondents, men, and those with lower levels of education who report lower levels of local news value.

The regression model for national news value produces a slightly different pattern of results. Higher national news value is similarly related to increased age, higher levels of education, and also identifying as a liberal. Or, to state the inverse, younger respondents, those with low levels of education, and those identifying as a conservative report lower levels of national news value.

Table 7.1 Regression model predicting audience attitudes about news

	Reporters are paid by their sources St. beta	Local news value St. beta	National news value St. beta	News fatigue St. beta
Age	−.051	.108**	.09**	−.164***
Sex (women)	−.001	.086*	.057#	.034
Race (white)	−.048	−.054	−.053	.029
Education	−.098**	.085*	.114***	−.2
Political ideology (conservative)	.194***	−.054	−.234***	.126***

$\# p \leq .1. * p \leq .05. ** p \leq .01. *** p \leq .001.$

Only two items in the model predicting news fatigue are significant—age and political ideology. Older respondents were *less* likely to say they were fatigued by news, while conservatives were *more* likely.

These findings provide a snapshot of the deep detachment among some groups of people regarding the low value of news. Is this cause for concern? My answer is yes. Especially when considering that these factors work to keep news exposure low, and this in turn corresponds with lower levels of civic and political participation. Perhaps even more worrisome is that certain groups—namely younger adults, those with lower levels of education, and Republicans—feel greater disconnect with news. These divides, if not addressed, will likely grow stronger and have serious implications on the state of news organization (and democracy) at local and national levels.

Turning Insight into Action: Asking BIG Questions

The above data analysis suggests some starting points for innovation both in terms of what needs innovating and among which audience segments. For example, the finding that 40% of survey respondents think that reporters are paid by the sources in their stories suggests that the public is largely unaware about the professional norms of journalism.[16] Calls for "radical transparency" in the news gathering and production process can be one way of doing this.[17] But these efforts need to also have specific audiences in mind—particularly younger audiences and those with lower levels of education. How can journalists and news organizations better communicate their professional values and rules to the public? One answer may rest in the compelling findings coming out of the Center for Media Engagement, which found that including an "explain your process" box alongside a news story resulted in more favorable evaluations.[18] However, the challenge remains in how to reach audiences that are unlikely to encounter the news story in the first place.

Another consideration is how to increase the value of news. Value is a powerful and complex concept (far more complex than the two-item measurements presented above). One reason for this complexity is that value is an audience-based concept, it lies in the eye of the beholder. How audiences determine whether news has importance, utility, or merit in their everyday life is key to growing its value. Findings from the data analysis suggest that certain audiences—namely older people from high-education backgrounds—are more likely to agree that news (local and national) covers topics they care about and that impact their lives. What can be done to increase news value among younger and low-educated audiences? Past academic research suggests that media has more value when it satisfies current needs, appeals to social and personal identities, or serves as a means of social connection.[19] As such, there is a need to better understand which topics are important to these audience segments and why, and the ways in which news exposure may conflict with their identities and daily routines.

Lastly, news consumption in today's media environment can carry a high cognitive cost. There is a constant churn of news content, coming from a wide range of sources and of varying quality. Navigating such a news media environment can be overwhelming, especially if one lacks the necessary skills. Strategies to reduce some of the cognitive cost of news consumption is another way to bridge the widening gap in overall levels of news consumption. That being said, proposed strategies should not be confused with simplifying an event/issue or turning a story into an easy-to-read listicle. These do little to reduce the fundamental costs that stand in the way of news exposure. Findings from the data analysis indicate that feeling "worn out" by the amount of local and national news is more common among young people and conservatives. Given this, what can be done to simplify the news exposure experience and stave off fatigue? What skills help audiences in not becoming "worn out" by news?

These are by no means simple questions to address. Efforts to convert low news consumers into more regular consumers of news will be no easy task. Learning how to tell important stories in a way that resonates with young adults, for example, will take work. But for these efforts to have any chance of succeeding, they need to be guided by audience insight. The data presented in this chapter is merely a starting point for where more attention, research, and creative energy needs to be devoted. For example, audience insight requires different methodological approaches. There is only so much survey data or website metrics that can tell you about the psychology of audience behavior. Qualitative research in which audiences are able to describe in their own words their relationship (or lack thereof) with news can provide critical insight to many of the questions asked.

Also critical is buy-in among stakeholders who are committed to addressing the growing inequality of news exposure. Convincing news organizations to target people who have not developed the habit of news consumption, and see little value and high cost in the activity, can be a hard sell.

For many journalism organizations, building new products and experiences for the already engaged seems like a more attractive business model. However, there is a real opportunity to apply the skills of audience insight to address the low value, high cost, and misconceptions about journalism among certain groups. Doing so will take partnerships across school curriculum, academic research, technology development, community organizations, and the news industry. These partnerships should not target adults only, but need to also focus on children and teenagers and the processes in which they are socialized into (or away from) news. Asking big questions is the first step. Building partnerships and solutions is the next.

Notes

1. Uwe Hasebrink and Hanna Domeyer, "Media Repertoires as Patterns of Behavior and as Meaningful Practices: A Multimethod Approach to Media Use in Converging Media Environments," *Journal of Audience & Receptions Studies* 9, no. 2 (2012): 757–779; Kim Christian Schrøder, "News Media Old and New," *Journalism Studies* 16, no. 1 (2015): 60–78.
2. Stephanie Edgerly, Esther Thorson, and Weiyue Cynthia Chen, "News Use Repertoires and News Attitudes during the 2016 Presidential Election" (conference paper, The Future of Journalism, Cardiff, UK, September 14–15, 2017).
3. Thomas B. Ksiazek, Edward C. Malthouse, and James G. Webster, "News-Seekers and Avoiders: Exploring Patterns of Total News Consumption across Media and the Relationship to Civic Participation," *Journal of Broadcasting & Electronic Media* 54, no. 4 (2010): 551–568; Markus Prior, *Post-Broadcast Democracy: How Media Choice Increases Inequality in Political Involvement and Polarizes Elections* (New York: Cambridge University Press, 2007).
4. Stephanie Edgerly, "Red Media, Blue Media, and Purple Media: News Repertoires in the Colorful Media Landscape," *Journal of Broadcasting & Electronic Media* 59, no. 1 (2015): 1–21.
5. Prior, "*Post-Broadcast Democracy*."
6. Judith Torney-Purta and Jo-Ann Amadeo, "Participatory Niches for Emergent Citizenship in Early Adolescence: An International Perspective," *The Annals of the American Academy of Political and Social Science* 633, no. 1 (2011): 180–200.
7. David T. Z. Mindich, *Tuned Out: Why Americans under 40 Don't Follow the News* (Oxford: Oxford University Press, 2005).
8. Stephanie Edgerly, Emily K. Vraga, Leticia Bode, Kjerstin Thorson, and Esther Thorson, "New Media, New Relationship to Participation? A Closer Look at Youth News Repertoiris and Political Participation," *Journalism & Mass Communication Quarterly* 95, no. 1 (2018): 192–212.

9. Nam-Jin Lee, Dhavan V. Shah, and Jack M. McLeod, "Processes of Political Socialization: A Communication Mediation Approach to Youth Civic Engagement," *Communication Research* 40, no. 5 (2013): 669–697.

10. Stephanie Edgerly, Kjerstin Thorson, Esther Thorson, Emily K. Vraga, and Leticia Bode, "Do Parents Still Model News Consumption? Socializing News Use among Adolescents in a Multi-Device World," *New Media & Society* 20, no. 4 (2018): 1263–1281.

11. Stephanie Edgerly, "A New Generation of Satire Consumers? A Socialization Approach to Youth Exposure to News Satire," in *Political Humor in a Changing Media Landscape: A New Generation of Research,* eds. Jodi C. Baumgartner and Amy B. Becker (New York: Lexington Books, 2018), 253–272.

12. Edgerly, Thorson, Thorson, Vraga, and Bode, "Do Parents Still Model News Consumption?"

13. Edgerly et al., "Do Parents Still Model News Consumption?"; Edgerly, "A New Generation of Satire Consumers?"

14. Mary Madden, Amanda Lenhart, and Claire Fontaine, "How Youth Navigate the News Landscape," *Data & Society* (2017): accessed July 6, 2019, https://datasociety.net/output/how-youth-navigate-the-news-landscape/.

15. Alan M. Rubin, "The Uses-and-Gratifications Perspective on Media Effects," in *Media Effects: Advances in Theory and Research*, eds. Jennings Bryant and Mary Beth Oliver (New York: Routledge, 2009), 165–184.

16. Editor's note: Journalists working for reputable, trusted news organizations do not pay their sources for information, while Hollywood tabloids or the National Enquirer might, although practices may be different outside of the Anglo-American context).

17. Joy Mayer, "Knight Commission Report Calls for 'Radical Transparency' in Journalism. Trusting News Can Help," last modified February 5, 2019, https://medium.com/trusting-news/knight-commission-report-calls-for-radical-transparency-in-journalism-trusting-news-can-help-95e3a7bd044f.

18. Gina M. Masullo, Alex Curry, and Kelsey Whipple, "Building Trust: What Works for News Organizations," accessed April 2, 2020, https://mediaengagement.org/research/building-trust.

19. Rubin, "The Uses-and-Gratifications Perspective on Media Effects."

8

Understanding Collaborative Journalism with Digital Trace Data and Crowdsourced Databases

Yee Man Margaret Ng

Introduction

News organizations have been increasingly collaborating with other, sometimes rival, newsrooms on reporting projects. The Pew Research Center declared the growth in journalism partnerships as a "recurring theme" and "a new era of interest."[1] Indeed, there are many webinars and conferences, such as the Collaborative Journalism Summit, to discuss how to make newsroom collaborations successful. Among all those present-day newsroom collaborations, perhaps the most well-known collaboration is the Pulitzer Prize-winning Panama Papers investigation in 2016, which revealed a vast collection of documents that explored a worldwide system of tax evasion and corruption. This global project was coordinated by the International Consortium for Investigative Journalism (ICIJ), involved nearly 100 international partners, and comprised more than 380 journalists working on six continents.[2] The investigation eventually prompted inquiries and audits in nearly half the countries that were the subject of reporting and has successfully driven new legislation and financial regulations in the United States and abroad.

Collaborative journalism is not just an adaptation to shrinking budgets. It also holds the promise of offering a more diverse mix of content, broader reach, and more in-depth investigations. Legacy media outlets are looking more than ever for ways to augment what they can produce with a depleted staff, and news startups are eager to get their work in front of a wider audience and figure out roads to sustainability. Particularly, pooling resources and sharing information is a powerful way to investigate and expose stories that

Yee Man Margaret Ng, *Understanding Collaborative Journalism with Digital Trace Data and Crowdsourced Databases*
In: *Journalism Research That Matters.* Edited by: Valérie Bélair-Gagnon and Nikki Usher, Oxford University Press.
© Oxford University Press 2021. DOI: 10.1093/oso/9780197538470.003.0009

politicians, corporations, and organized criminals are determined to keep in the shadows. What these collaborations mean for the public—at least in theory—is more transparent and accurate news coverage. Communication researcher Nikos Smyrnaios and his colleagues found that journalists who take part in collaborative projects feel more accountable and seldom have to issue corrections to amend stories' errors.[3] In addition to that, audiences trust collaborative news work more because those reports appear to be more independent.[3] In the era of "fake news" and declining public trust in media, collaborative work that seeks to serve the public becomes vital to preserving both public trust and editorial quality.

Academic studies and reports can serve as a guide for journalists when they start a collaborative project. However, most of these existing studies are focused on theoretical perspectives.[4] Existing studies also largely rely on qualitative methods that use case studies,[5] interviews, content analyses,[6] and ethnography[7] to investigate a fraction of the collaborative practices occurring in journalism. Empirical studies of real-world scale that examine collaborative trends and patterns within the journalism community are scarce. Thus, there is a need for more quantitative research to describe a broader picture of how collaborative journalism is performing, specifically answering questions such as how the various sizes, types, or sources of funding could shape the dynamic of modern-day newsroom collaborations.

Collaborative journalism deserves further inquiry in light of its growing importance, the resources devoted to it, and its role in creating more opportunities for news media in the face of economic and technological challenges. In the following sections, I first summarize what is generally meant by collaborative journalism and its history in the field. Second, I conceptualize collaborative practice and its current themes in the field of journalism. Changes in technology—specifically the transition from the analog age to the digital age—allow researchers to collect and analyze social data in new ways. Third, I identify two digital datasets—GitHub digital traces and crowdsourced databases—and illustrate their potential to quantify collaborative trends, thus to enhance the understanding of the breadth and depth of collaborations within and outside the United States. Lastly, I discuss the strengths and weaknesses of these approaches. Along with the discussion, I will address some preliminary results, but the main purpose of this chapter is to argue for a new research direction. Digital media provides new tools for journalists to work with, which in turn leads to new tools for academics to keep up with these innovations. The changing news landscape (and its practices) demands that researchers identify new data sources and employ new research methods to study and map journalistic flows. In the pursuit of filling this methodological gap, this work aims to show several new approaches that can better study the patterns and dynamics of collaborative action.

Collaborative Journalism Culture(s)

Collaborative journalism is commonly known as "a cooperative arrangement between two or more news and information organizations, which aims to supplement each organization's resource and maximize the impact of the content produced."[8] In contrast, other research has used the term *networked journalism*[9] and *news sharing*[10] to describe the partnerships among competing news organizations. The term *convergence* explains the need for collaborative practice "to meet a variety of technological, editorial, regulatory, and market-based opportunities and challenges."[11] I use the term *collaborative journalism* as a generic concept that broadly defines the practice of executing journalistic endeavors using a cross-entity approach.[12]

Collaboration is not a new practice in the news industry. The history of journalism includes varied forms of newsroom cooperation in daily production routines. One landmark example is the establishment of the Associated Press, the first wire service, by six major New York dailies in 1846 to share costs and resources to cover the Mexican-American War. Collaboration is not just preferable during the time of recession. Even during the time of profitability in the late 20th century, it was common for journalists on the same beat to collaborate by sharing notes and swapping tips.[9] However, working together across company lines has gone from an option to a critical component of any reporting effort in the last decade. The previously stable business model of "legacy media"—a mix of subscription, sales, and advertising—has been threatened by the dominance of Google (which also owns YouTube) and Facebook in the advertising market; the emergence of social media has immensely shifted media consumption habits of audiences. With the perfect storm of economic recession, technological transformation, and cultural change, journalists increasingly seek new funding and partnerships. "Byebye lone wolf" has become the motto, as journalism steps into the networked society and collaborations become regular work practices.[13]

Successful collaborations range in size, structure, and complexity. There are local and regional collaborations; for example, in 2019, a group of independent newsrooms pooled their resources to engage Chicago voters by creating a voting guide, Chi.vote.[14] There are collaborations that are cross-border and international. One example is the ProPublica-led Zero Tolerance (2019), which brings together ten newsrooms in four countries to cover how Trump's immigration policy impacts different countries.[15] There are collaborations on specific, time-bound projects that end with co-ordinated publication of major stories, such as the Panama Papers (2016). Other collaborations that enable newsrooms to share and to distribute each other's content aim to go on indefinitely. One example is The Local News Partnerships, an effort to leverage the reach and resources of the BBC to shore up the local press and fortify its role in democracy in the United Kingdom, which features more than 800 news outlets.[16]

Donors, both members of the public and foundations, seem to have an increased interest in funding these collaborative journalistic projects and assisting in coalition-building across newsrooms. These donors are international in scope and have different institutional backgrounds. In Europe, the Investigative Journalism for Europe (#IJ4EU) fund, backed by a European Commission grant, only supports journalistic investigations that involve journalists from at least two countries.[17] The Local Media Project, supported by the Knight Foundation, focuses on journalism-oriented collaboration that aims to strengthen local media ecosystems over the long term.[18] JournalismGrants, a media-funding project supported by the Bill & Melinda Gates Foundation, encourages applicants to "seek engagement and collaboration with local reporters on the ground." [19] The need for collaboration may have become a key component to secure funding. However, even as interest in collaboration grows, there are also a huge number of collaborations that do not end up seeing the light of day. French data journalist Nicolas Kayser-Bril openly discussed two of the unsuccessful collaborative projects he coordinated: the Belarus Networks (2014) failed because of a lack of involvement from a key partner; the project of Turkish Puppets (2016) failed because the publication partners showed disagreement in reporting direction.[20] Journalist turnover or intense news cycles are some other obvious challenges to making collaborations sustainable.[21] However, many journalists do not know how to begin nor run a productive partnership. Specifically, journalists have questions about what structural factors are likely to incubate a successful collaboration.

Scholarship has tended to focus on conceptualizing collaborative journalism rather than assessing it in practice or providing suggestions for innovation in these partnerships. For example, Heinrich refers to collaborative journalism as a new paradigm of a globalized news sphere that significantly differentiates from legacy journalism.[22] While the traditional journalistic sphere emphasized operational closure—the act of drawing clear boundaries between the professionals and the amateurs by upholding the former's journalistic expertise[23]—this has become increasingly difficult to sustain in the digital age and networked society.[24] Collaborative journalism, particularly in the field of data journalism—where actors with diverse backgrounds work closely together to collect, filter, share, and sift through documents and databases—is a valuable approach to gauge how journalists or news organizations work together to achieve a clear goal.[25] Such collaboration that transcends traditional and established boundaries not only occurs more often, but it is also increasingly accepted as a common form of reporting.

Researcher Carlos Martínez de la Serna tracked the development and identified three current themes in journalism collaborations:[26]

1) *Collaboration as a field repair,* a solution to the decline and erosion of journalism conditions
2) *Shared resources for journalism,* building on shared resources—public databases, open-source technology, networked communities—to fulfill journalism's core mission
3) *The expanding role of journalism schools, nonprofit organizations, and other players,* a surge in initiatives led by journalism schools and established nonprofit organizations.

In other words, the study regards collaborative journalism as a field solution that embraces a sharing economy and alternative players.

However, several questions remain open about the current state of collaborative journalism. Examining if certain types of collaborative journalism initiatives were more likely to get funded over the past decade—whether there were biases toward the types of subjects covered, organizations supported, and regions prioritized—could potentially reveal how these foundation–journalist relationships shape journalism.[27] Similarly, there are questions about the dynamics that facilitate successful collaboration. Collaboration is not a chaos-free process in which everyone has equal power and influence. Indeed, more generally, the notions of shared leadership and the softening of professional silos that underpin interprofessional teamwork could easily cause tension between collaborators.[28] Scholarship on collaboration finds that too much collaboration can mean no one takes responsibility for decisions and, as a result, there was limited accountability. Decision making can involve grueling rounds of discussions that inevitably turn contentious and unprofessional. While we may imagine that when high-powered news organizations get together to collaborate, they will reach consensus, there is also a possibility that the fact they are powerful can make it harder for them to collaborate. Therefore, understanding how structural factors, such as the size and type of a newsroom (plus other factors), shape the power dynamic of collaborations is necessary to evaluate and foster quality collaborations between various types of news organizations.

New Approach 1: Digital Trace Data in GitHub

Now that we have briefly discussed examples of collaborative journalism, what researchers have learned, and questions that can be asked, I want to elaborate how new digital research methods can push the research paradigm forward. Traditionally, social researchers have used surveys or qualitative research techniques such as focus groups, in-depth interviews, and observations to study cultural footprint (e.g., social behavior and psychological characteristics). However, given the growing amount of data generated by digital technologies, researchers have started to collect and analyze digital traces of human behavior. Digital trace data are records of activity undertaken through an online information system.[29] They can be unstructured information from emails, posts from online social media platforms, and activity logs of sensor data from mobile phones. Trace data offer strengths that qualitative methods do not: the data are geographically far-reaching, generated continuously, and also provide unique, unsolicited insight into human behavior and social processes.

In recent years, researchers have leveraged trace data as a tool to examine how people coordinate their large-scale collaboration efforts in open-source projects, such as Wikipedia.[30] Theoretically speaking, open-source is an aspiration toward open programming, grounded on the philosophical beliefs in social responsibility through freedom and openness.[31] In other words, the altruistic and collaborative spirit inherent in this open-source community is the willingness to share information, code, and tools.

Lewis and Usher have further developed four normative values for open-source culture in journalism[5]: transparency, participation, tinkering, and iteration. These arise from a broader understanding of openness in terms of sharing collected data, being transparent about their production, and being actively interactive with various actors such as journalists, hackers, and whistleblowers.[32]

GitHub, the largest online repository system in the world, has become a major digital space for open-source, collaborative journalism. It provides technological infrastructure that makes the logistics of creating, editing, and distributing collaborative content easy and feasible. Newsrooms are increasingly using GitHub to host their data and tools in the hopes of improving productivity and encouraging social collaborations. For example, St. Louis Public Radio released the code of "One Year in Ferguson," an immersive story that tells the story of Ferguson in both audio and visuals, on GitHub in 2016. The code was forked—or cloned—and then adapted as the foundation of the National Public Radio's story, "Life After Death." Quartz created a tool called Chartbuilder that allows anyone to make an exportable chart after uploading data in 2012. Several different newsrooms now use this chart tool (e.g., *The Wall Street Journal*, National Public Radio, etc.), some of which have customized their code. As such, on GitHub, newsrooms without dedicated developers can use open-sourcing tools built from other newsrooms for their reporting, whereas newsrooms with developers can extend collaboration-enabling tools that provide technological solutions for news work.

GitHub is also a social platform that offers researchers plenty of digital trace data to study collaboration networks. GitHub users can create profiles, follow other users, comment, fork (i.e., create a personal copy), watch (i.e., receive detailed notifications about events occurring within a repository), and star (i.e., add a repository to their favorites lists). GitHub records each user action as an event, and events are continuously generated as time elapses. These events allow modeling of the interactions between GitHub users who follow one another and share similar interests. In fact, there are a growing number of studies in the field of computer science examining the use of GitHub and its implications for social collaboration. For example, McDonald and Goggins found that collaborations on GitHub are not limited to people within the same organization but extended to people from other organizations and all over the world.[33] Further, Dabbish and colleagues explored the value of GitHub and found that the transparency in collaboration brought on by such mechanisms helps support innovation, knowledge sharing, and community building.[34] As users accumulate and collaboration compounds, GitHub continues to serve as a social platform to access a vast body of easily accessible, shared knowledge.[35]

For some, open source is a cultural movement with disputed ideologies, aims, and objectives. In Weber's book, *The Success of Open Source*, the phenomenon of free and open-source software is described as "the first and certainly one of the most prominent indigenous political statements of the digital world."[36] At its core, GitHub emphasizes community efforts and creates social affordances. The platform provides everyone access and promotes collaboration to help build something greater than what one could create alone. However, traditional concepts of divisions of labor do not apply to open-source development, and there is "no top-down allocation" of work within an ideal open-source project.[37] Many studies have found that there are relatively few people who contribute a lot, and most people contribute only one or two items.[38]

But who are the active contributors and followers in a journalism repository? What background do the active contributors have, and what does each person bring to the table? In general, what factors determine the success of those social collaborations? For example, Table 8.1 shows the top ten most popular journalism repositories in GitHub among 11,270 repositories among 190 news organizations in April 2019. At a glance, we notice that all popular repositories were created by national and international newsrooms that have invested heavily in teams to develop data-driven visual news applications. Further examination of forking, watching, starring, and committing actions for these repositories might reveal whether smaller newsrooms or non-journalists play a role in the development of open-source news tools. From a theoretical standpoint, these are research questions centering on activity within repositories. These questions explore how power dynamics affect the strategic choices made by each actor and institution—whether and with whom to collaborate, and to what level—across the GitHub ecosystem. These decisions directly influenced the outcomes of open-source participation.

New Approach 2: Crowdsourced Databases

Other valuable resources to study journalism collaboration include crowdsourced data. This crowdsourced data, based on collective reporting efforts by independent organizations, enables scholars and journalists to

Table 8.1 Top 10 GitHub journalism repositories (ranked by stars). April 2019

Rank	Newsroom	Repo Name	Description	Created at	Stars	Watchers	Forkers	Contributors
							Number of	
1	ftlabs	fastclick	Polyfill to remove click delays on browsers with touch UIs	2012-02-13	17343	542	2916	47
2	fivethirtyeight	data	Data and code behind the articles and graphics at FiveThirtyEight	2014-03-17	11957	1365	5596	37
3	newsapps	beeswithmachineguns	A utility for arming (creating) many bees (micro EC2 instances) to attack (load test) targets (web applications)	2010-06-29	5506	229	581	33
4	nytimes	objective-c-style-guide	The Objective-C Style Guide used by The New York Times	2013-07-31	5435	392	1202	45
5	guardian	frontend	The Guardian Dot Com	2012-05-18	5277	232	533	169
6	BBC-News	wraith	Responsive screenshot comparison tool	2013-01-23	4498	164	325	63
7	BBC-News	Imager.js	Responsive images while we wait for srcset to finish cooking	2013-08-07	3878	189	232	19
8	Financial-Times	polyfill-service	Automatic polyfill service	2014-06-26	3760	128	388	159
9	guardian	scribe	DEPRECATED: A rich text editor framework for the web platform	2013-11-11	3644	155	259	50
10	Quartz	bad-data-guide	An exhaustive reference to problems seen in real-world data along with suggestions on how to resolve them	2015-11-13	3537	216	299	19

consider field-wide questions and spot trends rather than just draw insights from successful (or unsuccessful) case studies. Two datasets that offer this potential include the crowdsourced dataset gathered by the Center for Cooperative Media (based at Montclair State University in New Jersey) that tracks collaborative journalism projects and the Foundation Maps for Media Funding, created by the Media Impact Funders and Foundation Center.

Launched in early 2018, the Center for Cooperative Media has been collecting, organizing, and standardizing information about collaborative journalism projects. The database is a collective effort aiming to serve as a central repository on collaborative journalism. As of July 2019, the Collaborative Journalism Database has recorded information of over 200 journalism collaborations, encompassing more than 1,500 newsrooms across nearly 100 countries. The database includes features such as when the partnership started, who was involved, funding sources, the tools that newsrooms used, whether the collaboration had a formal arrangement in place or someone in charge of the efforts, and some success metrics. Notably, the database assigns each collaboration into one of the six collaboration models, ranging from temporary partnerships in which organizations coordinate but work separately, to ongoing partnerships in which multiple organizations share resources.[10]

In an increasingly globalized world where stories jump borders, cross-border collaboration is a natural next step. When cross-border journalism started to gather momentum during the first decade of this century, journalism scholars were initially slow to pay attention.[13] However, when the first large-scale cross-border collaborative investigations began being published—such as the WikiLeaks' cables (2010), Offshore Leaks (2012), LuxLeaks (2014), Football Leaks (2016), Panama Papers (2016), and Paradise Papers (2017)—researchers started to analyze this growing phenomenon. For example, Grzeszyk's cultural study on cross-pollination reveals that cross-border journalism helps journalists within a given team to overcome their individual and national bias.[39] Other studies found that there was a wide adoption of technological infrastructure for collaboration since the mid-2000s from Google Docs (launched in 2006) to Slack (available since 2013), and the number of projects following formal versus informal agreements was similar.[18] However, there was not enough collaborative infrastructure, data security, or trust for true cross-border collaboration.[40]

The Collaborative Journalism Database could serve as a valuable data source for analyzing the trends and nature of *cross-border* and *cross-media* journalism collaborations. Using the database, researchers can further examine what kinds of projects were more likely to draw cross-border collaborations. They can see what tools were prevalent in cross-border collaborations, how often a non-traditional organization led an initiative, and to what extent the *size* of a newsroom affected the type of partnership (integrated or separate collaborations). A preliminary analysis by Stonbely found that these initiatives vary in their level of integration, commitment, and duration. However, they all seek to "produce content that is greater than what any individual journalist, newsroom, or organization could produce on its own."[10] Research on this line cultivates a better understanding of cross-border collaborative journalism.

Another crowdsourced database that helps study collaborations is the Foundation Maps for Media Funding. Foundations have played a critical role in funding, promoting, and sustaining these efforts and the overall diffusion of collaborative practices. For example, in 2014, the Knight Foundation funded eight pilot collaborations between news outlets and community contributors.[1] As national and global collaborative reporting projects receive millions of dollars, the Media Impact Funders and Foundation Center launched an interactive mapping and research tool that has revealed the full scope of philanthropically funded media projects worldwide since 2009. The Center regularly updates the map with information about funding trends, funder networks, types of grant-making, populations served, and much more, to promote transparency. Grant descriptions usually indicate projects with collaborative efforts.

Donors, both in the United States and across the globe, are putting increased pressure on grantees to produce impact metrics: to take on the mammoth task of proving that journalism is enhancing our world in some tangible, quantifiable way. As such, the database is a promising resource to explore relationships between funders, grantees, grants, and types of journalistic collaborations. This exploration answers questions like how relationships between foundations and journalists shape journalism, which are rarely held accountable by any democratic body.

Future Directions

Some stories are too big, too complex, and too global for one lone-wolf news organization to tackle. Collaboration is considered one of the most powerful adaptive strategies for journalism practice, empowering newsrooms to work together on quality work despite facing myriad challenges and declining resources. Since collaborative journalism now occurs on an international scale, this chapter provides several research directions—using digital trace data and crowdsourced databases—to advance study on this subject. There are still many possible studies: a more in-depth analysis of the power dynamic within journalists' collaboration networks, an examination of those collaborators' characteristics, whom they cater to or reach out to, and with whom they interact. The technological set-up of cross-border teams, the question of funding, and the pressures from funders are all topics also worth studying. Although the results discussed are only preliminary, they illustrate the potential of these digital platforms to track the evolution of collaborative journalism over time.

However, like other research methods, these new approaches are not without limitations. GitHub is only one of the platforms for social coding and does not represent *all* open-source collaborations within the journalism community. The issue of representativeness is not a new problem, nor is it unique to digital traces. For instance, bias may arise when using standard survey procedures such as phone-based sampling, which represents only non-institutionalized populations.[41] What this chapter wants to convey is that GitHub shows potential as a platform to bridge the intersection between non-journalist actors, institutions, and industries with journalism. Insights gained from analyzing GitHub digital trace data can lead to a better assessment of collaborative journalism's prominence, prevalence, story targets, and public interest impacts.

Crowdsourced data assumes that the source contains the best data. However, when working with crowdsourced data, researchers need to pay attention to data quality—whether there are quality controls to evaluate the validity of user-submitted information based on pre-defined criteria or whether there are diverse information sources for cross-checking. For the two databases discussed above, the Center for Cooperative Media has a team that screens and cleans submitted information before making it publicly accessible; the Foundation Center compiles data from 35 diverse information sources, including direct reporting of grants by funders, IRS information returns, funder websites, and other public sources. As seen, both databases have at least some degree of loose hierarchical authority to ensure that the data are useful for their intended purpose. These crowdsourced databases show great potential to quantify collaborative trends, enhance the understanding of the breadth and depth of collaborations within and outside the United States, and examine the impact of various sources of funding. In a practical sense, insights gained from analyzing these crowdsourced databases can help news organizations plan how to structure and organize their partnerships.

Going forward, I am sure that more collaborative practices will take advantage of open-source and digital technology to facilitate and manage peer production. Data generated from using digital tools will also dramatically increase in scale, enabling researchers to collect data that were off-limits in the past. At its best, academic research helps expose power dynamics and to inform managerial strategies to journalists of any level—either considering a partnership for the first time or looking to improve their collaborations—on what to consider when deciding to collaborate on a story, thus laying a solid foundation, avoiding pitfalls, and finishing strong.

Notes

1. Amy Mitchell and Rick Edmonds, "News Organization Partnerships and Collaborations," Pew Research Center, December 4, 2014, https://www.journalism. org/2014/12/04/journalism-partnerships/.
2. Kristen Hare, "How ICIJ Got Hundreds of Journalists to Collaborate on the Panama Papers," Poynter, 2016, http://www.poynter.org/2016/how-icij-got-hundreds-of-journalists-to-collaborate-on-the-panama-papers/405041/.
3. Nikos Smyrnaios, Sophie Chauvet, and Emmanuel Marty, 2017. "The Impact of CrossCheck on Journalists & the Audience Learning the Lessons from a Collaborative Journalism Project Fighting Disinformation Online During the French Presidential Election," hal-0198555 (November 2017), http://hal.univ-grenoble-alpes.fr/hal-01985555.
4. Alfred Hermida, "Tweets and Truth: Journalism as a Discipline of Collaborative Verification," *Journalism Practice* 6, no. 5–6 (2012): 659–668; Seth C. Lewis and Nikki Usher, "Trading Zones, Boundary Objects, and the Pursuit of News Innovation: A Case Study of Journalists and Programmers," *Convergence: The International Journal of Research into New Media Technologies* 22, no. 5 (January 2016): 543–560.
5. Peter Berglez and Amanda Gearing, "The Panama and Paradise Papers. The Rise of a Global Fourth Estate," *International Journal of Communication* 12 (October 2018), https://ijoc.org/index.php/ijoc/article/view/9141; Joy Jenkins and Lucas Graves, "Digital News Report: Case Studies in Collaborative Local Journalism," The Reuters Institute for the Study of Journalism, 2019, http://www.digitalnewsreport.org/publications/2019/case-studies-collaborative-local-journalism/.

6. Andrea Carson and Kate Farhall, "Understanding Collaborative Investigative Journalism in a 'Post-Truth' Age," *Journalism Studies* 19, no. 13 (July 2018): 1899–1911.

7. Lucas Graves and Magda Konieczna, "Qualitative Political Communication | Sharing the News: Journalistic Collaboration as Field Repair," *International Journal of Communication* 9, (June 2015), https://ijoc.org/index.php/ijoc/article/view/3381.

8. Sarah Stonbely, "Comparing Models of Collaborative Journalism," Center for Cooperative Media, (2017), https://centerforcooperativemedia.org/new-research-comparing-models-collaborative-journalism-released-sept-29/.

9. C.W. Anderson, Emily Bell, and Clay Shirky, *Post-Industrial Journalism: Adapting to the Present* (New York: Tow Center for Digital Journalism, Columbia University, 2012).

10. Lucas Graves and Magda Konieczna, "Qualitative Political Communication | Sharing the News: Journalistic Collaboration as Field Repair," *International Journal of Communication* 9 (June 2015).

11. Larry Dailey, Lori Demo, and Mary Spillman, "The Convergence Continuum: A Model for Studying Collaboration Between Media Newsrooms," *Atlantic Journal of Communication* 13, no. 3 (2005): 150–168.

12. Sarah Stonbely, "Comparing Models of Collaborative Journalism," Center for Cooperative Media, (2017), https://centerforcooperativemedia.org/new-research-comparing-models-collaborative-journalism-released-sept-29/.

13. Brigittee Alfter, *Cross-Border Collaborative Journalism: A Step-by-Step Guide* (New York: Routledge, 2019).

14. Joseph Lichterman, "These Chicago News Orgs Worked Together to Create a Collaborative Voting Guide," The Lenfest Institute for Journalism, 2019, https://www.lenfestinstitute.org/solution-set/these-chicago-news-orgs-worked-together-to-create-a-collaborative-voting-guide/.

15. Christine Schmidt, "Ten Newsrooms, 4 Countries, Thousands of Kids: ProPublica Launches a Project to Find Immigrant Children," Nieman Lab, 2018, https://www.niemanlab.org/2018/06/seven-newsrooms-4-countries-thousands-of-kids-propublica-launches-project-to-find-immigrant-children/.

16. BBC, "A New Era for Public Service Reporting," BBC, 2020, https://www.bbc.co.uk/lnp/.

17. The European Union, "Media Freedom and Investigative Journalism—Call for Proposals," The European Commission, 2019, https://ec.europa.eu/digital-single-market/en/news/media-freedom-and-investigative-journalism-call-proposals.

18. Liza Gross, "Collaboratives: You Have to Want to Be There," Knight Foundation, 2019, https://knightfoundation.org/articles/collaboratives-you-have-to-want-to-be-there/.

19. Journalism Grants, "What are the application criteria?", Journalism Grants, The Innovation in Development Reporting Grant Programme, 2020, https://innovation.journalismgrants.org/eligibility.

20. Nicolas Kayser-Bril, "Collaboration—One Tool among Many," in *Global Teamwork: The Rise of Collaboration in Investigative Journalism*, ed. R. Sambrook (Oxford: Reuters Institute for the Study of Journalism, 2017), 59–63.

21. Rachel Glickhouse, "Here's what ProPublica Learned about Managing a Collaboration Across Hundreds of News Organizations," Nieman Lab, 2019, https://www.niemanlab.org/2019/12/heres-what-propublica-learned-about-managing-a-collaboration-across-hundreds-of-news-organizations/.

22. Alfred Heinrich, *Network Journalism: Journalistic Practice in Interactive Spheres* (New York: Routledge, 2011).

23. Mark Deuze, 2008. "Understanding Journalism as Newswork: How It Changes, and How It Remains the Same," *Westminster Papers in Communication & Culture* 5, no. 2 (2008): 4–23.

24. Charlie Beckett and Robin Mansell, "Crossing Boundaries: New Media and Networked Journalism," *Communication, Culture & Critique* 1, no. 1 (2008): 92–104.

25. Bregtje van der Haak, Michael Parks, and Manuel Castells, "The Future of Journalism: Networked Journalism," *International Journal of Communication* 6, (2012), http://ijoc.org/index.php/ijoc/article/download/1750/832.

26. Carlos Martínez de la Serna, "Collaboration and the Creation of a New Journalism Commons," *Columbia Journalism Review* (March 30, 2018), https://www.cjr.org/tow_center_reports/collaboration-and-the-journalism-commons.php/.

27. Lucy Bernholz, Chiara Cordelli, and Rob Reich, "On the Agenda-Setting and Framing Influence of Foundations Relative to Social Challenges," in *Philanthropy in Democratic Societies: History, Institutions, Values*, eds. Rob Reich, Chiara Cordelli, and Lucy Bernholz (Chicago: University of Chicago Press, 2016).

28. Corinne B. Hart, "The 'Elephant in the Room': Using Emotion Management to Uncover Hidden Discourses in Interprofessional Collaboration and Teamwork," *Journal of Interprofessional Care* 25, no. 5 (2011): 373–774.

29. James Howison, Andrea Wiggins, and Kevin Crowston, "Validity Issues in the Use of Social Network Analysis with Digital Trace Data," *Journal of the Association for Information Systems* 12, no. 12 (2011): 767–797.

30. Aniket Kittur, Bongwon Suh, Bryan A. Pendleton, and Ed H. Chi, "He Says, She Says: Conflict and Coordination in Wikipedia," *CHI '07: Proceedings of the SIGCHI Conference on Human Factors in Computing Systems* (April 2007): 453–462; Ba-Quy Vuong, Ee-Peng Lim, Aixin Sun, Minh-Tam Le, Hady Wirawan Lauw, and Kuiyu Chang, "On Ranking Controversies in Wikipedia: Models and Evaluation," *WSDM '08: Proceedings of the 2008 International Conference on Web Search and Web Data Mining* (February 2008): 171–182.

31. Gabriella Coleman, *Coding Freedom: The Ethics and Aesthetics of Hacking* (Princeton: Princeton University Press, 2012).

32. Nikki Usher, *Interactive Journalism: Hackers, Data, and Code* (Urbana: University of Illinois Press, 2016).

33. Nora McDonald and Sean Goggins, "Performance and Participation in Open Source Software on GitHub," *CHI EA '13: CHI '13 Extended Abstracts on Human Factors in Computing Systems* (April 2013): 139–144.

34. Laura Dabbish, Colleen Stuart, Jason Tsay, and Jim Herbsleb, "Social Coding in GitHub: Transparency and Collaboration in an Open Software Repository," *CSCW '12: Proceedings of the ACM 2012 Conference on Computer Supported Cooperative Work* (February 2012): 1277–1286.

35. Ferdian Thung, Tegawende F. Bissyande, David Lo, and Lingxiao Jiang, "Network Structure of Social Coding in GitHub," *2013 17th European Conference on Software Maintenance and Reengineering* (March 2013): 323–326.

36. Steve Weber, *The Success of Open Source* (Cambridge: Harvard University Press, 2004), 7.

37. Steve Weber, *The Success of Open Source*, 62.

38. Antonio Lima, Luca Rossi, and Mirco Musolesi, "Coding Together at Scale: GitHub as a Collaborative Social Network," *8th International AAAI International Conference on Weblogs and Social Media, ICWSM 2014* (2014).

39. Tabea Grzeszyk, "Diversity Matters! How Cross-Border Journalism Calls Out Media Bias," *Journal of Applied Journalism & Media Studies* 8, no. 2 (2019): 169–189.

40. Eva Constantaras, "Data Journalism Should Thrive on Cross-Border Collaborations— Why Doesn't It?" Source, OpenNews, February 16, 2016, https://source.opennews.org/articles/data-journalism-should-thrive-cross-border-collabo.

41. Becky Pettit, *Invisible Men: Mass Incarceration and the Myth of Black Progress* (New York: Russell Sage Foundation, 2012).

9

The Business of Digital News

Understanding the Cross-Functional Orchestra

Damon Kiesow

Introduction

In news organizations today, editorial strategy is business strategy. The two
are entirely intertwined. Understanding either requires studying both.

I say this as a recent arrival into academia after 25 years in newsrooms and
boardrooms. Having seen both sides of the gap between practitioners and
scholars, neither is entirely prepared for how the industry is changing.

With the shift to digital, the process of publishing the news has transitioned
from a series of loosely coupled, sequential, and periodic production tasks to
a set of complex, overlapping, and stochastic outputs requiring significant
alignment and coordination to succeed.

For journalists, these changes are challenging newsroom norms and
driving an embrace of human-centered design practices and product
thinking. For academics it is an opportunity to study the remaking of organizational roles and relationships in the business of digital news, an effort that
is still in its infancy.

The Production of News

The transformation of organizational structures and boundaries is seen
most clearly in the production of news products and how print and digital
newsrooms observe the wall between editorial and business concerns.

In print, a designer fits columns of article text around empty boxes
denoting individual ad locations, ostensibly to avoid any active or passive
advertiser influence in the editorial process. But in digital newsrooms, the
influence of advertising is pervasive and integrated into every process. Web

Damon Kiesow, *The Business of Digital News* In: *Journalism Research That Matters.* Edited by: Valérie Bélair-Gagnon and
Nikki Usher, Oxford University Press. © Oxford University Press 2021. DOI: 10.1093/oso/9780197538470.003.0010

article pages are templated, and the number and location of ads are a key design decision. Editorial and advertising staff must negotiate these placements to balance storytelling and revenue needs.

The design of a web article page involves months of work with every department represented and implicitly focused on revenue priorities. And because more page views equals more ads which equals more revenue, the often-explicit goal of the newsroom becomes one of unyielding audience growth. This collaboration transforms what was a wall between advertising and editorial into a foundation that may favor revenue concerns and distort the editorial mission.

This pattern of boundary crossing and the related blending of skills between departments is repeated across the company, for example with newsrooms taking on analytics and development roles, and the former "circulation" group working on audience engagement and analyzing news coverage to understand what stories attract loyal readers.

News organizations are full of what were once semi-independently operating business functions that are now rapidly reconfiguring and renegotiating their digital existence. What once was a set of small jazz ensembles has become a cross-functional orchestra. And for the business of journalism to prosper, news workers must both influence and adapt to these changes and find their new seats on the stage. And for scholars to understand the music, it is not enough to just study the string section or woodwinds in isolation.

To understand digital news practice, academics must move away from a focus on legacy departmental structures and job titles and instead consider the developing interplay between the broad roles and skills and technologies required to produce and subsidize journalism.

Human-Centered Design and Process

Boczkowski and Siles have called for a "cosmopolitan" dialogue between research disciplines in rejection of the provincial focus of some scholarship.[1] They argue the use of diverse research methodologies is needed to understand the relationship between audiences, news work, and technology.

> Methodological cosmopolitanism may be defined as an empirical sensibility toward the use of multiple methods on the links between production and consumption, and materiality and content in the lifecycle of media

technologies. The goal of cosmopolitanism is not simply to add methods with different strengths within a single study but to combine them into an empirical apparatus that can capture the interpenetration of the relevant dimensions of media technologies within a given project.[2]

In journalism practice, this ethos is increasingly identified with the discipline of product management, which concerns itself with strategically aligning audience needs, technical resources, and economic sustainability. This alignment requires cross-functional teams that share empathy for readers and for internal goals and constraints.

These new audience-focused, product-thinking collaborations challenge news workers to break away from frames that defined the role and purpose of organizational structures in the pre-digital news industry. New frameworks of understanding are required, and a human-centered approach begins with a focus on the audience and examines how the process of producing the news navigates internal and external demands of the product solution stack:[3]

1. Desirability (reader need)
2. Viability (business need)
3. Visual Design (on brand and eloquent)
4. User Experience (function, usability)
5. Feasibility (including development effort)
6. Systems Integration (between disparate services and tools)
7. Workflow (the process for creating and publishing)
8. Culture (shared assumptions that govern behavior)

This approach does not presuppose a specific editorial philosophy or business model. It merely centers reader needs in the discussion and describes the interlocking motivations and limitations that must be navigated within an organization to best serve that audience.

The layers in this framework represent the people and processes necessary to support a digital newsroom including readers, salespeople, designers, developers, and journalists. Each has a stake in the process and in the news that is produced. Several were popularized by the consulting firm Ideo and Stanford University's Hasso Plattner Institute of Design, which has evangelized using human-centered design methodologies in business strategy.[4]

Design Thinking as a management tool highlights desirability, viability, and feasibility as the primary tensions involved in developing and bringing a product to market. The process asks, what is the customer need, can the organization develop a solution, and is that product or service economically viable?

For customers to receive the full benefits of a *desired* solution, it also must be aesthetically and functionally well designed for the purpose. And for a product to be both feasible and viable, a business requires the skills and time to develop it, the ability to integrate it with existing internal systems and workflows, and the cultural support of the broader organization to accomplish these tasks. *Viability* itself is often considered as an external measure—will people pay for—but includes strategic or indirect economic benefits as well as the internal cost of support.

Every product or service must pass the test of at least minimally satisfying the needs and expectations for each of the eight layers of this framework. And because the approvals include external stakeholders and cross legacy internal organizational boundaries, creative and strategic conflicts will arise. It is at the boundaries of those layers that innovation is often delayed or defeated. Those friction points, and the questions and issues that arise from them, are the focus of news product managers and must be the increased focus of academic study.

A Focus on the Business

The business of journalism depends on news organizations resolving these barriers to effective collaboration and in developing a new economic model for news. The rise of subscription and membership initiatives is one response to that need and has mirrored the failure of digital advertising to mitigate print revenue declines.

Human-centered design and product-thinking methodologies are entirely aligned with the demands of a reader revenue program. But internal process and collaboration gaps are often revealed in these efforts.[5]

A typical news website paywall limits access to content based on consumption habits. Having read five stories this month, you must subscribe and pay to read the sixth. The mechanism exposes an inherent interdepartmental conflict: The circulation team must limit access to encourage readers to become subscribers. But a paywall ostensibly limits page views, which the advertising team relies on to meet revenue goals. And the newsroom must now consider how to balance page view growth for advertising versus engaged and loyal reader growth for subscriptions. Resolving this tension requires traversing and answering the questions posed in each of the eight layers of the product solutions stack. Each also affords a range of research topics:

1. Desirability—No business strategy is possible without a product the community deeply values. It is the keystone of any product strategy, and the weaker the perceived value the less margin for error is possible in the layers below.
2. Viability—Understanding readers' "willingness to pay"[6] is central to operation of a paywall, including pricing and optimizing the balance between subscription and advertising revenue.
3. Design—Effective and informative visuals instill trust in the brand and the confidence of an informed purchase decision by the reader.
4. Usability—Making digital payment forms easier to use drives new subscriptions but requires a significant investment in research, design, and development work.
5. Development Effort—E-commerce is a relatively new focus for the news industry, and the complexity of the work is often underestimated. The time, skills, and priority applied will directly influence the usability and viability of the project.
6. Systems Integration—Digital subscription fulfillment requires data to be shared with credit card companies, print circulation databases, customer service call centers, and the content management system. Any inefficiency or failure in those connections may degrade the ability for customers to subscribe or access the site. Each system to be integrated may reside in different departments or with different external vendors, adding significant complexity to the development task.
7. Workflow—As new systems are integrated, staff from across the company must either adapt to new business processes or invest additional development time and expense to minimize process changes.
8. Culture—All of the above decisions and tasks must ultimately align with the values, beliefs, and organizational structure of the company. A product that effectively solved for desirability, viability, design, usability, feasibility, integration, and workflow but offered a subscription product that allowed subscribers to dictate news coverage would fail, as it would be immediately rejected by the ethical norms of the newsroom.

Each component task in the development of a digital news product is complicated, but the interdependencies between jobs and goals across departments make a successful effort wildly complex. News organizations are rushing to adapt, but too few recognize that a mastery of human-centered design and product-thinking methods is fundamental to a sustainable digital business.

The recent growth in product management and product-thinking practices in the industry is a good sign, but progress is uneven. News organizations need support to navigate the chaos of digital disruption, and academic researchers are just starting to recognize this opportunity.[7] Scholars must be invited in and allowed access to the proprietary studies and business data that drive digital strategy decisions. But those researchers must also commit to understanding the organization as a whole: audience, partners, technology, staff, incentives, goals, and culture as part of any study and explanation of its component parts.

Notes

1. Pablo J. Boczkowski and Ignacio Siles, "Steps toward Cosmopolitanism in the Study of Media Technologies," *Information, Communication & Society* 17 no. 5 (2014): 560–571.
2. Boczkowski and Siles, "Steps toward Cosmopolitanism," 566.
3. Damon Kiesow, "What It Takes to Shift a News Organization to Reader Revenue," American Press Institute, October 2, 2018, https://www.americanpressinstitute.org/reader-revenue/what-it-takes-to-shift-a-news-organization-to-reader-revenue/.
4. Ulla Johansson-Sköldberg, Jill Woodilla, and Mehves Çetinkaya, "Design Thinking: Past, Present and Possible Futures," *Creativity and Innovation Management* 22, no. 2 (2013): 121–146.
5. Kiesow, "What It Takes to Shift a News Organization to Reader Revenue," https://www.americanpressinstitute.org/reader-revenue/what-it-takes-to-shift-a-news-organization-to-reader-revenue/.
6. Daniel O'Brien, Christian-Mathias Wellbrock, and Nicola Kleer, "Content for Free? Drivers of Past Payment, Paying Intent and Willingness to Pay for Digital Journalism–A Systematic Literature Review," *Digital Journalism* (2020): 1–30.
7. Cindy Royal, Amanda Bright, Kristin Pellizzaro, Valerie Belair-Gagnon, Avery E. Holton, Subramaniam Vincent, Don Heider, Anita Zielina, and Damon Kiesow, "Product Management in Journalism and Academia," *Journalism & Mass Communication Quarterly* 97, no. 3 (2020), 597–616.

10

The Business of Journalism and Studying the Journalism Business

Nikki Usher and Mark Poepsel

Introduction

To those concerned with the fate of the global news industry, these are concerning times, with growing evidence that quality news and information is reaching a point of market failure. In this case of journalism, market failure describes "situations where public goods such as news and information are given inadequate support, having detrimental effects on society."[1] Across the world, Covid-19 has boosted attention to legacy, reputable sources of news, although this has not provided a comparable financial return.[2] In the United States, the crisis in journalism has become particularly acute, especially for newspapers: approximately one-fourth of US communities are now what some would call a "news desert," lacking regular access to local news and information. By the estimates of the US News Deserts project, the United States has lost "2,100 newspapers leaving at least 1800 communities that had a local news outlet in 2004 without any at the beginning of 2020."[3] Employment in journalism overall has declined drastically. According to Pew, newsroom employment dropped by 23% between 2008 and 2020, with newspapers losing more than half of their employees.[4] Note that 2008 reflects the beginning of the Great Recession; in the wake of Covid-19, many news outlets are under even more dire strain. One of the major issues facing scholars and journalists alike today is thus how to "save" journalism, although this is the wrong question to ask.

The goal of "saving" journalism is to return a semblance of financial sustainability and reporting strength to journalism that is presumed to now be worse in quality and coverage than it was before the digital disruption of the news business model. The "make journalism great again" approach is nostalgic for a journalism that had many flaws, including systematic misrepresentation

Nikki Usher and Mark Poepsel, *The Business of Journalism and Studying the Journalism Business* In: *Journalism Research That Matters.* Edited by: Valérie Bélair-Gagnon and Nikki Usher, Oxford University Press. © Oxford University Press 2021. DOI: 10.1093/oso/9780197538470.003.0011 of people of color and limited diversity within news outlets. This journalism was also often extractive, taking from communities rather than involving them as agential storytellers capable of telling their own stories.

Similarly, the hunt for a business model to save journalism is often best translated as a hunt for a business model that saves digital-first news outlets or newspapers. Extant best practices around membership models and engaged journalism has only begun to consider how requiring either time or money from audiences perpetuates or worsens class inequities in access to news and information. In the United States, efforts to return journalism to its trusted status are similarly nostalgic for a time when trust in journalism was also strongly correlated with distrust in major institutions (e.g., the US presidency), and there is, as of yet, little empirical data that "rebuilding trust" translates into economic returns.[5]

What is the right question to ask, then, for scholars and journalists interested in dealing with newspapers and the type of journalism that powers democracy when profit rarely follows? The question that we need to ask directly is, "How can digital journalism make more money?" This question brings the essential economic problem facing journalism to the forefront, providing a starting point that is focused on business practices rather than content.[6]

First, using examples from the United States, scholars and journalists need to be more holistically engaged with the economics of media more generally, and of different types of journalism beyond newspaper and digital-first outlets. Second, scholars and journalists need to be more intellectually honest about their aims in conducting this research. Is research on news business models aimed at propping up corporate-funded journalism? What is the purpose of critiquing current business models, and are the solutions proposed really tenable or equitable within current political and social landscapes? Third, universities should consider both their strengths and limitations in serving as potential "bubbles" for innovation, experimentation, and insulation from commercial pressures.

What Journalists and Journalism Studies Scholars Need to Know

Journalism Studies scholarship suffers from a disconnect to its strong tradition of media economics and media policy research. Similarly, most of the attention in scholarship about news business models is devoted either to functioning, independence, and innovation in public media[7] (largely outside the United States); to newspapers, which in the United States are presumed to be the single most important providers of local news and information; and to nonprofit journalism efforts—although the nonprofit sector in the United States has a legal structure vastly different from that of many international legal regimes, and thus is often not comparable or generalizable beyond its shores. However, to do research that matters, Journalism Studies scholars need to both engage more widely in research and consider more broadly what is happening in the news industry as a whole.

Research on media economics lives as a separate subfield, slightly adjacent to Journalism Studies, often focused on the formation and performance of media markets and sometimes nestled within media policy.[8] Additional scholarship that matters to understanding future business models for journalism is siloed within media industries research or distribution studies, which look more holistically at connections between media firms, ownership, and changes in user consumption.[9] Consider that within Journalism Studies, there have been few academic articles devoted to analyzing the technology systems that enable digital advertising or how the economics of digital content might impact news content and distribution.[10] There is, however, significant attention to the ways in which jobs and functions of journalists have changed, from the rise of product managers to the role of data journalists to the disappearance of the "wall" between editorial and business functions (especially in newspapers). This research tends to focus primarily on how roles and boundaries have changed, and less on the economic impact of these larger structural changes to news firms as a whole.

Scholars and news industry pundits need to also better acknowledge the news industry more holistically. While newspapers are faring particularly poorly, this does not mean that the news media industry in the United States has not been profitable. Until the Covid-19 global pandemic crisis, major cable networks like CNN, FOX, and MSNBC boasted record viewership, taking advantage of the Trump administration's media fodder. CBS's former chairman and CEO Les Moonves noted during the 2016 presidential campaign, "It may not be good for America, but it's damn good for CBS."[11] Talk radio, particularly on the Right, continues to draw strong and loyal audiences. Local television, unfettered by various loosenings of Federal Communication Commission (FCC) regulations on cross-ownership, continues to become less local and more consolidated—but it remains among the most trusted forms of journalism.

Similarly, podcasting is a thriving industry, though its future sustainability remains uncertain, especially given the tendency toward asynchronous listening (which impacts audience-size measurements) and limited (though growing) availability of digital measurement tools to assess audience size.

However, other attempts at innovation have been problematic. Misdirected pivots to video have resulted in massive layoffs. Even Vox, which began with much aplomb, is now requesting "membership contributions," although Vox is a for-profit media company, so these contributions are not tax-deductible. Similarly, talent at these large digital-first startups has shifted to legacy news organizations or other news media efforts, including the departure of Buzzfeed's Ben Smith and Shani Hilton to *The New York Times* and *The LA Times* respectively, and HuffPost's Lydia Polgreen to Gimlet Media, the podcasting company. Digital-first news media is faring less well than perhaps many had hoped, particularly as venture capitalists and new corporate owners tend to be less patient regarding expected returns on investment than a more benevolent newspaper baron of decades past.

National digital news audience size has remained remarkably stable, with the major news sites ranking roughly in the same "rank" of most-visited Internet sites as they have for about a decade. The continued growth of right-wing digital news sites—funded by right-wing family fortunes (e.g., Breitbart's benefactors are the Mercers), think tanks, and digital ad dollars—have received minimal attention from scholars. Partisan news, especially on the right, is thriving economically, and Facebook and YouTube's algorithms that favor highly emotional, partisan content are not the only reason why.

To wit, journalists and scholars are often consumed by the decline of newspapers and threats to digital-first outlets, without thinking about the news industry as a whole. This concern about the link between local news (via newspapers) and declines in democratic engagement are founded in empirical social science, although the normative expression of this link is more robust than the data itself. There is an irony about mourning the decline of a commercial, capitalist funding model and connecting its dissolution, almost uncritically, to the performance of American democracy. And these normative presumptions require that Journalism Studies engage with research more widely and consider the news industry broadly.[12]

Calls for Intellectual Honesty

An important call to action for conducting research on the news industry that matters requires intellectual honesty from both journalists and scholars as to the aims of the research and the limitations of new funding streams as they pertain to equity and power. There are also broader questions about what role the academy, especially traditional tenure-track and tenured scholars working outside the center model (see Chapter 2, by Holcomb), should play in conducting applied scholarship that helps companies make more money or keeps nonprofit revenue streams in the black. Scholars have the time to conduct independent research that is not tied to the performance of quarterly earnings and other measures of impact, but what to do with this independence and how to ask questions that matter requires additional reflexivity.

In many other fields, particularly business, marketing, and communication's own advertising subfield, this explicit academic focus on helping companies make more money is not frowned upon. However, there is a distinct likelihood that even if scholars and news organizations could co-operate, we would have different goals for publication and different metrics of success (for more on this issue, please see Chase Davis' practitioner reflection in Chapter 15). If the burning question before journalists and scholars is how to get people to pay for news (presuming the advertising model is untenable), it is surprising how little research has actually been conducted within Journalism Studies on consumers' willingness to pay for journalism. A 2020 systematic literature review of this research in *Digital Journalism* found only 37 published academic articles between 2000-2019 that provided a variable-level assessment as to why people pay for journalism; the authors note "[i]n general, the amount of research...remains relatively scarce."[13] The vast majority of this research has been in the United States, Germany, and in Nordic countries with significant cultural capital and purchasing power, while the lack of consistent measurements leaves the results as a whole relatively inactionable and ambiguous. There is no consistent takeaway from academic literature over 20 years of study about why people pay for news, and their willingness to do so (although we do know more about their motivations for paying *attention* to the news; see Stephanie Edgerly in Chapter 7). Arguably this failure deserves some recrimination within the field: despite all our resources and stated concern for the survival of quality news and information, we have used very little of our privileged academic independence to explore these questions.

There is some blame to be placed upon news organizations who are unwilling to share data, especially outside of the center model for applied research. For example, in 2011, one of the authors began conversations with data analysts at *The Washington Post* to begin looking at "willingness to pay." However, roadblocks immediately ensued; there was a resistance to letting the author directly examine the data, and restrictions discussed around publishing and peer review. Individual partnerships with various news organizations do not yield generalizable results, although Weber et. al's report on the Minneapolis-St. Paul market for the News Media Alliance provides insight into how individual markets might be systematically analyzed.[14] However, this partnership with the *Minneapolis Star-Tribune* is mediated by a news industry association, and the data was published outside the traditional academic model (see Holcomb's discussion of opportunities and benefits of this research, earlier in Chapter 3). Even in the best partnerships, it is likely that publication of these studies would face an uphill battle in traditional scholarly publication models because of the small samples and, often, lack of engagement with theory based within Journalism Studies. Publishing in a peer-reviewed journal might limit the efficacy and distribution of the findings, too.

There are other questions and issues related to the commercial viability of journalism that require additional intellectual honesty from scholars and journalists alike. First, scholars situated within Journalism Studies have been reluctant to pursue scholarly narratives that blame news industry business decisions for their current financial problems. While scholars are quick to ascribe a fear of innovation to newsrooms, there has been limited discussion about how news consolidation, the rise of chains, and the inefficient advertising monopolies many local newspapers had over their markets contributed to vulnerabilities that made it easier for a competitor to disrupt the market (first digital ad agencies, later Google and Facebook). Much of this scholarship peaked in the 1980s and 1990s as newspaper monopolies consolidated, but there has been little post-Internet scholarship that has considered how management decisions, public ownership, and questions of debt and pension management have created challenges for the survival of local newspapers in particular. While the takeover of newspaper chains by hedge funds has been maligned by scholars and news industry pundits alike, scholarly research on the impact of hedge funds on content, subscriptions, audience perspectives, and beyond has been almost nonexistent. This research, then, lives in journalism trade publications and is often covered as a beat.

The most intellectually honest scholars would also likely admit the gaps in their knowledge of corporate transactions and mergers, how to read public disclosures, how boards of directors function, and what factors impact the pricing and valuation of news firms. Similarly, without significant uphill effort, understanding how venture capital functions, what private equity firms do, and how monopoly power impacts markets are outside our scholarly purview, at least at present, minus a few exceptions in contemporary scholarship.[15] Yet without this basic knowledge, which most of us would not have been exposed to in graduate school, it becomes difficult to truly assess the impact of current news business strategy.

There are other difficult questions related to news business models that require intellectual honesty and considering intellectual independence against the promise of funding support. While scholars are eager to research on Google, Facebook, Twitter, and other big tech platforms, we have not engaged in an open debate about how taking money from these organizations to do our research might compromise our research questions. The debate over access to Facebook data lives largely in the computational social science arena. Journalism schools have largely uncritically accepted funding from Facebook (consider City University of New York administering $14 million of Facebook's money). Similarly, journalism schools have pursued partnerships with Facebook, Instagram, and Google to hire students for internships or to develop programming, training, and other opportunities. If Google offers a free training on its software to students, why not take them up on it? But the encroaching dependency of training journalists on more Google products has received less attention. However, Google alone has put $527 million into journalism worldwide, with Facebook pledging $300 million. Both big tech companies have promised even more money for journalism in the wake of Covid-19, with a focus on local news.[16]

There are also questions to ask about news philanthropy more generally. The Knight Foundation has provided significant funding, especially of late, to scholars studying questions about the future of journalism. Similarly, it is one of the biggest funders of journalism innovations in the United States, with $300 million pledged in 2018. It is unlikely that a scholar working at a major research university has been untouched by Knight funding, even if not directly. Knight funds research chairs at universities, helps set up funding for small pilot projects, and supports other granting organizations that then fund journalism school projects such as the Online News Association. Knight's recent infusion of $50 million, enabling centers at George Washington University, Carnegie Mellon, New York University, the University of Washington, and UNC-Chapel Hill provides the chance to pursue new research. But critical interrogation of Knight's power within the journalism academy and journalism itself has largely been limited to research on some of its initial Knight Challenge grants.[17] Knight itself is largely under-explored in scholarly research as an object of study, which is problematic given its influence. There are other questions that emerge as well from this connection between funding and the academy more broadly. In particular, the role of universities in shaping the future of journalism requires additional interrogation if the aim is to produce journalism research that matters. Regardless of the specific case, intellectual honesty as to the aims of the research and the limitations of new funding streams as they pertain to equity and power is required from both journalists and scholars.

Universities and the Future of Journalism

As the business model for journalism remains uncertain, particularly for the kind of news that powers democratic life, universities have an opportunity to play an important role in charting its future. Journalism schools are facing uncertain times, too, with concerns about dwindling enrollment—and while there was a Trump-bump, parents and students alike know that the path to a steady job in journalism is more uncertain than in other fields. Nonetheless, this book features some examples of how universities can serve as foundational institutions in supporting the future of news. There is the role of centers that universities can house, as noted, but there are other opportunities to consider: universities as academic incubators, universities as "teaching hospitals" for journalism, and universities as safe homes for public media and investigative nonprofits.[18]

Universities can and do serve as incubators for news innovations. Some of these incubator opportunities come out of fellowships for practicing journalists and scholars. The JSK Stanford fellowship program brings together journalists interested in technology to work on new projects, and other fellowship programs, such as Nieman (at Harvard), Knight-Wallace (at Michigan), and Klein-Berkman (also at Harvard) give journalists a chance to experiment and launch new ideas. However, these fellowships help individuals, who may in turn create products for journalism that scale, or they may go back to their newsrooms as more seasoned journalists with new skills. The hope of incubating new news startups and encouraging research on innovation can live at a university and often does, such as in the case of the Missouri's Reynolds Journalism Institute and CUNY's social journalism and entrepreneurial journalism programs. However, these programs often function as an extension of a professionals' skill set and are rarely connected to the student experience, unless journalists happen to engage with students who are taking some of their university classes. Universities can be incubators, but more research is needed on how to best structure and scale these innovations.

Similarly, the "teaching hospital" model of journalism school is ideally suited to university collaborations with journalists. The model imagines young journalists working as trainees but with real responsibilities to cover the news for the public, much like a teaching hospital gives medical students and young doctors chances for on-the-job training. This is particularly important, as student labor can provide an important dose of energy to coverage areas that are not well supported by the market. Similarly, being housed in a university provides a certain level of shelter from ups and downs in fundraising; a university's budget would dwarf any teaching hospital effort.

One long-running example is the University of Maryland's Capital News Service, which provides much-needed State House coverage of Maryland's capital, Annapolis, and gives students bylines in major news outlets thanks to cooperative news agreements; another is the University of Southern California's Neon Tommy, which provides digital-first coverage to neighborhoods and issues overlooked by bigger outlets in Los Angeles. Similarly, the News21 project housed at Arizona State University (ASU) is a competitive program open to students at ASU and across the nation to learn investigative journalism techniques. Another high-profile example focused on digital storytelling is George Washington's Planet Forward, another intercollegiate effort to encourage environmental coverage.

As seen in Mourão in Chapter 11, Michigan State has long provided supplementary local coverage to Michigan communities. But there were chances to revise how this coverage was done, with particular attention to digital storytelling. One finding emerged that holds trenchant lessons for those moving forward: journalists working in professional newsrooms do not always have the time or the mind-space to partner, even with the most ambitious of journalism projects. On the other hand, as Moore shows in her work with "One River, Many Stories" (Chapter 16), universities can provide crucial resources and new skills to help communities with solutions-oriented journalism. These efforts were not intended to create large, institutional supplements for local journalism, but instead augmented coverage through project-oriented student efforts.

But there are challenges to these projects. All of these projects, and many new efforts, require the careful stewardship of journalism professors and often adjunct journalism professors, and this labor does not always count toward professional advancement or tenure. These projects also require the connections and continued fundraising of the journalism schools and professors that house them. Moreover, not every student is capable of doing professional-level coverage. One way forward is to continue doing research about what works when journalism schools try to step in to fill gaps.

A related but similarly important role of public universities is serving as homes to public broadcasting stations. Two-thirds of the public radio stations nationwide are affiliated with colleges.[19] Many Midwestern state universities, as noted in Chapter 1, house some of the most historic public broadcasting television and radio stations. These public broadcasting efforts are similarly insulated from the harshest of market pressures with university infrastructure and support. However, their connections to the university life as a whole can be mixed, and whether students are involved as trainees often depends highly on the individual organizational cultures of these newsrooms. Furthermore, there are some downsides of being housed in a university: questioning the university itself becomes uncomfortable, and journalists have to go through the same university bureaucracy when it comes to hiring and to ethics.

The University of Illinois provides an instructive example of some of these tensions. Illinois public media, also known as WILL, offers public television and public radio, including original local programming, to the Urbana-Champaign market. WILL is an NPR and PBS member station, bringing national programming to the area. WILL is technically housed in the College of Media, home to the journalism, advertising, and media and cinema department, but is housed in a different building away from the main campus, creating structural barriers to regular staff and faculty interaction. What would seem to be obvious, mutually beneficial connections between the journalism department and WILL have often floundered, in part because of the tremendous labor that comes with supervising students, while WILL has professional public broadcasting standards that can be difficult for student journalists to attain. Similarly, WILL journalists have not played significant roles in teaching courses, despite their ample experience. To move beyond these difficulties, the College of Media at Illinois invested in hiring two individuals to help supervise student journalists and facilitate better integration.[20]

However, while being housed at a university can provide benefits such as infrastructure, labor, and a steady, larger institutional budget that may come to the rescue in serious times of need, there are additional complications that can compromise independent reporting. When journalists at Illinois NPR (as part of a reporting collaboration with WILL) and ProPublica Illinois began investigating the university's mishandlings of sexual assault and sexual harassment, the university attempted to require them to reveal their sources by name. Technically, WILL employees, like most faculty and staff, are mandatory reporters of sexual assault and help facilitate a report of the assault and the victim through the university's various offices related to Title IX. This, of course, threatened to compromise sourcing and independent reporting critical of the university, although ProPublica Illinois *could* pursue this sourcing. The situation drew national attention from news organizations including *The New York Times*, drawing additional attention to scandals the university had mishandled. Journalists were concerned that the university's actions amounted to a "gag order" with a dangerous precedent set. The situation diffused as the university made changes to strengthen its sexual assault policies.

The threat to any journalism running through a university is clear; independent journalism is welcome but may run up against the might of the university providing the literal roof over the newsroom. Similarly, universities may not always see the value of public radio or public media. To raise funds in 2015, Howard University considered selling the license to its broadcasting spectrum in an FCC auction, which would have effectively eliminated its public television station WHUT, the only Black-owned public media station in the United States.[21] Pressure mounted from community members, alumni, and students, and the university pulled out of the auction, noting that it would not have received the profit windfall it had initially expected. Thus, while universities can provide insularity against market forces, universities themselves are prone to financial instability and may not be committed to holding on to public media outlets.

More research is required about the strengths and limits to the relationships between public media and universities, with attention toward limitations in independent journalism, organizational leadership and cohesion with journalism education, and financial relationships with the larger university bureaucracies. These issues may also extend to other journalism efforts housed in journalism schools, including incubators and teaching hospital efforts, and researchers need to be at the forefront of journalism research that matters to understand how their own universities may play a critical role in supporting journalism that powers democracy outside of market pressure.

Business of News Research That Matters

This chapter aimed to point out some of the strengths and weaknesses when it comes to how Journalism Studies has studied the business of journalism. With a focus on the United States, this chapter showed what Journalism Studies as a field needs to know about journalism and commercial profits, called for intellectual honesty, and asked for journalism schools to highlight the strengths and limits of partnerships. These efforts would bolster journalism research that matters to both the news industry and the study of journalism. There are many missed opportunities because of failures to cooperate with news organizations. However, for journalism researchers, this applied research presents challenges, particularly when it comes to scholarly publishing. A rethinking of how to make scholarly incentives more amenable to this research and how to facilitate better partnerships is required, and this volume offers some insight into approaches toward working together.

To do research that matters on the business of news, Journalism Studies researchers and journalists alike also need to be more intellectually honest about the aims of research into the revenue model for journalism. If this research is ultimately motivated by the quest to make more money for news outlets, either as commercial entities or as nonprofit ones, that is a perfectly acceptable rationale. While financially sustainable journalism may facilitate the kind of quality journalism that is needed for democratic life and cultural cohesion, it is one step removed from the basic question of how to make news organizations more money. To be able to consider these questions about the financial models for journalism, it is best to do so as a commercial problem and a commercial transaction first, in order to provide maximum clarity to key questions. Similarly, Journalism Studies researchers need to acknowledge what they do not know: this requires substantial engagement with adjacent subfield research and a better understanding of corporate finance and governance.

Finally, Journalism Studies researchers can help build critical bridges between universities and missing coverage gaps that have emerged as news organizations have cut back their reporting. More research on best practices are needed, as well as closer looks at how universities may also hinder journalistic independence. Journalism Studies can provide new and valuable research to help journalism survive and thrive in ways that are not nostalgic but forward-looking and pragmatic.

Notes

1. Victor Pickard, "The Violence of the Market," *20th Anniversary Special Issue: The Challenges Facing Journalism Today* 20, no. 1 (2019): 155.
2. Nic Newman with Richard Fletcher, Anne Schulz, Simge Andı, and Rasmus Kleis Nielsen, "Digital News Report," Reuters Institute, 2020, http://www.digitalnewsreport.org/.
3. Penelope Muse Abernathy, "The Local News Landscape in 2020: Transformed and Diminished," UNC Hussman School of Journalism and Media, 2020, https://www.usnewsdeserts.com/reports/news-deserts-and-ghost-newspapers-will-local-news-survive/the-news-landscape-in-2020-transformed-and-diminished/.
4. Elizabeth Grieco, "U.S. Newspapers Have Shed Half of Their Newsroom Employees since 2008," Pew Research Center, April 20, 2020, https://www.pewresearch.org/fact-tank/2020/04/20/u-s-newsroom-employment-has-dropped-by-a-quarter-since-2008/.
5. Raymond J. Pingree, Brian Watson, Mingxiao Sui, Kathleen Searles, Nathan P. Kalmoe, Joshua P. Darr, Martina Santia, and Kirill Bryanov, "Checking Facts and Fighting Back: Why Journalists Should Defend Their Profession," *PloS ONE* 13, no. 12 (2018): e0208600, https://journals.plos.org/plosone/article?id=10.1371/journal.pone.0208600.
6. Henrik Örnebring, "Journalism Cannot Solve Journalism's Problems," *Journalism* 20, no. 1 (2019): 226–228.
7. See for example, Stephen Lacy, "The Financial Commitment Approach to News Media Competition," *Journal of Media Economics* 5, no. 2 (1992): 5–21; M. Burns and N. Brugger, *Histories of Public Service Broadcasters on the Web* (London: Peter Lang, 2012); S.K. Evans, "Making Sense of Innovation: Process, Product, and Storytelling Innovation in public Service Broadcasting Organizations," *Journalism Studies* 19, no. 1 (2018): 4–24.
8. Though see the scholarship of Robert Picard, *The Economics and Financing of Media Companies* (New York: Fordham University Press, 2011) and James Hamilton's work, including *All the News that's Fit to Sell: How the Market Transforms Information into News* (Princeton: Princeton University Press, 2004).
9. See for example: Amanda D. Lotz, *The Television Will Be Revolutionized* (New York: NYU Press, 2014).
10. Though see: Joshua A. Braun and Jessica L. Eklund, "Fake News, Real Money: Ad tech Platforms, Profit-Driven Hoaxes, and the Business of Journalism," *Digital Journalism* 7, no. 1 (2019): 1–21.

11. Paul Bond, "Leslie Moonvies on Donald Trump," *Hollywood Reporter*, February 29, 2016, https://www.hollywoodreporter.com/news/leslie-moonves-donald-trump-may-871464.

12. Daniel Kreiss and J. Scott Brennen, "Normative Theories of Digital Journalism," in the *Sage Handbook of Digital Journalism Studies*, eds. Alfred Hermida, C. W. Anderson, David Domingo, and Tamara Witschge (New York: Sage, 2016): Chapter 20.

13. Daniel O'Brien, Christian-Mathias Wellbrock, and Nicola Kleer, "Content for Free? Drivers of Past Payment, Paying Intent and Willingness to Pay for Digital Journalism– A Systematic Literature Review," *Digital Journalism* (2020, online before print): 1–30.

14. Matthew S. Weber, Jonathan Anderson, Eugene Lee, Renee Mitson, Allison J. Steinke, Sarah Kay Wiley, and Hao Xu, "Connecting the Dots: Digital Subscriptions," *News Media Alliance* (2019), https://www.newsmediaalliance.org/release-new-study-reveals-connection-entertainment-news-media-subscriptions/.

15. But see the work of Rodney Benson, Victor Pickard, and, for venture capital/startups, Matt Carlson and Nikki Usher.

16. "Google's Media Takeover," Tech Transparency Project: Google Transparency Project, Campaign for Accountability, October 9, 2019, https://www.techtransparencyproject.org/articles/googles-media-takeover.

17. See Seth C. Lewis, "From Journalism to Information: The Transformation of the Knight Foundation and News Innovation," *Mass Communication and Society* 15, no. 3 (2012): 309–334.

18. These partnerships can be fraught as well because of issues about privilege (what organizations get to be a part of the university) and legal issues that must be agreed upon.

19. This draws from an interview by the author with Maurice Bresnahan, CEO of WILL TV, AM, and FM, April 19, 2019. Bresnahan was invited to write an essay for the book but declined.

20. Vivian McCall, "News Outlets Call University of Illinois Policy a Reporter Gag Order," will.radio.tv.online, November 14, 2019, https://will.illinois.edu/news/story/news-outlets-call-university-of-illinois-policy-a-reporter-gag-order.

21. Joseph Lichterman, "Howard University Decides It Won't Sell WHUT in Spectrum Auction," *Current*, February 17, 2017, https://current.org/2017/02/howard-university-decides-it-wont-sell-whut-in-spectrum-auction/.

PART III
JOURNALISM RESEARCH'S HIDDEN CHALLENGES

11

Rebuilding Trust through
Journalism Education

Teaching Multimedia Reporting with
Local Communities

Rachel R. Mourão and Soo Young Shin

Introduction

Every year, Professor Joe Grimm starts his multimedia reporting class by taking students to visit the rural, suburban, and urban areas that surround Michigan State University (MSU). From town halls and chambers of commerce to ice cream shops and local libraries, he carefully introduces students to the communities they will serve for the next months. Grimm has taught this class more than 25 times, and these interactions focus on the residents' answers to three questions: *What should people know about this place? What are some of the stories that should be told about your community? How can we help telling those stories?*

This chapter traces the development of a multimedia reporting class offered at a land-grant institution surrounded by a resource-strapped community. Our main argument is that opportunities for researchers to engage with communities and the local news industry are unevenly distributed, and such disparities must be addressed before we ask academics to jump on the engagement bandwagon. These inequalities manifest in many ways. For example, when it comes to research, some questions are more attractive than others for a news industry that has long been under economic duress. It is no surprise that willingness to partner on revenue-generating research is more appealing than engaging with projects dealing with systematic social issues, for example (as Kilgo details in Chapter 13).

In this chapter, we focus on inequalities related to *opportunities* for engagement, both when it comes to newsrooms and academic settings. In

Rachel R. Mourão and Soo Young Shin, *Rebuilding Trust through Journalism Education* In: *Journalism Research That Matters*. Edited by: Valérie Bélair-Gagnon and Nikki Usher, Oxford University Press. © Oxford University Press 2021.
DOI: 10.1093/oso/9780197538470.003.0012

particular, we discuss research-informed solutions to the challenges faced by a public affairs undergraduate reporting class that combines innovation with a decades-long tradition of local engagement. Results from our mixed-method approach combining historical data, in-depth interviews, and a field experiment provide a framework for connecting journalism education with communities that surround universities.

Here, we understand community engagement as part of MSU's land-grant mission. For decades, our journalism program has aspired to bridge the town–gown divide with reporting assignments that push students to develop emotional and intellectual investments in the lives of people living in communities that often receive little attention from mainstream newsrooms and face major socioeconomic challenges. Engagement journalism techniques inform our approach, but the mission of community engagement has a deeper history and a purpose that goes beyond journalism education and pedagogy.

With support from the Online News Association (ONA), we had the opportunity to experiment with a "teaching hospital" model in collaboration with the local news media, trying out engaged journalism techniques and innovations in multimedia reporting. In this experiment, we used one of the sections of the class to focus exclusively on the issue of schools of choice, adding mapping, data, and video to the curriculum. The other classes worked as control groups and used the old curriculum that had no specific topic requirements and focused primarily on writing. However, we quickly realized that we had to adapt our expectations when it came to partnerships with the local news media. We found it to be unrealistic to expect that local newsrooms in a shrinking market would have the resources to dedicate to engagement experiments, including the time and staff required to mentor students and oversee their work. In our case, it was not that journalists did not want to engage, but they just could not prioritize it in their daily activities.

We believe our engagement experiment does provide a framework for connecting research, journalism education, and local communities. In this chapter, we first detail the course's historical evolution from in-house writing assignments to providing a multimedia news service for local communities in Michigan. Then, we present the results of the ONA-funded field experiment. Findings reveal some improvement on student experience and diversity of sources and media, but shortcomings when it comes to basic writing skills. Finally, we provide some recommendations for a curriculum that responds to the needs of a multimedia-driven industry while maintaining a strong shoe-leather reporting tradition connected to local residents.

The Course

The ONA project was the latest iteration of a series of transformations that have shaped the course, Multimedia Writing and Reporting (henceforth JRN300) since the early 2000s. To retrace the course's trajectory, we analyzed syllabi and interviewed faculty members and students. The syllabi ranged from Spring 2008 (the oldest available version) to Fall 2018 and were compared in terms of course objectives and assignments, providing a broader context for interviews. Interviewees include the school's director, three instructors, and five students. One of the faculty interviewees has taught the class since 2008, providing a deeper knowledge of the course's transformation.

Course objectives have always focused on public affairs at the hyperlocal level, which have gradually received less attention from local news outlets over the years. Students build knowledge about various types of stories and platforms by becoming more comfortable with reaching out to community members and covering local governments, local businesses, and public schools. Every semester, student reporters are assigned a single community that becomes their geographic "beat," where they will cover official meetings—such as township board and city council—local features, businesses, and community events. Daily coverage often requires localizing statewide, national, or international events to their assigned community. To give the sense of a real newsroom, students must report regularly (seven weekly stories), keep deadlines, interview community members, and publish stories on multimedia news websites.

In early years, students submitted their print in-class assignments only to course instructors. Two major transformations were made between 2009 and 2010: the inclusion of multimedia elements to the course and the creation of an online space for student work to be published. These transformations were formalized in 2016--2017, when the term "multimedia" was added to the course description, and student stories were posted on a single reformulated website (The Spartan Newsroom).

The push for online publishing started in 2009 with experiments involving personal student blogs, followed by separate community blogs, and finally the single news portal. According to interviewees, the fact that stories are published and read by local people gives students a sense of real journalistic reporting and responsibility. According to instructors, students try to produce better work because they want to get published and know community members might be reading. Community member's feedback (i.e., people calling to correct errors or giving compliments) also motivates students to be more vigilant about reporting.

From a skills perspective, the course slowly evolved from a basic news writing class in the 1990s to a multimedia reporting class by the 2010s. In 2008, for example, students learned the basics of storytelling using blogs that needed to include photos and links to related stories. Gradually, new techniques such as Google Maps, search engine optimization, video, and infographics were added to the curriculum. Students were also pushed to gather and disseminate information via social media. In 2016, students were formally required to turn in at least two different media components for every assignment and use a minimum of three platforms for their final project. Those changes were made as a response to the evolution of market requirements for young reporters, and the goal was to learn about packaging stories for print, online, and video "in the most effective combination," as Joe Grimm, professor of the course since 2008, said.

These changes did not come without shortcomings. As the curriculum expanded to include photo, audio, video, maps, and data journalism, less time could be devoted to basic reporting and writing, a challenge that must be addressed in future iterations of the course. This is a weakness that we will return to when discussing findings from the ONA project.

Community Engagement

Since its inception and in line with MSU's land-grant philosophy, the course has required that students report on the communities surrounding the university, with campus-based stories generally being prohibited. The benefits of community engagement are twofold: (1) training students on various forms of "real" reporting, and (2) helping them become more civically engaged as they learn about the political system. The class rotates, covering 13 communities in mid-Michigan. Students, instructors, and community members agreed that one of the biggest strengths of the course is the relationship students develop with local residents. This relationship is a two-way street: It benefits the students by giving them real-world experience, and it also benefits residents by filling community information needs in places that receive less professional reporting. Instructors endeavor to encourage students to reach out to and interact with their beat (i.e., the assigned community) as professional journalists do in various ways. For example, professor Frederick Fico, who taught JRN300 in the 2000s, called community sources every week in order to fact-check information and ask about students' performance.

Several of the stories produced have a real impact on local affairs. For example, a student in Professor Joy Visconti's 2018 section wrote stories on the polarization between two communities, and how one of them is marginalized by the local leadership. Community members used stories as evidence of their needs being ignored when asking for more resources. "I think the student who wrote the story realized its impact," Visconti said.

In our interviews, students said that building community relationships makes the course more demanding and intensive, but also noted that getting out of their comfort zones made them better reporters. The main difficulties mentioned by students refer to the requirement for all stories to be about public affairs, and speaking with diverse groups of citizens in places that they have never been before. According to one student, the course taught her how to communicate with people, which gradually made her experience more enjoyable. Others emphasized that instructor involvement was key to getting those relationships started: "My professor helped me to formulate meaningful emails, calls, and messages to my sources, which helped me understand the steps a powerful reporter needs to take to write a great, newsworthy story," a student said. Generally, community members welcome student reporters. Jane Greenway, the parks and land management coordinator for Meridian Township, is regularly contacted by students asking about park development projects and is "impressed with their level of questioning."

Toward Issue-Oriented Reporting: The Online News Organization Challenge Fund

Until 2016, stories have largely focused on events such as local political meetings (town hall, school board meetings, etc.) and soft news. While these are undoubtedly important, instructors started conducting small experiments to move the course toward more in-depth coverage of specific issues. In 2017, one of the sections focused exclusively on issues related to the First Amendment. In the following semester, another section focused on issues of diversity. These experiments served as the foundation for the ONA-funded project implemented in 2018.

Every year, the ONA provides money for experimental projects that test innovative ideas to enhance the journalism curriculum through its Challenge Fund. Part of their requirement is that these projects follow a "teaching hospital" model partnering with the local news media. Our project focused on "schools of choice," a policy at the forefront of national conversations about the U.S. education system after the 2016 election. Michigan approved its first school of choice law in 1994, and the ONA project had three goals: first, we sought to humanize a largely statistical phenomenon through journalistic storytelling. Second, we incorporated multimedia and data journalism to shoe-leather reporting. Finally, we used "schools of choice" as a framework to move our curriculum toward issue-oriented journalism education.

Because MSU has several sections of JRN300, the grant allowed for a randomized field experiment setting. This project was applied in one of these sections, which became the treatment group. The results we present here come from a content analysis of the stories produced for the class, open-ended class feedback, and semi-structured interviews with students. In 2018, data from four classes were collected: one experimental (taught by Grimm), two controls taught by different instructors, and one control taught by Grimm. Full instruments and datasets can be provided upon request.

We content-analyzed 292 weekly stories produced by treatment and control groups focusing on source diversity, types of stories (event-driven or features), and generic frames (episodic or thematic). Source diversity is critical to coverage of civic affairs, with scholars arguing that official sources, such as politicians or the police, are the most represented in the news.[1] The overreliance on official sources was further articulated in the theory of "indexing," which predicts that the range of debate about political issues in the news depends on the range of elite debate about the issue.[2] It is, thus, crucial to create a model for journalism education that fosters diversity of viewpoints and access to the news via sourcing patterns that go beyond official narratives.

For story types, prior studies suggest that civic affairs reporting often dedicates more attention to event-driven stories with immediate impact (e.g., accidents, protests) or scheduled events sponsored by official sources (e.g., press conferences). This pattern has led scholars to suggest that general journalistic framing could be broadly separated into episodic and thematic frames. *Episodic* coverage is faster to produce and focuses on individual behaviors, episodes, and singular events, thus drawing less attention to systemic or societal problems.[3] *Thematic* framing, on the other hand, relates individual stories to larger contextual issues. Thematic stories tend to be longer and provide more context and viewpoints related to the issue, its cause, and potential solutions.

Intercoder reliability was performed with randomly selected stories following the recommendation of Riffe et al. (2005) for 85% Assumed Level of Agreement in Population. Krippendorff's alphas ranged from 0.79 to 0.98 and were calculated using Recal.[4]

Sources

Stories were coded for the number of sources directly quoted among the following categories: government officials, education officials, business owners, teachers, parents, students, NGOs, and other (residents, other experts, etc.). We measured the share or proportions of all voices reported belonging to each group by adding all sources mentioned (N total) and calculating a proportion for each group (N group/N total).

When comparing both groups, we found a statistically significant difference when it comes to quotes from education officials, government officials, business owners, students, NGOs, and others. To control for instructor style and meet the assumption of independence for comparing means, a two-way ANCOVA was performed including instructor and student name as fixed terms. Results reveal a statistically significant difference between experimental and control groups, such as that the experimental group ($M = .31$, $SD = .04$) had more official sources overall (ratio) than the control groups ($M = .20$, $SD = .04$) [$F(1) = 4.97$, $p < .05$]. It is important to note that these numbers reflect the sum of education officials and politicians for the treatment group. Further, we noticed that although the treatment group had a higher ratio of official sources, it also had a wider range of sources within the education beat: officials, parents, students, teachers, and others (e.g., librarians). In the control group, most quotes came from two groups: elected politicians and "person on the street" interviews.

Type of Stories

Cross-tabulations reveal that stories from the treatment group were more human-centered than the control groups. Results show that 20.7% of the stories from the control groups were event-driven hard news, and this number was reduced to 9.4% in the treatment class [$\chi^2(1, N = 224) = 4.92$, $p <. 05$]. One of our goals for this course was to move beyond topical event-driven reporting and toward humanizing public affairs issues, and these results reflect those efforts. See Table 11.1.

Additional tests were conducted entering the instructor variable as a layer, which allows us to verify if these differences are happening because of different teaching styles, but results could not be computed because one cell had less than five observations, violating chi-square assumptions.

There was no statistically significant difference between control and treatment groups when it comes to episodic/thematic coverage, with both averaging about 60% episodic. However, these numbers could also be reflecting the impact of different instructors on course outcomes. To control for that, we tested the two courses taught by the same instructor: Spring 2018 experimental class and Fall 2018 control course. Results reveal a statistically significant difference between treatment and control groups, with 23% of stories from the control group being thematic versus 40% of the treatment group (schools of choice class) [$\chi^2(1, N = 124) = 3.38, p <. 05$].

In sum, stories from the treatment group had a more diverse range of sources, relying less on government state officials (politicians) and more on education officials, and a wider range of non-official sources: educators, teachers, students, and parents. Stories from the control groups relied on government officials, mainly traditional politicians, and residents (vox populi quotes). Stories from the treatment group also brought more in-depth human content and features, while the control group had more traditional public affairs hard news.

Table 11.1 Type of stories by group

	Control	Treatment	$\chi^2(1, N = 224)$
Hard news (event-driven)	20.7%	9.4%	4.92*
Feature (human-driven)	79.3%	90.6%	n.a.

*p < .05.

Students, Instructors, and the Public

Qualitative interviews with students and instructors showed that their overall attitude about the "schools of choice" experiment was positive, but that the move toward issue-oriented multimedia reporting does not come without shortcomings. In particular, as the curriculum expanded to include photo, audio, video, maps, and data journalism, less time could be devoted to basic reporting and writing, a challenge that must be addressed in future iterations of the course.

Initially, the challenge with the issue-oriented class was that students were unfamiliar or not particularly excited about the topic (i.e., school of choice). According to a student:

The class was focused on the topic of schools of choice, and most of the writing done in the class focused on this particular subject. It was challenging for me because I was unfamiliar with the topic of schools of choice at first. As the class progressed, I gained and established valuable relationships with my sources and colleagues and the topic of schools of choice (treatment group).

Another important issue reported by students was the fast pace of the experimental course, which was sometimes overwhelming. In their words:

The organization [was my least favorite thing]. Everything was very fast paced, and we weren't sure what to do most of the time (treatment group).

At the beginning of class I was very confused on how this class was going to work but toward the end I believe it did make sense (treatment group).

The control groups, however, also had a similar issue:

Writing every week and trying to contact people for sources while taking all my other classes was very stressful. And we started writing articles without having a clear understanding of what we're supposed to be covering (control group).

This is an issue that journalism educators have to reflect on when it comes to making a course like this a curriculum requirement. Our goal is to expose students to the reality of being a reporter, and we believe having weekly stories is beneficial to them. Further, we want to provide a reliable news website for residents. However, we must be mindful that students have other classes, career paths, and commitments, many of which do not prioritize hyperlocal public affairs. Our data analysis, however, still indicated that most students enjoyed getting published in our website and being "forced" to engage with the communities:

> [My favorite part was] That our stories got published in the Spartan Newsroom. We could actually make a difference and tell a story (treatment group).
>
> I really enjoyed being pushed out of my boundaries. I was forced to speak to many people I never thought I would've. I felt like I learned the most when I did this. I faced fears and accomplished many things I never thought I could have done (treatment group).

For the ONA experimental group, we also identified an important result related to teamwork: rather than create teams based on access to transportation and using demographic considerations such as gender and race, the ONA class also identified interests and distributed groups by skills, ensuring to have a video producer, mapmaker, and writers on each team. As a result, students reported greater satisfaction working on teams. According to one student:

> [My favorite part was] the final project for sure. Seeing everything come together and tell a tough story like Lansing losing students was something that was well worth the reporting in the beginning (treatment group).
>
> It was the hardest, but it was also the most fun project I've ever done it at MSU. I think because I was so engaged with the students in the community. So, I actually got to experience what they were going through. I went to a lot of these places and I watched all these kids do these things for two months . . . I really liked that project a lot and that kind of made me want to report more about places that don't get a lot of spotlight (treatment group).

Finally, results also show that the ONA project expanded the course's transmedia capabilities by sending out narratives across many different platforms: print, web stories, StoryMaps, and video. From the students' perspective, this added visibility to their work.

Engaging with Local News: Challenges and Opportunities

In our proposal for ONA, we detailed an ideal partnership between the university and the local newspaper: their reporters would come to the classroom to help us with planning and mentor our students in exchange for us providing content to help replace some of what the paper was losing through staff cuts. As the weeks progressed and breaking news happened (Parkland shootings and protests), it became evident that our local newspaper was understandably limited in the amount of time they could dedicate to coaching our students to produce content that the paper actually needed. From our perspective, it seems like the teaching hospital model that ONA incentivizes is much more feasible in partnerships that involve larger media partners and smaller universities.

It is worth mentioning that our partnership was nonetheless valuable. Visiting the newsroom was informative for students, and the newspaper education reporter came to class a few times to help with story ideas. However, time, space, and bureaucratic processes were big obstacles preventing student work from being published in the newspaper. Fortunately, Michigan State has the resources to present student content in other platforms, including The Spartan Newsroom (student media), social media, and ArcGIS Storymaps library. We have also produced a print magazine to share with community members, Michigan senators and state representatives, school boards, and ONA.

We are fortunate enough that our experiment benefited from decades of community engagement conducted by educators in this specific institution. Before we recommend our formula to everyone, we must consider that these opportunities vary immensely across different universities and academic cultures. We recognize that this project was only possible because we are privileged in many ways, including a low turnover of professors of practice who act as a bridge between researchers and professional journalists.

Finally, the field experiment we detail in this chapter was only possible with support from the ONA Challenge Fund, which provided, among other things, resources for equipment, data collection, and incentives. Once again, this opportunity is unevenly distributed as some projects are more attractive to grantors than others, and funding available may vary over the years. Overall, we found that opportunity inequality is a big challenge for engagement in financially strapped states where the university is the biggest hub for journalism.

Creating Greater Trust

Reclaiming the role of journalism and Journalism Studies is critical at a time when journalists and academia are both under attack. We argue that journalism education should also take a central role in rebuilding citizen's trust in local reporting. We offer three key recommendations for making this kind of partnership between universities and communities possible and beneficial to students: minimizing instructor turnover, active administrative support from the university, and recognizing tradeoffs when it comes to prioritizing particular journalism skills in the classroom.

Our historical analysis detailed how a course can move from in-house writing assignments to providing a news service to communities that became more and more underserved by the local news media over the years. Crucial to this development has been the involvement of key faculty members who steward the creation and maintenance of a student news outlet, have deep knowledge of local communities, and serve as the gatekeepers for students who are unfamiliar with the people and issues they are going to cover. While there is always a risk associated with sending novice journalists into various unfamiliar communities, we believe that experienced instructors can mitigate it. In our interviews, instructors reported being very hands-on when it comes to verification and ethics, often calling sources to check on the work of their students. That expectation, however, places a heavier burden on instructors of this class as compared to other courses in our curriculum: they need to be familiar with the community and with a wide range of local issues, policies, and civic groups, while constantly checking on students' work to ensure journalistic error does not jeopardize the trust between the university and local citizens. Our first recommendation, therefore, cautions against high turnover of faculty in charge of undergraduate reporting classes, especially when those classes involve local community engagement. Often, basic reporting classes are underestimated vis-à-vis graduate seminars or upper-level advanced reporting, but administrators must see their outreach value and their significance to student development when assigning instructors. Here, consistency is key.

A second related recommendation refers to the feasibility of having students provide a reliable and efficient news service to the community. This once again requires a significant investment from school administrators, who ought to dedicate resources to the enterprise (e.g., faculty course releases, funding for web development and management, etc.). In other words, running a newsroom cannot be considered just another task for professors teaching undergraduate reporting courses. Similarly, we found it was much easier to engage with community members than with the local newspaper. This was not a result of journalists' unwillingness to engage with the class, but it is a reality when reporters simply do not have the time or resources to dedicate to mentoring and monitoring student work.

Finally, through our experiments we found some challenges when introducing innovation to basic reporting and writing courses. As schools adapt their curricula to the industry demands, educators struggle with the question of how to foment a multimedia mentality without losing gains associated with basic reporting and writing. With time as a scarce resource, our ONA-funded experiment revealed losses in writing in the treatment section that followed a more multimedia-oriented curriculum. Here, one option could be splitting public affairs reporting classes in two parts, guaranteeing that equal efforts are dedicated to shoe-leather reporting, writing, and multimedia training, as well a longer period for students to work on their beat and build relationships with local sources.

One obvious limitation of this analysis is that it focuses on a single case study in a very specific geographical context and, as such, results cannot be generalized. Further, limitations include the influence of exogenous factors on our field experiment. For example, the Stoneman Douglas High School shooting happened while we were conducting our ONA experiment, and we opted to deviate some resources from the "schools of choice" issue to cover the marches. Despite these limitations, we believe the lessons learned here can be adapted to many institutions that share the same land-grant vision of Michigan State.

Connecting Journalism Studies research to the practice means also including research-informed strategies to professional training in journalism schools. In this chapter, we start with the assumption that coursework can be used to both train students and to engage with local communities, who are often underserved by the local news media. Our analysis of a public affairs reporting class revealed some challenges, but also exciting opportunities to rebuild trust through the ground up, with students and instructors working closely with community members in a much more inclusive journalistic production process. We believe our project was a good start for a relationship with the local news industry, but the question remains: How do we make meaningful collaborations that are beneficial to academics and professional reporters when there is disparity in resources across the two groups?

Notes

1. Herbet J. Gans, *Deciding What's News* (Chicago: Northwestern University Press, 2004).
2. W. Lance Bennett, Regina G. Lawrence, and Steven Livingston, *When the Press Fails* (University of Chicago Press, 2008).
3. Shanto Iyengar, *Is Anyone Responsible? How Television Frames Political Issues* (University of Chicago Press, 1994).
4. Deen Freelon, "ReCal OIR: Ordinal, Interval, and Ratio Intercoder Reliability as a Web Service," *International Journal of Internet Science* 8, no. 1 (2013): 10–16.

12

What Is Data Literacy?

And Why Should We Count on It Changing the News?

Jan Lauren Boyles

Introduction

Pie charts that total more than 100 percent. Scatterplots with strange and mysterious outliers. Column and row figures that are transposed. News consumers and scholarly researchers can generally spot such egregious examples of flawed data. But what about a report that cherry picks data points to support an author's argument? Or what about a study that mistakes correlation for causation? Or, still further, what about a dirty dataset that has so much "noise," yet is still publicly presented as valid and accurate? Compelling visualizations and narratives can make data appear so beautiful that they become believable. Detecting these faults necessitates higher levels of computational comprehension beyond fundamental math and statistics; it mandates a deeper understanding of how data work.

While journalists serve an instrumental role in explaining data to the general public, they are not the sole entity shaping society's engagement with data today. New players—both humans and machines—are mediating (and in many cases reformulating) the data-driven information that publics receive. A multitude of new stakeholders—from technologists/developers and civic hackers/activists to marketers/researchers—interface with data with varying levels of expertise. With the accelerating datafication driven by these actors, understanding the behind-the-scenes operations of big data grows ever more important for all actors within today's digital news ecosystem. Training in how to effectively deal with data is inconsistent, however. In the absence of formal education, scholars, practitioners, and the public often learn how to interact with data on the fly. In dealing with data, such knowledge cleavages—if left unchecked—carry the dangerous capacity to further bifurcate the public into classes of "data-haves" and "data-have-nots."

Jan Lauren Boyles, *What Is Data Literacy?* In: *Journalism Research That Matters.* Edited by: Valérie Bélair-Gagnon and Nikki Usher, Oxford University Press. © Oxford University Press 2021. DOI: 10.1093/oso/9780197538470.003.0013

As data-driven storytelling continues its ascent, these societal shortfalls in knowledge around data can be problematic—leading to possible mistakes, misinterpretation, and misinformation. Taken together, persistence of these knowledge gaps around data know-how carry the potential to further erode levels of public trust around journalistic production. And at their most extreme, these data-driven intellectual divides may ultimately hamper the ability of citizens to fully engage with the news.

Addressing these challenges of big data's entry into news circulation, this chapter defines and examines capacity-building efforts around *data literacy*—conversation and/or engagement that takes place around how a dataset is formed, processed, and interpreted by both the press and the public. This work first defines data literacy. A set of barriers that have prevented data literacy's wide-scale adoption to date are also discussed. Sample low and no-cost approaches are presented, which data practitioners (journalists and scholars) can incorporate toward building data literacy within news communities.

Defining Data Literacy

Perhaps the most significant shift around knowledge manufacture in the digital age surrounds the entry of big data. Data streams and datasets represent core inputs into public storytelling today. Asymmetrical knowledge often exists between those in academia, civic institutions, or industry who construct the data, and those who interpret it.[1] Algorithms that shape the news, which are constructed by technologists who are often removed from day-to-day knowledge production, can be difficult for non-technologists to understand.[2] In other cases, bad actors can engage in "statactivism"—a wide set of "creative strategies deployed by different publics to align statistical data with their concerns."[3] In these situations, expertise is needed to spot when the collection, analysis, or presentation of data is faulty.

The concept of *data literacy* can help facilitate a better understanding between journalism practitioners and audiences about how big data can be used to shape public knowledge. Data literacy stands as an outgrowth of *media literacy*, which encompasses how information is packaged and processed for public circulation,[4] and *news* media literacy, which is centered upon teaching best practices by which citizens can critically evaluate journalistic products.[5] Described as "developing critical understandings of the language, audience and representations of data,"[6] data literacy spotlights how stakeholders develop insights from a given dataset.[7] Data literacy encompasses more than mere numeracy, or the application of general mathematical awareness to an information product.[8] While numeracy can be a facet of data literacy, the concept as a whole tackles a wider spectrum of activity that spans from the capture/collection of data to its ultimate rendering in public-facing products.

Prior academic research has articulated varied and wide-reaching visions of data literacy.[9] Some scholars suggest that merely understanding how the data functions itself is not enough; publics must also grasp how critical infrastructures are constructed by developers to retrieve, house, and parse the data.[10] Other scholars extend data literacy into broadening societal comprehensions of privacy/security protections and the consequences of algorithmic power, as well as identifying human and machine-generated communication biases that can exist in code.[11] While these are all worthy directions for future concept explication, data literacy in this chapter will be defined as conversation and/or engagement that takes place around how a dataset is formed, processed, and interpreted by both the press and the public. Data literacy initiatives can provide a greater explanation of data's societal role.

As part of data literacy outreach efforts, scholars have suggested that journalists can be reoriented into a new, collaborative role around data. In this effort, news practitioners can join with civic technologists and educators (among others) to highlight when data should or should not be trusted.[12] To achieve this end, however, these actors must do more than just provide public access to the data. As Dourish and Gómez-Cruz argue, "data must be narrated—put to work in particular contexts, sunk into narratives that give them shape and meaning, and mobilized as part of broader processes of interpretation."[13] There may be a delicate balance in practice around journalists contextualizing data for the public, though. Audiences may see journalistic interpretation of datasets as "paternalistic," shaping news for audiences.[14] Initial research has suggested that audiences may find this top-down data storytelling approach to be ideologically narrow and limiting.[15] Striking the right balance between providing information and interpretation around data rests as a central challenge for data actors (including journalists) today. Presentational matters aside, engagement with data clearly requires new knowledge. Disciplines like data/computer science and statistics have not typically been at the heart of news production and/or consumption. Data literacy efforts, as a result, need to better account for how "the origins, the textures, and the implications of Big Data" interplay into information processing for both news producers and consumers.[16]

In the late 2010s, intense scrutiny was placed upon how media narratives—at their most unethical—could be manipulated by those wishing to deceive the public.[17] For the profession of journalism, the stakes are high: Without the public's trust in news production, the legitimacy and authority that undergirds journalistic practice itself stands at risk.[18] Given the circulation of fabricated content across digital platforms, audiences must dedicate greater efforts to decipher and to interpret content, in order to make judgment calls between what they perceive to be true or false.[19] Journalists have attempted to intervene by providing fact-checks and offering what they perceive as independent, fair reporting; but thus far, even though journalists provide critical civic information, they are not directly engaging citizens in civic decision making.[20] In this light, data literacy has also been identified as a potential lever to bolster press–public engagement around the news in the digital age.[21] In the last decade, philanthropic foundations have significantly invested into public-facing news media literacy projects (particularly those based in urban centers), which often attempt to (re)train the public to "think like journalists."[22] Proponents of recent news media literacy initiatives advocate that their outreach projects help break down informational barriers between news producers and consumers.[23] To date, however, little academic research within the field of Journalism Studies has applied notions of data literacy to journalistic practice. In the limited literature available, data literacy outreach efforts have been heralded as a possible strategy to combat the public's high levels of skepticism around news production.[24] Despite its promise, several barriers have impeded wide-scale adoption of data literacy approaches to date.

Data Literacy Roadblocks

Several types of roadblocks—educational, institutional, and cultural—exist that prevent the diffusion of data literacy across society. Early socialization forces, such as parents and schools, have been identified as potential shaping factors that can help cultivate adulthood understandings of how data operates. Teachers in K–12 schools more readily adopt statistical reasoning approaches that explain, for instance, why measures of central tendency may hide outliers.[25] These concepts, however, are often presented in abstraction without ties to real-world examples.[26] On the whole, efforts to infuse data literacy into K–12 classrooms in the United States have been uneven, with notable demographic and geographic achievement gaps.[27] At the college level, schools of education that train future teachers have generally been slow to integrate data literacy across their curricula, too.[28] In training prospective developers who create the code that drives algorithms and other computational products, university computer science programs have traditionally taught students that documenting their workflows in open source environments can help detail how data works.[29] Open source environments, however, tend to provide a digital space for technologists to trade talents with one another, rather than an explanatory forum for sharing those talents with the public.[30] Globally, the greatest energy toward integrating data literacy into higher education can be currently witnessed within library and information science programs, which see data literacy as an extension of their historic responsibility of curating scholarly research.[31]

To date, few journalism schools have invested in discipline-specific math or statistics courses offered by cross-campus colleagues.[32] Some trace this general reticence to fears that emphasizing statistical content could "risk alienating 'math phobic' journalism students."[33] Journalism students have historically exhibited high levels of math anxiety—or a general reluctance to embrace basic numeracy concepts.[34] Despite this tendency against adopting statistically driven coursework, two-thirds of j-school administrators surveyed agreed that students who are trained in data literacy "enjoy a leg up in the journalism job market."[35]

Aspiring news workers who graduate from journalism schools generally receive limited data literacy instruction. While journalism school administrators have long promoted data literacy as an essential skill for their graduates, the development of data-driven coursework has taken hold within American and Western European colleges and universities quite slowly.[36] Journalism school deans and directors who have advocated for faculty-led development of data literacy programming indicate that the adoption is a direct response to shifts in news industry labor demands.[37] Others highlight that more pervasive bureaucratic obstacles—such as adherence to accreditation standards, (re)training of tenured faculty, and/or realignment of internal strategic priorities—serve as more substantial impediments toward more fully integrating data literacy across j-schools.[38] Administrative leaders often wrangle whether data literacy merits a module within an existing course, an entire class, or a sequence of classes within the curriculum.[39] Roughly half

(48 percent) of America's accredited journalism schools offer a standalone class in data journalism, which provides foundational skills in data literacy.[40]

In the absence of wide-scale educational adoption of data literacy, journalism school graduates often acquire data skills (and abilities in data literacy) in their first positions on the job. Internal communication bottlenecks within the newsroom can slow how news workers adopt new skills, however. Newsroom innovation with data often remains siloed within specialist teams, rather than being shared by practitioners across the organization.[41] Based upon prior education and current training, levels of practitioner self-competency in working with data vary heavily. Media practitioners who display higher levels of confidence in their knowledge of data are more likely to employ data-driven approaches within their own journalistic works.[42] Newsroom-wide adoption of such approaches also takes managerial leadership to advocate for the work's value.[43] Yet, as news organizations operate with bootstrapped budgets and lean staffs, newsroom leaders—particularly those at small community newspapers—struggle to allocate resources toward data literacy opportunities and programming.

Balancing the imperative for heightened data literacy with the imperiled financial climate for journalistic practice can prove difficult for newsroom leaders. At the same time, convening community among data actors can also prove challenging because of knowledge gaps around computation.[44] Both pressures are particularly palpable for legacy news providers—publications that are struggling with sagging revenues and shrinking staffs. In response, local news publications often must target smaller data literacy outreach ideas that are more feasible to implement. To this effort, journalism researchers can also help move the needle toward more collaborative engagement around data-driven news.

Small Experiments with Big Data

To foster data literacy within news communities, several small-scale, low (and no) cost strategies can be employed. Such outreach can act as a catalyst toward convening key community stakeholders who care about data.

Locally based educational efforts around data can act as a first step. Historically, industry trade groups such as the Newspaper Association of America Foundation sponsored news media literacy initiatives to partner community newspapers with elementary educators through projects such as hosting visiting journalists in classrooms or donating used newspapers to schools.[45] Revisiting these initiatives for the data-driven age, renewed outreach around data literacy can better reach frontline personnel—including K–12 educators, journalism school faculty, civic technologists/developers, and professional news workers—who play vital roles in educating the public about data. To this end, written and digitally delivered manuals with hands-on exercises—prepared by the National Institute for Computer-Assisted Reporting (NICAR) conference and Investigative Reporters and Editors (IRE), among others—can provide an entry point for these data literacy education efforts. Informative guides around data reporting have also been developed by members of the scholarly community. University departments in statistics and computer science (particularly those from land-grant institutions with extension and outreach missions) can further build upon these materials by developing online data literacy training modules for K–12/university students, practitioners, and the general public. Creators of these guides need to be wary of borrowing terms from the tech community—such as *manipulating data*—that can acquire other shades of meaning that harken to how mis/disinformation spreads online.

Stronger relationships can also be forged with community actors who already engage in open data efforts. University librarians and statisticians would be logical initial partners. Community media outlets may find additional support by tapping into technology incubators and/or co-working spaces where local technologists gather. Other local community initiatives around code—such as Hacks/Hackers chapters[46] or Code for America's nationwide brigade network—are spurring greater community-driven participation around data. Building upon this energy, local publications can also serve as co-sponsors or conveners for community tech events, such as hackathons.[47] Such gatherings can stimulate conversation among academicians, technologists, journalists, and the public. With time, these exchanges can perhaps serve as the foundation for building stronger computational communities around data.

Expanded efforts around data literacy don't have to break the bank. Data literacy approaches can also leverage simple low- and no-cost tactics to reach newsroom staff and their audiences. Through a collaborative project with Arizona State University's Walter Cronkite School of Journalism and Mass Communication's News Co/Lab, the *Kansas City Star* has been testing new approaches to audience engagement. The paper, for instance, has been experimenting with explainers that detail how the data behind the story was analyzed.[48] In essence, this content acts like a "mini-methods" section similar to that which one would find within an academic journal article. Even though this small step may occupy extra time from a reporter, the result provides added transparency to the final news product. Inviting local experts into the newsroom for brown bag lunch sessions can also serve as an initial no-cost forum for knowledge exchange.

Journalism researchers also have a role to play. Across all these press–public–academic experiments in heightening data literacy, additional academic research can help assess the effectiveness of these interventions. However, one challenge is that scholars have not yet coalesced around how to measure or evaluate engagement around data literacy. To this end, future research by Journalism Studies scholars could subsequently evaluate the effectiveness of these training tools in facilitating practitioner and public understanding of data. Academic inquiry could also help illustrate the degree to which audiences find data explanation to be a help or a hindrance. In addition, Journalism Studies scholars can provide value in determining the extent to which community-based collaborations around data literacy actually work. Such efforts can extend Journalism Studies research beyond the ivory tower and beyond the newsroom, into the spaces where news engagement occurs today.

Beyond conducting scholarly studies on the effectiveness of these press–public–academic interventions, journalism educators are also experimenting with better ways to infuse data into the curriculum for doctoral students (many of whom will transition to tenure-track positions to research journalism's societal role). The Ph.Digital Bootcamp at Texas State University, for instance, provides immersive weekly sessions for early career researchers to better understand how data operates.[49] Journalism researchers can also bolster data literacy by providing open source access to the datasets that undergird their scholarly publications.[50] For data literacy to truly acquire traction, though, numerous parties—news providers, tech communities, university experts, and the public—must vigorously collaborate on these projects.

As society grows ever more "datafied" in the digital age, knowledge exchange around data literacy has become ever more vital for both news producers and consumers. Surface-level numeracy is insufficient; all actors instead need to be trained in how data functions. This outreach stands essential to cultivating shared data knowledge among publics. In their best incarnation, data literacy initiatives can perhaps counterbalance the effects of misinformation. And at their most optimistic, these interventions may ultimately bring stakeholders together in broader civic conversation within news communities. For now, the small-scale initiatives highlighted here (among others) can potentially serve as first steps toward fuller public understandings of big data, in the hope of fostering a more data-literate society.

Notes

1. Luci Pangrazio and Neil Selwyn, "'Personal Data Literacies': A Critical Literacies Approach to Enhancing Understandings of Personal Digital Data," *New Media & Society* 21, no. 2 (2019): 420.
2. Kate Crawford, Kate Miltner, and Mary L. Gray, "Critiquing Big Data: Politics, Ethics, Epistemology," *International Journal of Communication* 8 (2014): 1668.
3. Jonathan Gray, Carolin Gerlitz, and Liliana Bounegru, "Data Infrastructure Literacy," *Big Data & Society* 5, no. 2 (2018): 7.
4. Tibor Koltay, "The Media and the Literacies: Media Literacy, Information Literacy, Digital Literacy," *Media, Culture & Society* 33, no. 2 (2011): 215.
5. Emily K. Vraga, Melissa Tully, and Hernando Rojas, "Media Literacy Training Reduces Perception of Bias," *Newspaper Research Journal* 30, no. 4 (2016): 71.
6. Pangrazio and Selwyn, "Personal Data Literacies," 422.
7. Jake Carlson and Lisa R. Johnston, *Data Information Literacy: Librarians, Data, and the Education of a New Generation of Researchers*, Vol. 2. (West Lafayette: Purdue University Press, 2015), vii.
8. Gray, Gerlitz, and Bounegru, "Data Infrastructure Literacy," 2.
9. Tibor Koltay, "Data Governance, Data Literacy and the Management of Data Quality," *International Federation of Library Associations Journal* 42, no. 4 (2016): 307–308.
10. Gray, Gerlitz, and Bounegru, "Data Infrastructure Literacy," 2–3.
11. Jennifer Pybus, Mark Coté, and Tobias Blanke, "Hacking the Social Life of Big Data," *Big Data & Society* 2, no. 2 (2015): 4.
12. Andrew Schrock and Gwen Shaffer, "Data Ideologies of an Interested Public: A Study of Grassroots Open Government Data Intermediaries," *Big Data & Society* 4, no. 1 (2017): 2.
13. Paul Dourish and Edgar Gómez-Cruz, "Datafication and Data Fiction: Narrating Data and Narrating with Data," *Big Data & Society* 5, no. 2 (2018): 1.
14. Ester Appelgren, "An Illusion of Interactivity: The Paternalistic Side of Data Journalism," *Journalism Practice* 12, no. 3, (2018): 308.
15. Rodrigo Zamith, "Transparency, Interactivity, Diversity, and Information Provenance in Everyday Data Journalism," *Digital Journalism* 7, no. 4 (2019): 470–489.
16. Zizi Papacharissi, "The Unbearable Lightness of Information and the Impossible Gravitas of Knowledge: Big Data and the Makings of a Digital Orality," *Media, Culture & Society* 37, no. 7 (2015): 1095–1100.

17. Edson C. Tandoc, Jr., Zheng Wei Lim, and Richard Ling, "Defining 'Fake News': A Typology of Scholarly Definitions," *Digital Journalism* 6, no. 2 (2018): 143.

18. Nikki Usher, "Re-Thinking Trust in the News: A Material Approach through 'Objects of Journalism,'" *Journalism Studies* 19, no. 4 (2018): 565–566.

19. Edson C. Tandoc, Jr., Richard Ling, Oscar Westlund, Andrew Duffy, Debbie Goh, and Zheng Wei Lim, "Audiences Acts of Authentication in the Age of Fake News: A Conceptual Framework," *New Media & Society* 20, no. 8 (2018): 2757.

20. Lucas Graves, *Deciding What's True: The Rise of Political Fact-Checking in American Journalism* (New York: Columbia University Press, 2016), 6.

21. Dan Gillmor, "Toward a (New) Media Literacy in a Media Saturated World," in *Journalism and Citizenship: New Agendas in Communication*, ed. Zizi Papacharissi (New York: Routledge, 2009), 11.

22. Momin M. Malik, Sandra Cortesi, and Urs Gasser, *The Challenges of Defining "News Literacy"* (Cambridge: Berkman Center Research, 2013), 5.

23. Renee Hobbs, "The State of Media Literacy: A Response to Potter," *Journal of Broadcasting & Electronic Media* 55, no. 3 (2011): 423.

24. Paul Mihailidis and Samantha Viotty, "Spreadable Spectacle in Digital Culture: Civic Expression, Fake News, and the Role of Media Literacies in 'Post-Fact' Society," *American Behavioral Scientist* 61, no. 4 (2017): 449.

25. Joan Garfield, "The Challenge of Developing Statistical Reasoning," *Journal of Statistics Education* 10, no. 3 (2002): 4.

26. Garfield, "The Challenge of Developing," 6.

27. Roslyn Arlin Mickelson, Martha Cecilia Bottia, and Richard Lambert, "Effects of School Racial Composition on K–12 Mathematics Outcomes: A Metaregression Analysis," *Review of Educational Research* 83, no. 1 (2013): 121.

28. Ellen B. Mandinach and Edith S. Gummer, "A Systemic View of Implementing Data Literacy in Educator Preparation," *Educational Researcher* 42, no. 1 (2013): 30.

29. Catherine D'Ignazio and Rahul Bhargava, "DataBasic: Design Principles, Tools and Activities for Data Literacy Learners," *The Journal of Community Informatics* 12, no. 3 (2016): n.p.

30. Jan Lauren Boyles, "Deciphering Code: How Newsroom Developers Communicate Journalistic Labor," *Journalism Studies* 21, no. 3 (2020): 349.

31. Tibor Koltay, "Data Literacy for Researchers and Data Librarians," *Journal of Librarianship and Information Science* 49, no. 1 (2017): 6.

32. Christine Cusatis and Renee Martin-Kratzer, "Assessing the State of Math Education in ACEJMC-accredited and Non-accredited Undergraduate Journalism Programs," *Journalism & Mass Communication Educator* 64, no. 4 (2010): 356; Justin D. Martin, "A Census of Statistics Requirements at US Journalism Programs and a Model for a 'Statistics For Journalism' Course," *Journalism & Mass Communication Educator* 72, no. 4 (2017): 470.

33. Louise Yarnall, J.T. Johnson, Luke Rinne, and Michael Andrew Ranney, "How Post-secondary Journalism Educators Teach Advanced CAR Data Analysis Skills in the Digital Age," *Journalism & Mass Communication Educator* 63, no. 2 (2008): 159.

34. Patricia A. Curtin and Scott R. Maier, "Numbers in the Newsroom: A Qualitative Examination of a Quantitative Challenge," *Journalism & Mass Communication Quarterly* 78, no. 4 (2001): 720; Scott R. Maier, "Numeracy in the Newsroom: A Case Study of Mathematical Competence and Confidence," *Journalism & Mass Communication Quarterly* 80, no. 4 (2003): 921; An Nguyen and Jairo Lugo-Ocando, "The State of Statistics in Journalism and Journalism Education–Issues and Debates," *Journalism* 17, no. 1 (2015): 3.

35. Robert J. Griffin and Sharon Dunwoody, "Chair Support, Faculty Entrepreneurship, and the Teaching of Statistical Reasoning to Journalism Undergraduates in the United States," *Journalism* 17, no. 1 (2016): 109.

36. Bahareh Heravi, "3WS of Data Journalism Education: What, Where and Who?" *Journalism Practice* 13, no. 3 (2019): 349.

37. Sharon Dunwoody and Robert J. Griffin, "Statistical Reasoning in Journalism Education," *Science Communication* 35, no. 4 (2013): 535.

38. Charles Berrett and Cheryl Phillips, *Teaching Data Journalism and Computational Journalism* (Columbia University School of Journalism and Stanford University, 2016), 74; Robin Blom and Lucinda D. Davenport, "Searching for the Core of Journalism Education: Program Directors Disagree on Curriculum Priorities," *Journalism & Mass Communication Educator* 67, no. 1 (2012): 80–83.

39. Jonathan Hewett, "Learning to Teach Data Journalism: Innovation, Influence and Constraints," *Journalism* 17, no. 1 (2015): 131.

40. Berrett and Phillips, "Teaching Data Journalism," 77.

41. Jan Lauren Boyles, "The Isolation of Innovation: Restructuring the Digital Newsroom through Intrapreneurship." *Digital Journalism* 4, no. 2 (2016): 241.

42. John Wihbey and Mark Coddington, "Knowing the Numbers: Assessing Attitudes among Journalists and Educators about Using and Interpreting Data, Statistics, and Research," *International Symposium on Online Journalism* 17 (2017): 17.

43. George Sylvie, *Reshaping the News: Community, Engagement, and Editors* (New York: Peter Lang, 2018), 4.

44. Mike Ananny, "Press–Public Collaboration as Infrastructure: Tracing News Organizations and Programming Publics in Application Programming Interfaces," *American Behavioral Scientist* 57, no. 5 (2013): 637.

45. Jim Abbott, *Newspaper in Education: A Guide for Weekly and Community Newspapers* (Washington, DC: Newspaper Association of American Foundation, 2005), 3.

46. Seth C. Lewis and Nikki Usher, "Code, Collaboration, and the Future of Journalism," *Digital Journalism* 2, no. 3 (2014): 386.

47. Jan Lauren Boyles, "Laboratories for News? Experimenting with Journalism Hackathons," *Journalism* (2017): Preprint, 1.

48. Mike Fannin, "We Need Each Other. So Let's Keep the Conversation Going," *The Kansas City Star*, August 26, 2018, https://www.kansascity.com/news/local/article217302265.html.

49. Cindy Royal, "PhDigital Bootcamp: 2019 Evaluation Assessment," July 24, 2019, http://phdigitalbootcamp.com/report/PhDigital_evaluation_report_final2019.pdf.

50. Tobias Dienlin et al., "An Agenda for Open Communication," *Journal of Communication* (2020): Preprint, 1.

13

Engaging the Academy

Confronting Eurocentrism in Journalism Studies

Brian Ekdale

Introduction

From the passing of Brexit in the United Kingdom to the elections of populist, anti-immigrant leaders in the United States, Brazil, Hungary, the Philippines, and India, we are witnessing a global turn toward ethno-nationalism and xenophobia. While this phenomenon is much larger than academia, it raises important questions about what those of us engaged in knowledge production are doing to implicitly or explicitly perpetuate ethnocentrism and nationalism. Scholarly knowledge production exists within systems of power that have material consequences on which kinds of knowledge are produced and valued.[1] From designing course syllabi to choosing which conferences to attend, scholars make a variety of decisions that contribute to what Appadurai terms the "academic imagination."[2] Within the discipline of communication, this imagination is built on an enduring legacy of sexism, racism, homophobia, transphobia, and ethnocentrism.[3] While inequities within our discipline are intersectional in nature, my specific focus here is on the problem of Eurocentrism, and Americentrism more specifically, in journalism and mass communication research. The point here is not to reduce the world into geopolitical binaries but rather to recognize that, as Medie and Kang argue, "a diverse academy is more likely to pose a broader array of research questions, adopt diverse methods and have access to a greater variety of sources."[4]

Public engagement typically focuses on producing and sharing scholarly knowledge with audiences outside of academia. But it is important to acknowledge that scholarly knowledge is imperfect, itself imbued with structural, ideological, and individual biases. These biases are reflected in the scholarship we read, the topics we study, the theories we test, and the methods we employ. If we want journalism research to matter, and if we

Brian Ekdale, *Engaging the Academy* In: *Journalism Research That Matters*. Edited by: Valérie Bélair-Gagnon and Nikki Usher, Oxford University Press. © Oxford University Press 2021. DOI: 10.1093/oso/9780197538470.003.0014 believe it is important to share our findings, suggestions, and critiques with practitioners, we need to be open and responsive to critiques of our own professional practices. Therefore, it is important for scholars to engage each other, not merely through our shared objects of analysis, but in the very nature of scholarly knowledge production.

To make the case for this reflexivity with journalism research, this chapter offers an overview of inequities that emerge from Eurocentric knowledge production, and recommendations for how to think about future research. First, I document inequities in scholarly knowledge production between the Global North and Global South. I then offer a brief contextualization of the structural nature of these inequities. Finally, I recommend specific practices journalism scholars based in the Global North can do to become better allies of our colleagues in the Global South, and highlight recent efforts to engage the academy around the issue of inequities in scholarly knowledge production.

I should note that I write from a position of significant privilege. I have benefited from racial, ethnic, and gender hierarchies in life and in academia as a white, heterosexual, cisgender American man who is a first-language English speaker. I am still learning to acknowledge my privilege, and I have contributed to the marginalization of others. In short, I have made mistakes, and I certainly will make more. My goal is not to claim a self-righteous stance or to encourage others to adopt a scholar savior complex. The purpose of this chapter is to acknowledge failings within journalism and mass communication studies, to provide context for the systematic marginalization of scholars based in the Global South, and to offer scholars in the Global North specific strategies they can use to challenge the enduring legacy of Eurocentrism in academia.

Global Inequities in Scholarly Knowledge Production

Global inequities in scholarly knowledge production are evident across academia. Of social science journals indexed by Web of Science, 90% are published in Europe and North America, and two-thirds are published in just four countries: the United States, United Kingdom, Germany, and the Netherlands.[5] Scholars based in the Global South are also underrepresented on journal editorial boards. One study found that in development studies, an inherently international field, 61% of editorial board members were based in the United States and United Kingdom, while only 8.5% were from developing countries.[6] Within the discipline of communication, Chakravartty and colleagues found that 86% of editorial board members at 12 communication journals were affiliated with U.S. institutions. These imbalances on editorial boards demonstrate how "colonial legacies of White supremacy permeate scholarly and public debates" within our discipline.[7]

Scholarship about the Global South and by scholars based in the Global South is also underrepresented in the pages of peer-reviewed academic journals. Gingras and Mosbah-Natanson found that less than 2% of social science journal articles indexed by Web of Science were published by scholars based in Latin America (1.3%), Africa (0.4%), and the Commonwealth of Independent States (0.1%) combined.[8] Within communication, one content analysis of 5,228 articles published in top communication journals between 2004 and 2010 found that only 39 articles (0.7%) focused on Africa and only 25 (0.5%) were authored by Africa-based scholars.[9] Similarly, although a systematic review of comparative Journalism Studies published in 22 peer-reviewed journals between 2000 and 2015 found an increase in "collaborations between researchers based in Western and non-Western institutions" over time, the same study found a consistent small proportion of articles first-authored by scholars based in non-Western countries (~10%), as well as a decline in articles authored exclusively by researchers based in non-Western countries.[10] Further, scholarship about the Global South or by scholars based in the Global South often is published in less prestigious journals. For example, Elega and Özad report that none of the 32 Africa-focused research articles about blogs published between 2006 and 2016 appeared in top-tier digital media journals like *New Media & Society* and *Journal of Computer-Mediated Communication*.[11] Similarly, Wasike found that less than a quarter of Africa-based studies published between 2004 and 2014 were published in journals ranked in the top 50 of the *Thomson Reuters Scientific Journal Ranking* for Communication.[12]

It is worth noting that scholarly knowledge production within and about the Global South is unevenly distributed. Specifically, research about the Global South is disproportionately published by scholars based in the Global North. Not only is this evident in journalism and mass communication studies, but it is also true for international fields like development studies, gender and politics, and area studies.[13] Yet, this imbalance is not necessarily the result of fewer submissions from scholars based in the Global South. Briggs and Weathers reported a 20-year decline in African politics research published by scholars affiliated with African institutions, even though the share of articles submitted by Africa-based scholars had increased during the same time period.[14] Even when research about the Global South is published, some nations and sub-disciplines are featured more prominently than others.[15] The net effect of this discrepancy is that certain parts of the world become doubly marginalized in academic literature.[16]

Academic conferences also reveal and reinscribe global inequities in scholarly knowledge production.[17] Most disciplinary conferences, even area studies conferences, are held in North America and Europe. As a result, scholars based in the Global South who wish to attend the premiere conferences in their respective fields bear a disproportionate financial and logistical burden, made worse by recent changes to visa requirements in the United States.[18] While hosting decisions are based on a variety of factors, the choice of where to host an annual conference reflects an organization's values. Since its founding in 1912, the Association for Education in Journalism and Mass Communication (AEJMC) has hosted only five conferences outside the United States, all of which have been in Canada (1975, Ottawa; 1992, Montreal; 2004, Toronto; 2014, Montreal; 2019, Toronto). As for the International Communication Association (ICA), between its founding in 1964 and 1996 the organization hosted only one conference outside of the United States (1987, Montréal). Since 1997, ICA has traveled to several different countries in North America, Europe, and Asia, though it is yet to host its annual conference in South America or Africa.[19] In contrast, the International Association for Media and Communication Research (IAMCR) has been true to its name, hosting annual conferences in 19 different countries and five continents between 2000 and 2020.[20]

Academic conferences are also spaces where scholars' contributions to the field are recognized by their peers in the form of prestigious awards given out by divisional and organization leadership. At journalism and mass communication conferences, these awards disproportionally have been bestowed upon scholars based in the Global North. For example, Hanitzsch notes that while more than half of ICA's Journalism Studies Division members work at institutions outside the United States, the division has given all of its book, dissertation, and outstanding article awards between 2011 and 2018 to "scholars from universities located in the West," including 13 of the 20 major awards given to scholars based in the United States.[21] Compare these numbers with what Hanitzsch, Löffelholz, and Weaver articulated as the division's (then an interest group) founding goal of global inclusivity:

Even though English has become the *lingua franca* in the social sciences, a Journalism Studies Interest Group should thus attract scholars from non-English-speaking countries in order to contribute their national potentials to the international scientific discourse. Mastering proper English, though essential for publication, should not be made a criterion that prevents potential papers from being presented at international conferences.[22]

While the awards bestowed on behalf of ICA's Journalism Studies Division may not reflect these noble intentions, academic Eurocentrism, or more precisely academic Americentrism, has been most evident at AEJMC.

Founded in 1912, AEJMC is the oldest and largest scholarly organization in the field of journalism and mass communication.[23] As such, it has the ability to establish standards of excellence, socialize emerging scholars, and shape research agendas for the field. Although AEJMC seeks to internationalize, and the organization has more than 200 faculty and 50 graduate student members from 50 countries outside the United States, many view AEJMC as a American organization.[24] To test this presumption, I decided to look at who the organization has recognized through its many awards. Using conference award history posted on AEJMC's website, I coded each award recipient by country based on their institutional affiliation at the time of recognition.[25] Table 13.1 summarizes the geographic locations of AEJMC award winners condensed into three groups: the United States, Europe, and "Beyond," which comprises anywhere else in the world. Of the 18 award categories listed here, only three (i.e., Krieghbaum Under-40 Award, AEJMC Presidential Award, and AEJMC-Knudson Latin America Prize) have ever been awarded to scholars based outside of the United States. In total, 98.9% of the individual awards coded here were given to scholars affiliated with institutions in the United States, 0.5% to scholars based in Europe, and 0.6% to scholars based anywhere else in the world. It is also worth noting that prior to 2015, only one individual award had been given to a scholar based outside the United States.[26]

AEJMC journals also lag behind their peers when it comes to publishing articles written by scholars based outside of the United States. Although U.S.-based scholars are overrepresented in ICA journals, Waisbord points out that their dominance has declined in recent years. Waisbord coded lead authors of articles published in five ICA journals by country/institutional affiliation, finding that between 2010 and 2017, U.S.-based scholars comprise 64% of lead authors in *Journal of Communication*, 46% in the

Table 13.1 Geographic location of AEJMC award winners based on institutional affiliation

Award	United States	Europe	Beyond
Krieghbaum Under-40 Award	36	2	1
Baskett Mosse Award for Faculty Development	27	0	0
AEJMC Presidential Award	47	0	1
Charles E. Scripps Award for JMC Administrator of the Year	12	0	0
Charles E. Scripps Award for JMC Teacher of the Year	12	0	0
Paul J. Deutschmann Award for Excellence in Research	30	0	0
Eleanor Blum Distinguished Service to Research Award	16	0	0
Nafziger-White-Salwen Dissertation Award—Student	35	0	0
Nafziger-White-Salwen Dissertation Award—Advisor[a]	35	0	0
AEJMC Tankard Book Award	13	0	0
AEJMC-Knudson Latin America Prize	5.5	0	0.5[b]
AEJMC Equity & Diversity Award	11	0	0
Dorothy Bowles Public Service Award	8	0	0
Outstanding Contribution to Journalism Education	25	0	0
Robert Knight Multicultural Recruitment Award	31	0	0
MaryAnn Yodelis Smith Research Award	22	0	0
Lionel Barrow Jr. Award for Distinguished Achievement in Diversity Research	11	0	0
Lee Barrow Doctoral Minority Student Scholarship	44	0	0
Total	**420.5**	**2**	**2.5**

[a] Although the Nafziger-White-Salwen Dissertation Award is only awarded to doctoral students, I also coded institutional location of advisors, because the award serves as a symbol of prestige for doctoral advisors and programs.

[b] In 2017, the AEJMC-Knudson Latin America Prize winning book was co-authored by a scholar based in Argentina and a scholar based in the U.S.

Journal of Computer-Mediated Communication, 67% in *Communication, Culture, & Critique,* 66% in *Human Communication Research,* and 60% in *Communication Theory.*[27] I similarly coded the country/institutional affiliation of lead authors in AEJMC's two primary research journals during the last decade. Between 2010 and 2019, 78% of articles published in *Journalism and Mass Communication Quarterly* and 90% of monographs published in *Journalism & Communication Monographs* listed a U.S.-based lead author. For an organization that claims to "encourage the implementation of a multi-cultural society in the classroom and curriculum,"[28] AEJMC has much room to grow when it comes to the awards it bestows and the scholarship it publishes.

My goal here is not to shame individuals and organizations but rather to demonstrate the pervasiveness of Eurocentrism in academia broadly and in journalism and mass communication studies specifically. As Shohat and Stam argue, Eurocentrism "thinks of itself in terms of its noblest achievements— science, progress, humanism—but of the non-West in terms of its deficiencies, real or imagined."[29] The inequities discussed above demonstrate that academic Eurocentrism is alive and well in journalism and mass communication studies. Next, I briefly consider the structural explanations for past and present Eurocentrism in academia.

Understanding Eurocentrism in the Academy

It is impossible to discuss global inequities in scholarly knowledge production without considering the impact of colonialism, which was predicated on the inherent intellectual superiority of colonizers over the colonized. During the colonial era, Western empiricism was privileged as the one true path to enlightenment, while all other modes of inquiry were dismissed as backward.[30] The enduring legacy of European epistemic supremacy persists today not only in the Global North but also in the Global South, evident by the "knowledge colonialism" of African journalism students being trained with American textbooks.[31] English has become the *lingua franca* of scholarly knowledge production, and theories and methodologies developed in the Global North routinely are tested and employed throughout the world.[32] Moreover, as Hanitzsch points out, "Western researchers often take it for granted that their work is relevant to readers around the world, while researchers from non-Western contexts often have to defend their choice of countries and country-specific literatures."[33] Global North scholars, particularly those in North America, are far more likely to cite colleagues based in the Global North than those in the Global South, while university curricula and course syllabi demonstrate a clear favoritism toward the history and intellectual merits of Western civilization.[34]

There is also a significant resource gap between Global North and Global South institutions of higher education, the result of a variety of factors including uneven development and neoliberalization.[35] Due to this resource gap, many Global South institutions provide their faculty with outdated equipment, limited library collections, little to no research funding, and few training and mentoring opportunities.[36] At the same time, faculty in the Global South earn smaller salaries than their Global North colleagues while taking on heavier teaching loads.[37] To supplement their income, many faculty members choose to teach additional classes at nearby universities or do consultancy work for NGOs and foundations, all which take time away from building an independent research agenda.[38] In addition to these resource limitations, some Global South institutions have experienced a crackdown on academic freedom as well as a declining interest in local knowledge production due to the growth in foreign ownership of previously public industries.[39]

In response to these structural barriers and the marginalization of Global South scholarship, there has been an increase in local and regional journals, many of which are hosted at Global South institutions.[40] While these journals provide welcome publication opportunities for Global South faculty and serve as venues that celebrate scholarly knowledge produced in the Global South, they have limited reach.[41] Most of these journals have few readers outside of the region, resulting in the further marginalization of scholarship produced in the Global South. In short, global inequities in scholarly knowledge production are structural, intertwined with both the enduring legacy of colonialism and the ongoing resource gap between Global North and Global South institutions of higher education.

Engaging the Academy

Engaging the academy means turning the critical gaze inward to question the choices, big and small, scholars make during the process of knowledge production. Critical introspection is particularly important for those of us who are beneficiaries of significant identity, prestige, and resource privilege, as well as those in positions of professional power. Shakuntala Rao argues journalism and communication scholars should adopt an intersectional approach to "mindful inclusiveness" to address the structural inequities in scholarly knowledge production.[42] Mindful inclusiveness avoids the trappings of tokenism and quotas by focusing on ensuring many different bodies, voices, and perspectives are included in the field's conversations, journals, conferences, and syllabi. Such efforts will likely face resistance from critics and skeptics, but that makes this work all the more valuable.

In recent years, there have been a number of important efforts to raise the visibility of groups that have been historically and structurally marginalized within academia. This is evident in online campaigns like #womenalsoknowstuff and #pocalsoknowstuff that not only challenge the overrepresentation of white, male experts in popular media coverage but also critique the marginalization of women and people of color in scholarly knowledge production.[43] Other initiatives have taken an intersectional approach to questioning the very logics that guide our field. A recent example is *Data & Society*'s #unsettle program that seeks to "center Indigenous, Black, Feminist, and Queer cosmologies" by interrogating the marginalizing logics that structure sociotechnical systems of power.[44]

Within the communication discipline, ICA will host a Global Knowledge Exchange pre-conference at its upcoming ICA in Africa regional conference in Cape Town, South Africa.[45] This pre-conference has been designed to facilitate mutually beneficial knowledge exchange without reinforcing systemic inequities in academia, by assembling research teams composed of one emerging scholar based at an African institution, one senior scholar based at an African institution, one emerging scholar based outside the continent, and one senior scholar based outside the continent. Unlike traditional mentoring programs that assume a knowledge giver and knowledge receiver, this pre-conference is designed to recognize the various ways participants can contribute to and benefit from each other. To acknowledge and address the financial strain experienced, in particular by emerging and Africa-based scholars, ICA has committed $20,000 in travel grants to support the pre-conference.

In April 2020, *Digital Journalism* associate editors Edson Tandoc Jr., Kristy Hess, and Scott Eldridge II, along with editor-in-chief Oscar Westlund, penned an editorial about what the journal is doing to recognize and address inequities in scholarly knowledge production.[46] Seeking to embrace Rao's suggestion of "mindful inclusiveness,"[47] the editorial team acknowledged the journal's geographic imbalance when it comes to authorship as well as countries studied. They then describe specific practices the journal has put into place not only to welcome but to seek out "the voices of those who are not often heard, and who may have never been asked for their input."[48] These practices include appointing International Engagement Editors, refusing to reject a submission based solely on English proficiency, training reviewers to overcome their biases, and working to open up the journal archive to authors with outdated literature reviews.

Each of these initiatives represent forms of engagement that engage the academy rather than the general public. Public engagement in the academy is not just the process of co-producing knowledge or sharing insights with practitioners; public engagement also includes academics challenging members of the academy to address structural inequities in scholarly knowledge production. In addition to these efforts, below is a list of specific practices that scholars based in the Global North can adopt to better serve as allies of their colleagues in the Global South. These suggestions are organized by the different roles scholars perform in their professional careers.

Behind the scenes at journals. Invite scholars based in the Global South to join journal editorial boards, and mentor these scholars into editorial positions. Reach out to new scholarly networks to encourage faculty and graduate students based in the Global South to submit manuscripts. Track submission and acceptance rates by country of origin, and use these metrics to evaluate the journal's commitment to geographic diversity, equity, and inclusion. Several journals affiliated with ICA already track this data and include it in their annual reports.

Behind the scenes at conferences. Consider the organization's core values when making conference hosting decisions. If the organization is unable or unwilling to host annual conferences in underrepresented areas, support regional conferences that reduce the financial and logistic burden for scholars based in the Global South. For example, in the past few years ICA has hosted regional conferences in Chile, China, Ghana, India, Kenya, and Malaysia, while AEJMC held a 2015 regional conference in Chile. Attend regional conferences outside your home country. If we expect our colleagues in the Global South to travel to North America or Europe to attend annual conferences, we must be willing to return the favor. Subsidize the costs of attendees traveling from the Global South, and support programs that welcome all attendees into the community of scholars.

In your scholarship. Read and cite scholars based in the Global South. Outside of the journals you regularly pay attention to, seek out journals based in the Global South and those with more balanced editorial boards. Here is an abridged list of journals that publish high-quality journalism and mass communication scholarship from scholars based in the Global South: *African Journalism Studies, Arab Media & Society, Asian Journal of Communication, Communicatio, Cuadernos, Journal of African Media Studies, Journal of Arab & Muslim Media Research, Journal of Latin American Communication Research,* and *Media Asia.* Broaden your personal networks by connecting with scholars based in the Global South on social media. Look for opportunities to collaborate with colleagues based in the Global South.

As an educator. Assign scholarship about the Global South and by scholars based in the Global South. Reading lists reveal our biases about which places and voices are worthy of attention. If our syllabi, particularly those for graduate seminars, present a Eurocentric "canon," we reinscribe the enduring colonial legacies of our discipline. Ask colleagues with expertise in different parts of the world for relevant suggestions. Everyone has blind spots. We need to acknowledge and face our limitations head on.

As a reviewer. Approach the reviewing process as a "coach" rather than a "critic."[49] Don't think of yourself as a gatekeeper to an elite scholarly club; instead, consider how to nurture the valuable seeds planted within a manuscript. Remember that English is not the first language for many scholars. Focus on the manuscript's contribution to theory, methods, and global understanding rather than any perceived deficiencies in spelling and grammar. Recognize that many colleagues have limited institutional resources and cannot be expected to produce a sample size equivalent to scholars affiliated with resource-rich universities and foundations.

As a colleague. When evaluating your peers, acknowledge citation bias in terms of gender, race, and nationality. Recognize the value of presenting at regional conferences as an effort to truly internationalize our field. Recruit and mentor graduate students from outside of North America and Europe. Invite emerging scholars from the Global South or based in the Global South to give research talks at your university. Write reviews of books published by scholars based in the Global South. Nominate senior scholars based in the Global South for research, teaching, and service awards.

Most importantly, listen and be humble. Ask colleagues based in the Global South what you can do to be helpful as well as what to avoid. And be receptive to critique when you have fallen short.

Conclusion

In January 2019, Steve King, a Republican congressman from my home state of Iowa, was stripped of his committee assignments after he said the following to a reporter from the *New York Times*: "White nationalist, white supremacist, Western civilization—how did that language become offensive? Why did I sit in classes teaching me about the merits of our history and our civilization?"[50] Most Americans rightly were appalled that an elected official would openly proclaim such affection for white nationalism and white supremacy (King would later go on to lose his primary race in 2020); yet, how many of our syllabi reflect the very same values King articulated? Journalism and mass communication faculty, particularly those based in the Global North, need to ask ourselves: whose merits are we teaching?

This chapter has focused on the enduring legacy of Eurocentrism in journalism and mass communication studies. Media scholars who see themselves as critics and evaluators of cultural production must also recognize our own role in knowledge production. While "studying journalism without any sort of ethnocentric bias is an epistemological impossibility,"[51] this chapter has offered several recommendations to help scholars in the Global North become better allies of our colleagues in the Global South. Creating more diverse, equitable, and inclusive forms of scholarly knowledge production broadens our understanding of our world and has representational power for aspiring researchers in the Global South.

Although public engagement typically focuses on sharing scholarly knowledge with audiences outside of academia, scholars need to be open and responsive to critiques of our own professional practices. Therefore, it is important for scholars to engage each other, not merely through our shared objects of analysis but in the very nature of scholarly knowledge production. While turning the lens on ourselves represents a different form of engagement, the current political moment makes it clear that engaging the academy is of great importance and consequence. We are witnessing a global turn toward ethno-nationalism and xenophobia that raises important questions about what those of us engaged in scholarly knowledge production are doing to implicitly or explicitly perpetuate ethnocentrism.

Notes

1. Wendy Willems, "Provincializing Hegemonic Histories of Media and Communication Studies: Toward a Genealogy of Epistemic Resistance in Africa," *Communication Theory* 24, no. 4 (2014): 415–434.
2. Arjun Appadurai, "Grassroots Globalization and the Research Imagination," *Public Culture* 12, no. 1 (2000): 1–19.

3. Paula Chakravartty, Rachel Kuo, Victoria Grubbs, and Charlton McIlwain, "#CommunicationSoWhite," *Journal of Communication* 68, no. 2 (2018): 254–266; Paula M. Gardner, "Diversifying ICA: Identity, Difference, and the Politics of Transformation," *Journal of Communication* 68, no. 5 (2018): 831–841; Thomas Hanitzsch, "Journalism Studies Still Needs to Fix Western Bias," *Journalism* 20, no. 1 (2019): 214–217; Vicki Mayer, Andrea Press, Deb Verhoeven, and Jonathan Sterne, "How Do We Intervene in the Stubborn Persistence of Patriarchy in Communication Scholarship?" in *Interventions: Communication Research and Practice*, eds. Adrienne Shaw and D. Travers Scott (New York: Peter Lang, 2018), 53–64.

4. Peace A. Medie and Alice J. Kang, "Power, Knowledge and the Politics of Gender in the Global South," *European Journal of Politics and Gender* 1, no. 1–2 (2018): 41.

5. Yves Gingras and Sébastien Mosbah-Natanson, "Where Are Social Sciences Produced?" in World Social Science Report, 2010 (Paris: UNESCO Publishing, 2010), 149–153.

6. Sarah Cummings and Paul Hoebink, "Representation of Academics from Developing Countries as Authors and Editorial Board Members in Scientific Journals: Does This Matter to the Field of Development Studies?" *European Journal of Development Research* 29, no. 2 (2016): 369–383.

7. Chakravartty et al., "#CommunicationSoWhite," 255.

8. Gingras and Mosbah-Natanson, "Where Are Social Sciences."

9. Ann N. Miller, Christine Deeter, Anne Trelstad, Matthew Hawk, Grace Ingram, and Annie Ramirez, "Still the Dark Continent: A Content Analysis of Research about Africa and by African Scholars in 18 Major Communication-Related Journals," *Journal of International and Intercultural Communication* 6, no. 4 (2013): 317–333.

10. Folker Hanusch and Tim P. Vos, "Charting the Development of a Field: A Systematic Review of Comparative Studies of Journalism," *International Communication Gazette*, Advance online publication, 11, doi:10.1177/1748048518822606.

11. Adeola. A. Elega and Bahire E. Özad, "New Media Scholarship in Africa: An Evaluation of Africa-Focused Blog Related Research from 2006 to 2016," *Quality and Quantity* 52, no. 5 (2018): 2239–2254.

12. Ben Wasike, "Africa Rising: An Analysis of Emergent Africa-Focused Mass Communication Scholarship from 2004 to 2014," *International Journal of Communication* 11, no. 1 (2017): 198–219.

13. Cummings and Hoebink, "Representation of Academics"; Haythem Guesmi, "The Gentrification of African Studies," *Africa is a Country*, December 22, 2018, https://africasacountry.com/2018/12/the-gentrification-of-african-studies; Medie and Kang, "Power, Knowledge."

14. Ryan C. Briggs and Scott Weathers, "Gender and Location in African Politics Scholarship: The Other White Man's Burden?" *African Affairs* 115, no. 460 (2016): 466–489.

15. Elega and Özad, "New Media Scholarship"; Wasike, "Africa Rising."

16. Rashmi Luthra, "Transforming Global Communication Research with a View to the Margins," *Communication Research and Practice* 1, no. 3 (2015): 251–257.

17. Gardner, "Diversifying ICA"; Mayer et al., "How Do We Intervene."

18. Vik Sohonie, "The Most Powerful Currency Today," *Africa is a Country*, December 12, 2018, https://africasacountry.com/2018/12/the-most-powerful-currency-today.

19. As will be discussed later, the International Communication Association has hosted regional conferences in South America and Africa.

20. Of note, the 2003 conference was cancelled due to a SARS outbreak, and the 2020 conference was moved from Beijing, China to Tampere, Finland due to a coronavirus outbreak.

21. Hanitzsch, "Journalism Studies Still."

22. Thomas Hanitzsch, Martin Löffelholz, and David Weaver, "Building a Home for the Study of Journalism: ICA Creates a Journalism Studies Interest Group," *Journalism* 6, no. 1 (2005): 107–115.

23. Steyn, Elanie, "Scholarly Organizations in Journalism," in *The International Encyclopedia of Journalism Studies*, eds. Tim P. Vos and Folker Hanusch (John Wiley & Sons, 2019), 1–5.

24. In 2012, then-AEJMC President Kyu Ho Youm appointed the Task Force on AEJMC in the Global Century to study how AEJMC can better position itself within a global context. The task force's report (available at http://www.aejmc.org/home/wp-content/uploads/2015/04/Global-Task-Force-Report-4_22_15.pdf), which was completed in Summer 2014, offers several suggestions for how AEJMC can internationalize.

25. I collected the data in March 2020 from https://www.aejmc.org/home/scholarship/award-recipients. AEJMC also has several divisional awards that are not included here because I was unable to locate a complete list of recipients. I also did not include the First Amendment Award, which is awarded to professional journalists, not academics. I did not code for awardee's race, ethnicity, or country of origin, only their institutional affiliation at the time of receiving the award.

26. Silvia Pellegrini from Pontificia Universidad Catolica de Chile, Santiago, received the AEJMC Presidential Award in 2008.

27. Silvio Waisbord, *Communication: A Post-Discipline* (Malden, MA: Polity, 2019).

28. http://www.aejmc.org/

29. Ella Shohat and Robert Stam, *Unthinking Eurocentrism: Multiculturalism and the Media* (New York: Routledge, 1994), 5.

30. V.Y. Mudimbe, *The Invention of Africa: Gnosis, Philosophy, and the Order of Knowledge* (Bloomington: Indiana University Press, 1988); Georgette Wang and Vincent Shen, "East, West, Communication, and Theory: Searching for the Meaning of Searching for Asian Communication Theories," *Asian Journal of Communication* 10, no. 2 (2000): 14–32.

31. Arnold S. de Beer, "Looking for Journalism Education Scholarship in Some Unusual Places: The Case of Africa," *Communicatio: South African Journal for Communication Theory and Research* 36, no. 2 (2010): 213–226.

32. Hayes M. Mabweazara, "Charting Theoretical Directions for Examining African Journalism in the 'Digital Era,'" *Journalism Practice* 9, no. 1 (2015): 106–122; Hu Zhengrong, Zhang Lei, and Ji Deqiang, "Globalization, Social Reform and the Shifting Paradigms of Communication Studies in China," *Media, Culture and Society* 35, no. 1 (2013): 147–155.

33. Hanitzsch, "Journalism Studies Still," 214.

34. Gingras and Mosbah-Natanson, "Where Are Social Sciences"; Peter K.J. Park, *Africa, Asia, and the History of Philosophy: Racism in the Formation of the Philosophical Canon, 1780–1830* (New York: SUNY Press, 2014); Minna Salami, "Philosophy Has to be About More Than White Men," *The Guardian*, March 23, 2015, https://www.theguardian.com/education/commentisfree/2015/mar/23/philosophy-white-men-university-courses.

35. Amina Mama, "Is It Ethical to Study Africa? Preliminary Thoughts on Scholarship and Freedom," *African Studies Review* 50, no. 1 (2007): 1–26.

36. Ann N. Miller, Mary N. Kizito, and Kyalo W. Ngula, "Research and Publication by Communication Faculty in East Africa: A Challenge to the Global Community of Communication Scholars," *Journal of International and Intercultural Communication*, 3, no. 4 (2010): 286–303.

37. Rodrigo Arocena and Judith Sutz, "Changing Knowledge Production and Latin American Universities," *Research Policy* 30, no. 8 (2001): 1221–1234; Miller et al., "Research and Publication."

38. Johann Mouton, "The State of Social Science in Sub-Saharan Africa," in *World Social Science Report, 2010* (Paris: UNESCO Publishing, 2010), 63–67.

39. Philip G. Altbach, "Academic Freedom: International Realities and Challenges," *Higher Education* 41, no. 1–2 (2001): 205–219, https://link.springer.com/article/10.1023/A:1026791518365; Arocena and Sutz, "Changing Knowledge Production."

40. Briggs and Weathers, "Gender and Location."

41. Silvio Waisbord, "De-Westernization and Cosmopolitan Media Studies," in *Internationalizing "International Communication,* ed. Chin-Chuan Lee (Ann Arbor: University of Michigan Press, 2015), 178–200.

42. Shakuntala Rao, "Commentary: Inclusion and a Discipline," *Digital Journalism* 7, no. 5 (2019): 698–703.

43. womenalsoknowstuff.com; pocexperts.org

44. https://datasociety.net/announcements/2020/03/03/unsettle-braiding-the-network.

45. This regional conference was scheduled to take place in November 2020 but was postponed due to travel concerns related to the coronavirus pandemic. At the time of this writing, no new conference date has been set.

46. Edson Tandoc Jr., Kristy Hess, Scott Eldridge, and Oscar Westlund, "Diversifying Diversity in Digital Journalism Studies: Reflexive Research, Reviewing and Publishing," *Digital Journalism* 8, no. 3 (2020): 301–309.

47. Rao, "Commentary."

48. Edson et al., "Diversifying Diversity," 303.

49. Patricia A. Curtin, John Russial, and Alex Tefertiller, "Reviewers' Perceptions of the Peer Review Process in Journalism and Mass Communication," *Journalism and Mass Communication Quarterly* 95, no. 1 (2018): 278–299.

50. Trip Gabriel, "Before Trump, Steve King Set the Agenda for the Wall and Anti-Immigrant Politics," *New York Times*, January 10, 2019, https://www.nytimes.com/2019/01/10/us/politics/steve-king-trump-immigration-wall.html.

51. Hanitzsch, "Journalism Studies," 214.

14

Beyond Ferguson

Re-Examining Press Coverage of Protests of Police Brutality

Danielle K. Kilgo

Introduction

A rise in the demand for democracy from citizens in countries across the globe has increased public and media attention to protests and grassroots collective action efforts. Technology has changed how these groups organize and mobilize, but it has not eliminated the essential needs of social movements, such as the need for exposure in traditional news media. This particular need is a catch-22 though, as the analyses of mainstream news coverage have concluded time and time again. In a pattern often referred to as the protest paradigm, advocates stage events and protests to get media attention. Then, journalists superficially cover these events and emphasize trivializing and negative aspects instead of the grievances and agendas of the protesters. Even as technology shifts have changed journalistic practice and production routines, the paradigm has remained intact . . . for some protests anyway.[1]

Much of my research has contributed to this conversation by uncovering patterns of media portrayals in the context of Black civil rights protests and the Black Lives Matter movement, beginning with the protest that followed the death of Trayvon Martin in 2012. Unarmed and alone, the teenager was murdered in Florida by George Zimmerman, a neighborhood watch volunteer. Zimmerman was acquitted of all charges.

This chapter builds on that foundation of research, analyzing the 2018 protests that followed the death of Stephon Clark, a Black 23-year-old man shot by police in his grandmother's backyard. Using data collected from a content analysis of local, metropolitan, and national newspaper coverage, I give an overview of how the media portrayed these protests. Additionally,

Danielle K. Kilgo, *Beyond Ferguson* In: *Journalism Research That Matters.* Edited by: Valérie Bélair-Gagnon and Nikki Usher, Oxford University Press. © Oxford University Press 2021. DOI: 10.1093/oso/9780197538470.003.0015 news coverage is linked with the number of times it was publicly shared across social media platforms, and I provide a look into the patterns of social media sharing and, thus, distribution on social media sites.[2]

This journalism research matters because it provides empirical evidence to call to account systematic bias and implicit (and sometimes explicit) racism in the news media. We need to do more of this research, even though the work is challenging, hard to publish within academic contexts, and extremely difficult to change in the profession. Media coverage affects public opinion and government policy, and these effects are amplified when issues are unobtrusive to the everyday lives of the general public, as protests often are. Though media coverage does not write policy or pull triggers, the continuous delegitimization of protests through news media can stifle social progress and privilege narratives that reinforce social disparities. Further, the analysis of press coverage is important in this context because the effects of structural and institutional forces like racism can sometimes be challenging to diagnose.

Likewise, these critiques can be difficult to digest, particularly in professions like journalism and academia that profess allegiance to truth-seeking. I know from experience as a Black woman and scholar: When I've worked with journalists and editors, initial reactions are frequently defensive, and several have aggressively attacked the motive and validity of my research as a self-protective measure. I've experienced similar responses from scholars in the blind-review process. Nevertheless, we cannot make better what we refuse to see, and therefore the continual assessment and critique of press patterns are just some of the many ways we as scholars, journalists, educators, and communicators can engage and develop our crafts and reduce the consequences communication can have on others.

Black Lives Matter, from Florida to California

In 2012, a teenager named Trayvon Martin was leaving a convenience store carrying a now-infamous bottle of tea and package of Skittles candy. Community watch volunteer George Zimmerman viewed Martin as a threat and confronted him against the instructions of emergency personnel. Zimmerman then said he feared for his life, which ultimately led to Martin's murder. Protests across the United States called for justice for Martin. When Zimmerman was acquitted one year later, protests assembled across the United States, and these events were the origins of the modern-day Black civil rights movement (often referred to as the Black Lives Matter movement), a decentralized but nationally organized movement against the wrongful deaths of Black people and the lack of prosecution of their attackers, and in support of civil rights for marginalized populations.[3] The hashtag #BlackLivesMatter first appeared in this context.

The shooting deaths and assaults of Black people didn't start or stop with Martin's death. For decades, Black communities in the United States have been concerned about issues related to the excessive use of force by enforcement agencies and police, "driving while Black," unjust criminal punishments, and mass incarceration.[4] However, it was the shooting death of Michael Brown in Ferguson, Missouri (and the subsequent events) that brought the issue into the international spotlight. Brown was unarmed when he was shot and killed by a police officer. Within 24 hours, on-the-streets protests began, and hashtag activism efforts carried the #BlackLivesMatter conversation throughout the world. The events that unfolded flooded the news cycle: protesters in Ferguson were met with dramatic and militant government reaction; journalists were arrested; and protesters engaged in occasional radical tactics that sometimes included violence.

The deaths of Martin and Brown contributed to a broader discourse about the impact on Black communities of institutional, systematic, overt, and covert racism. The cyclical narrative of unarmed Black people being shot by authorities and police, police acquittals/non-indictments, confrontations with police, and protests continued to headline newspapers and feed the news cycle. Additionally, public discourse and social media conversations strengthened and complicated the reach of such news, which appeared alongside a debate about racial injustice narratives and colorblind ideological positions.

On March 18, 2018, when Stephon Clark was murdered in his grandmother's backyard in Sacramento, California, media professionals and the public had extensive exposure to the ongoing issue of police use of force in Black communities and the corresponding protests. Clark was holding a cell phone that was mistaken by two police officers as a gun. Clark was shot multiple times in the back. Protests nationwide were reported by March 22, 2018, just one day after the police body camera footage was released. Though efforts gradually reduced in size, protests continued for more than six months after Clark's death, reigniting after the non-indictment of the police officers in 2019.

Noting that journalists have had more time to learn from and recon-
cile problematic coverage from previous event cycles, this work explores
the coverage of the first wave of Stephon Clark protests. After the death of
Stephon Clark, journalists were more familiar with these kinds of events, including the narratives, the government, community, legal responses, and the
protests. *Was the coverage of protests that mobilized after the death of Stephon
Clark more legitimizing than protest coverage of past incidents?* In other words,
did journalists' coverage of the contemporary Black civil rights movement
improve as journalists had greater experience with covering these types of
stories and more context to understand advocacy efforts?

How the Media Sees and Shows Black Lives Matter

Before exploring the patterns of coverage of the Sacramento protests, it is
important to look at the overall patterns that characterize similar events.
My previous work found that protests of police brutality are often framed in
delegitimizing ways more so than legitimizing. These patterns are a product
of established journalism practices and routines and thus appear in coverage
of other protests as well. Many grassroots protests like BLM and other Black
civil rights efforts are what we call "status quo–challenging" protests, and
their agendas push against the political or societal norms and expectations.
In the past, researchers routinely found that the mainstream media covers
status quo–challenging movements in marginalizing ways.[5] Delegitimizing
press coverage contributes to the broader narrative scholars refer to as the
protest paradigm, which describes the paradoxical process that facilitates
the following chain of events: (1) social movements need media coverage
to project their voice and signal their strength; (2) media organizations require movements to engage in newsworthy activity to be worthy of coverage;
(3) protests engage in deviant, sensational, or dramatic behavior to attract
media attention; and (4) the media covers the violent, combative, sensational, and dramatic behavior (delegitimizing features) instead of the protest
and movement's substance (legitimizing features).

More recent empirical inquiries have found that the protest paradigm
patterns don't hold up as well in the diverse media ecosystem that accom-
panies the digital era. For example, research looking at the social media
news coverage of non-U.S. protests shows instances where more legitimizing
features appeared in coverage.[6] Scholars have found that other considerations

also help explain press coverage deviations, including the news organization's ideology[7] and ideological affiliation with the government.[8] This scholarship doesn't suggest that the paradigm was "overthrown," but it did leave many researchers wondering if the conceptual framework that guides our under-standing of press coverage was useful in the digital era.

My research suggests these protest paradigm patterns do still remain rel-evant. Black Lives Matter coverage has generally appeared to be resistant to this change. Nestled in this diverse ecosystem, media coverage of protest efforts related to the extrajudicial police killings of Black people was quite problematic, consistently aligning with the patterns prescribed by the pro-test paradigm. For Black Lives Matter protests in Ferguson, these patterns were prominently documented in mainstream newspapers[9] and digital news coverage.[10] From both longitudinal and comparative perspectives, my work suggests that standard journalistic practice techniques are employed differ-ently for Black Lives Matter protests than they are for other protests. One inquiry used a comparative approach, analyzing the protests that followed the death of Trayvon Martin and the death of Michael Brown.[11] Both sets of protests were subject to marginalization, and legitimizing coverage was withheld. In another study, I found that Black civil rights protests, like the protests against Confederate monuments in 2017, were also characterized more through marginalizing narrative features than legitimizing features.[12] In other words, the overall patterns of media production surrounding Black Lives Matter show little change. Ultimately, the continued inquiry into press patterns is necessary because the issues surrounding police shootings and protests are unobtrusive—issues that do not affect the majority of people, and thus individuals tend to learn and make judgments about these issues from the news.

To explore how the media covered the protests that followed the death of Stephon Clark, a systematic quantitative content analysis was conducted. I selected a sample of coverage from the first wave of protests (March 20, 2018 through September 20, 2018) from nationally circulated newspapers (*Washington Post, The New York Times*), California metropolitan newspapers (*San Francisco Chronicle, San Diego Tribune, Los Angeles Times, Mercury News*) and the local Sacramento paper, *The Sacramento Bee*. The coverage was pulled from Newswhip, a database that collects all unique URLs from these news organizations' websites. Public shares of these unique URLs are also tracked within the APIs of major social media networks, and these an-alytics are used to assess social media engagement. The initial sample was collected using the keyword search term "Stephon Clark."[13] Then, the selection was further refined. Coverage that centered Stephon Clark but did not cover the associated protests was removed. Editorials and opinion pieces were removed (10.5%, n = 32), and articles that could no longer be retrieved from a working website were removed from the study.[14] A final sample of 175 articles was analyzed.

The coding scheme included the prominent devices that align with the most common frames of the protest paradigm. Delegitimizing frames include the riot (protester violence, disruptive protesters), confrontation (confrontations with police and arrests), and spectacle frames (engaged in odd/unusual behavior, emotional behavior), while legitimizing coverage includes the debate frame (protesters engaged in peaceful, non-disruptive collective action, and mentions of protester demands and agendas). Each component of these frames was assessed independently for more descriptive analysis. In addition, the coding protocol included advocate-sponsored themes that give more information about the substance of demands, and the potential penetration of advocacy messages. Unlike the coding protocol of protest frames, which reflect direct descriptions and attributions of protests, the advocate-sponsored themes were coded from the article in general (i.e., themes didn't have to come directly from protesters or advocates). These were adapted from the advocacy frames used in prior work.[15] I coded the sample with an outside graduate student coder, and we held five training sessions to assist us with reaching exceptional interrater reliability. To measure reliability, Cohen's kappa statistic was used, and the final kappa variables reached reliability scores in ideal ranges (.92—1.0).[16]

#StephonClark Protests: The Angry, Disruptive Protests of Police Actions

Across the board, no differences were found in the prevalence of any of the devices in coverage from local, state, or national papers, consistent with research findings analyzing like-protest coverage.[17] Table 14.1 includes the breakdown of narrative features that were present in news coverage. In terms of delegitimizing coverage, protest coverage was saturated in spectacle frame features: protesters were described as angry (81.1%) more often than they were described as sad or in mourning (10.9%). The riot frame appeared more often as protesters disrupting everyday life (66.9%) than protesters engaged

Table 14.1 Presence of marginalization devices in news coverage

	State %(n)	National %(n)	Local %(n)	Total %(n)	Chi-Square
Riot					
Violent Behavior	18.6 (8)	5.3 (1)	8.8 (10)	10.9 (19)	3.75
Disruptive Behavior	62.8 (27)	68.4 (13)	68.1 (77)	66.9 (117)	0.43
Spectacle					
Angry Emotional State	88.4 (38)	94.7 (18)	76.1 (86)	81.1 (142)	5.64
Sad Emotional State	16.3 (7)	21.1 (4)	7.1 (8)	10.9 (19)	5.01
Oddity/Unusualness	62.8 (27)	68.4 (13)	69.0 (78)	67.4 (118)	.56
Confrontation	16.3 (7)	5.3 (1)	12.4 (14)	12.6 (22)	0.48
Legitimizing					
Peaceful/Legal Behavior	44.2 (19)	68.4 (13)	61.9 (70)	58.3 (102)	4.92
Grievances/Agendas	74.4 (32)	78.9 (15)	81.4 (92)	79.4 (139)	0.94
Advocacy-sponsored Themes					
Police Accountability	100 (43)	94.7 (18)	96.5 (109)	97.1 (170)	1.851
Racial injustice	7 (3)	15.8 (3)	6.2 (7)	7.4 (13)	0.334
Economic Inequality	0	0	1.7 (3)	1.7 (3)	n.a.
Gun Violence	0	0	0	0	n.a.

in violence (10.9%), and mentions of confrontation with police and arrests appeared in about a quarter of the articles. Legitimizing features were quite prevalent in coverage, with mentions of the protesters' peaceful/legal protest activity appearing in 58.3% of coverage, and at least one grievance and agenda item appeared in almost four-fifths of all coverage. Importantly, while there are significant mentions of the grievances and demands of protesters, these mentions predominantly emphasized justice for Clark (a component of the police accountability advocacy-sponsored theme). Meanwhile, congruent advocacy-sponsored themes were neglected, specifically those that linked police use of force with other systemic and ongoing factors, such as racial injustice, economic inequality, and gun violence. The connection with Clark and gun violence was not found in the news coverage analyzed. Coverage patterns indicate that journalists took an episodic approach to the inclusion of the debate frame features, and thematic issues were left out of most coverage.

In sum, these results show that though delegitimizing features were present quite often, particularly features of the riot and spectacle frame, legitimizing devices appeared regularly also. *Ultimately, this could be a sign of progress.* Because Clark's death was so similar to those that had received international news coverage in years prior, journalists might have benefited from increased familiarity with the subject matter. Additionally, the recurrences of these issues in recent years, alongside new accountability efforts to empirically track police shootings like *The Washington Post*'s police shootings database, may have made the demands and agendas of protesters more transparent and credible for journalists to report. However, progress does not mean there is not still work to be done. This inquiry shows that these demands were episodically centered, focusing primarily on reiterating that the protests were about Clark's death, and not the larger context that helps explain why systematic change is so essential.

Social Media Complicates News Circulation

While news organizations filter information for public consumption, social media audiences have now assumed significant media power as creators and circulators of news information. Of the many ways that individuals can engage with news on social networking sites, the "share" features are important and powerful, as they indicate information has been intentionally redistributed throughout networks. In this way, engagement through sharing expands the reach of narratives and privileges the information within. News organizations have not underestimated the power of social media in recent years, particularly as people have increasingly retrieved their news from social media networks.

The shared coverage can recreate the patterns of narratives put forth by the press, and it has in the past. For example, in the Ferguson protests, social media audiences on Facebook were significantly less likely to share articles with the spectacle frame,[18] reducing the reach of that coverage. As a continuation of this work, I explored if the absence or presence of legitimizing and delegitimizing features affects news audience sharing patterns.

Sharing frequencies and descriptive statistics indicated that the sharing data was not normally distributed, and this was corrected by removing the extreme outliers, which were analyzed separately ($n = 6$). Regression analyses were run on the remaining data. Accounting for media outlet type, the regression analysis showed that the legitimizing and delegitimizing narratives coded in this study aren't the best predictors of audience sharing.

On Facebook, the final model was not significant [$f(12, 169) = .96$, p = .49]. On Twitter, the final model was significant [$f(12, 169) = .012$, p < .05], but the analysis indicated that the organization type was the only predictor of sharing—coverage from national news organizations receives considerably more shares on Twitter than other news organizations.

The outliers told an enlightening story, however. Outliers represent the most viral coverage from this incident, and the sharing numbers indicate these messages had the broadest reach in their respective social networks. All outliers were articles from national newspapers. The major theme that emerged from most of these outliers was the emphasis on injury and violence. Three of the articles shared updated details of the shooting and autopsy report and often included visual representations that reinforced these narratives. Protests were discussed as a response to these updates. One article from The New York Times titled "Stephon Clark Was Shot 8 Times Primarily in His Back, Family-Ordered Autopsy Finds" was shared more than 8,000 times publicly on Twitter and 11,000 times on Facebook. It included a video that combined police camera footage with graphic representations of how Clark was killed. Images of crowds of protests appear throughout the article, but the text doesn't mention them until the end, and the emphasis is predominantly on the size of the protest.

Another outlier from The Washington Post titled "Sacramento sheriff's vehicle hits woman during Stephon Clark protest and drives away, video shows" discusses a police vehicle that struck and injured a non-compliant protester (confrontation). Two other protest-related outlier stories led with details about the crowd size and celebrity involvement of protests and discussed police control preparation and efforts. The emphasis of police preparation tells a more compelling story about comparative differences in protests of police violence and, for example, the Women's March, where coverage of police preparation tactics was notably absent from the massive, disruptive, and international assemblies.[19]

Small Changes, More Needed

From the perspective of journalists and media producers, the continued inclusion of legitimizing and delegitimizing features is an approach to reporting about protest that leans toward the often-idealized value of objectivity. This analysis indicates that, to some degree, journalists are progressing toward more balance than previous content analyses of Black Lives Matter coverage have found. However, the results also show areas that align with the paradigm's prediction. For example, overall, protesters were still most frequently described as angry. And while protests were routinely associated with their goals and agendas—most notably the call for police justice for Clark (a feature of police accountability)—they failed to connect other relevant grievances and goals. Clark's death occurred just days after the mass shooting at Marjorie Stoneman Douglas High School in Parkland, Florida, on February 14, 2018.

The massive March for Our Lives protests were planned for March 24, yet this connection between shootings in high schools and police shootings of unarmed people was not made in news coverage. Instead, it was discussed in the opinion sections of the papers, which notably were excluded from this analysis. Moreover, the broader issues of racial inequality in policing and the economic inequality in the community were rarely included in news coverage. These connections should not be made only as a form of opinion in the media, just as Black Lives Matter protests should not be separated from the issue of guns. Identifying and sourcing knowledgeable protesters and activists, consistently engaging with marginalized communities, and maintaining and actively engaging in efforts to diversify newsrooms should help these connections develop more naturally.

Media producers should also remember that in general, the delegitimizing and legitimizing features aren't the core indicators for social media sharing, but the coverage of violence is a consistent factor of viral narratives. On Facebook, local and metropolitan news were shared just as often as national news. This wasn't the case on Twitter, however. Social media users were significantly more likely to retweet coverage from national newspapers. This could be because of the prominent role Twitter plays in journalistic practice, and the elite crowd frequently using the platform, including journalists and policymakers.

The most circulated individual articles included a theme of police-provoked violence against Black people and protesters. It's challenging to make sense of why these rose to the top over other articles with similar features, and algorithmic manipulations are an integral consideration for the interpretation and general understanding of social media engagement. However, the outliers still show that visualized violence against Black people, and not necessarily violence of protesters, is a major theme in the most shared articles. As a collective group of media creators, editors, producers, and content redistributors, we should consider the costs and consequences of including and circulating narratives about graphic violence. At the very least, journalists can strive to continually make the connections of immediate violence with the historical foundations of violence that have marginalized and oppressed Black communities (and beyond).

Where Do We Go from Here?

So, where do we go from here? The obvious answer is to take stock in the legitimizing features of a protest. Find newsworthiness in the profound connection of social grievances and the systemic injustices that maintain the status quo in our society. Much more than merely a hashtag reference, the consistent attention to the depth of grievances should be considered essential to news coverage. Consistent linkages of police brutality to the economic and racial inequalities *are vital* for helping the public understand protesters' perspectives. As Dr. Martin Luther King, Jr. noted many years ago, "A riot is the language of the unheard." Without careful attention to the depth of the unheard, journalists undercut the meaningfulness of those grievances and contribute to the maintenance of the status quo.

From here, we also have to look at the norms and routines that are central for reporting the context of these grievances. For example, issues of police brutality against Black people are linked with racist policies and ideas. However, reporting about racism can be challenging for journalists, as racism's conceptualization and operationalization are debated in the journalistic profession, just as it is in academia and in society. Challenging does not mean impossible. We must continue to develop new reporting protocols that adapt to modern forms of racism. Recent progress on this matter includes Associated Press's 2019 recommendations for the use of the term "racist" in obnoxiously overt cases of racism instead of "euphemisms." However, as has been illustrated by scholars across many fields, racism goes far beyond racist tweets and inappropriate political statements. We have to develop norms, routines, and policies that account for this nuance. Such standards could increase journalists' willingness to cover difficult subjects.

We can't settle for a one-size-fits-all approach because other factors, such as the underrepresentation of racial minorities in newsrooms and classrooms and the debatability of racism's parameters generally, are affecting how news is produced and how coverage patterns persist. Scholars, practitioners, educators, and activists must continue to have extensive, thoughtful, reiterative evaluations and conversations about the often-cyclical practices and patterns of production. By doing so, we are better equipped to step away from the unintended outcomes of journalistic impartiality that continue to threaten people around the globe, and step toward the goal of striving to produce narratives of the truths that are important to *all* its citizens.

Notes

1. Danielle K. Kilgo and Summer Harlow, "Press, Protests and the Hierarchy of Social Struggle," *International Journal of Press/Politics* 24 (2019): 508.
2. Sharing data was collected from an archive that pulls aggregate data from the public application program interfaces of Facebook and Twitter.
3. Deen Freelon, Charlton D. McIlwain, and Meredith Clark, "Beyond the Hashtags: #Ferguson, #Blacklivesmatter, and the Online Struggle for Offline Justice," *Center for Media & Social Impact, American University* (2016).
4. Beth Richie, *Arrested Justice: Black Women, Violence, and America's Prison Nation* (New York: New York University Press, 2012); Michelle Alexander, *The New Jim Crow: Mass Incarceration in the Age of Colorblindness* (New York: The New Press, 2010).
5. Joseph M. Chan and Chin-Chuan Lee, "The Journalistic Paradigm on Civil Protests: A Case Study of Hong Kong," in *The News Media in National and International Conflict*, eds. Andrew Arno and Wimal Dissanayake (Boulder: Westview Press, 1984): 183–202; Douglas M. McLeod and James K. Hertog, "Social Control, Social Change and the Mass Media's Role in the Regulation of Protest Groups," in *Mass Media, Social Control and Social Change: A Macrosocial Perspective*, eds. David Demers and Kasisomayajula Viswanath (Ames: Iowa State University Press, 1999): 305–330.
6. Summer Harlow and Thomas J. Johnson, "Overthrowing the Protest Paradigm? How the New York Times, Global Voices and Twitter Covered the Egyptian Revolution," *International Journal of Communication* 5 (2011): 1–18.; Summer Harlow et al., "Protest Paradigm in Multimedia: Social Media Sharing of Coverage about the Crime of Ayotzinapa, Mexico," *Journal of Communication* 67 (2017): 328–349.
7. David A. Weaver and Joshua M. Scacco, "Revisiting the Protest Paradigm: The Tea Party as Filtered through Prime-Time Cable News," *The International Journal of Press/Politics* 18 (2013): 61–84.
8. Saif Shahin et al., "Protesting the Paradigm: A Comparative Study of News Coverage of Protests in Brazil, China and India," *International Journal of Press/Politics* 21 (2016): 143–164.
9. Danielle K. Kilgo et al., "From #Ferguson to #Ayotzinapa: Analyzing Differences in Domestic and Foreign Protest News Shared on Social Media," *Mass Communication and Society* 21 (2018): 606–630.
10. Kilgo et al., "From #Ferguson to #Ayotzinapa."

11. Kilgo, Mourão, and Sylvie, "Framing Ferguson."

12. Kilgo and Harlow, "Press, Protests."

13. Stephon Clark had to appear in the title, metadata, or article description or first paragraph to appear in this sample.

14. These tend to be Associated Press articles that are not permanently archived to news websites.

15. Rachel R. Mourão, Danielle K. Kilgo, and George Sylvie, "Framing Ferguson: The interplay of advocacy and journalistic frames in local and national newspaper coverage of Michael Brown," *Journalism* (2018).

16. Matthew Lombard, Jennifer Synder-Duch, and Cheryl Campanella Bracken, "Content Analysis in Mass Communication: Assessment and reporting of intercoder reliability," *Human Communication Research* 28 (2002): 587. Note that in the training and intercoder reliability testing for this chapter, economic inequality, gun control, and racial injustice infrequently appeared. However, 100% agreement was reached.

17. Kilgo, Mourão, and Sylvie, "Framing Ferguson."

18. Kilgo et al., "From #Ferguson to #Ayotzinapa."

19. Kilgo and Harlow, "Press, Protests."

PART IV
JOURNALISM PRACTICE MATTERS

15

How Academics Can Work with Journalists (Hint: They Already Have)

Chase Davis

To journalists of a certain type—data-savvy investigative reporters, mainly—the story of Philip Meyer's work on the 1967 Detroit riots conjures the same near-mythical retellings as Watergate.

Touched off by a police raid on an unlicensed bar, the riots grew over five days to be among the most violent and deadly in American history, leaving 43 people dead and more than 1,000 injured.

Journalists covering the story struggled to understand the motivations of the rioters and how the situation escalated so quickly. That is, until Meyer, then a correspondent with the Knight Newspapers bureau in Washington, arrived on the scene and circumvented the implicit and explicit racial bias at work with what was then a brand-new journalism technique.

Rather than simply gathering quotes from people on the street, or relying on experts to characterize the events, Meyer proposed a solution that was considered radical for its day: draw a sample of residents from the most affected neighborhoods, conduct a survey, and tabulate the results on a computer.

The results upended many of the popular theories about who took part in the riots, why, and the underlying grievances many poor black residents had with police. And they gave birth to a new specialty in journalism long known as computer-assisted reporting, but now more popularly referred to as data journalism.

Less often celebrated, however, is the role that academics played in that story. In his own telling, Meyer was inspired to begin experimenting with computers and social science research methods during his Nieman Fellowship at Harvard in 1966. His work on the riots enlisted the help of researchers at the University of Michigan and Wayne State University, who

Chase Davis, *How Academics Can Work with Journalists (Hint: They Already Have)* In: *Journalism Research That Matters.* Edited by: Valérie Bélair-Gagnon and Nikki Usher, Oxford University Press. © Oxford University Press 2021. DOI: 10.1093/oso/9780197538470.003.0016 helped to design the survey, devise a sampling procedure, and otherwise provide advice.

Though likely not the first of its kind, Meyer's early collaboration helped pave the way for countless partnerships between journalists and academics that have led to blockbuster stories, new reporting tools, and even business-side advancements that will help sustain the industry.

We journalists remain hungry for those collaborations. But for researchers, professors, and others outside the media industry, it can be difficult to know the most effective ways to engage with journalists.

I and many of my close friends and colleagues in journalism have worked closely with academics over the years. Both of our tribes stand to gain much from working together, but ours is rife with inscrutable rules and customs. The hope here is to demystify some of those and provide some friendly advice in order to make future collaborations a little easier for everyone.

Define the Rules of Engagement, Early

We journalists are sticklers for our own unique professional ethics. Our careers and professional identities live or die based on the trust we build with our sources and our audience. The last thing we want to do is burn someone—especially someone trying to help us.

Which is why it is crucial to define the rules of engagement early on in any collaboration. As with most successful partnerships, the most important thing is to make sure everyone is on the same page—and it helps if academics understand the different kinds of roles journalists might ask of them.

To a journalist, an academic might be a source—called upon to provide quotes, context, and information, either on the record or off. You might fill the role of consultant, helping supply advice, checks, and balances on the methodology of an analysis. Or you might be a full-blown collaborator, working alongside journalists to publish a story that combines your shared expertise.

Other issues reflect differences in how academics and journalists understand academic expertise. You might have some data that interests a journalist for its news value, but that data might also not be appropriate to make public. Or maybe you share a paper pre-publication, but you don't want a journalist to publicize it before it comes out. Or you are approached to provide advice in a professional capacity that you would normally charge for as a consultant.

Most of the time, if something goes awry, it's because of a misunderstanding, not malice.

But no matter what the situation is, you should make it as explicit as possible, as early as possible, as often as possible, and in terms so clear that no human being could possibly misunderstand them.

What role does each party play? What is on the record versus off? Who can publish what, and when? How is credit assigned—through bylines, contributor credits, or just quotes and source citations? What data, if any, should be made public?

The specific questions will depend on the nature of the collaboration, but every party involved should have no doubt about the terms, no matter how basic.

Academic Research Differs from How Journalists Use Research for Storytelling

Journalists are all about the story. And a good story is often very different from a good academic paper. Both are rigorous in their presentation of the facts, but serving a general-interest audience generally doesn't demand the same level of precision as peer-reviewed research.

Obvious as that sounds, the question of how to frame and present findings resulting from academic collaborations almost inevitably leads to tension.

Journalists are trying to walk a fine line. They need to ensure facts and conclusions are represented accurately, but they also need to make their stories interesting and relatable. Often that means relating findings through anecdotes, metaphors, and other literary tools that might—in the eyes of a detail-oriented academic collaborator—muddy their precision.

At the same time, the ability to relay complex phenomena in human terms is one of a journalist's greatest strengths, and one of the most helpful things they can bring to a collaboration.

In 2018, *The New York Times* published a series of hypnotic interactive visuals showing how black children typically end up less financially well-off than white children as adults, regardless of whether they grew up rich or poor. The project was based on data provided by a group of academics who had studied the issue and published their findings in a paper entitled

"Race and Economic Opportunity in the United States: An Intergenerational Perspective."

The paper is more than 100 pages long, filled with complex equations, and clearly not intended to be summer reading at the beach. *Times* journalists distilled that work into words and images that people could not only understand, but also were compelled to share.

Negotiating out how much precision is too much, or not enough, is something else that should be done early in a collaboration. Don't assume your work will be rendered with full academic fidelity. A journalist is a translator, and inevitably some nuance will be lost along the way.

Journalists Appreciate REAL Academic Partnerships, Not Self-Promotion

This is a quick one: If you're going to approach a journalist about a collaboration, do it authentically—not with an eye toward self-promotion.

Journalists are bombarded all day, every day, by pitches and press releases. When we get a cold call from someone "eager to discuss my latest research" or touting "new breakthrough findings" we usually just ignore it.

Even if we don't, we will be skeptical and a little self-conscious about being hoodwinked.

Not exactly the most solid ground on which to build a real collaboration.

The solution to this is to do what journalists do: cultivate real relationships. Rather than cold emailing someone, ask them out to coffee. Have an understanding of their work and be able to explain how your expertise might fit in. Help them see how you can help them.

Help journalists figure out sustainable business models.

Up to this point, the implied nature of these collaborations has been primarily journalistic. But the actual business of news needs help, too—probably more than ever.

The "business side," as journalists often call it, is the part of a news organization charged with making enough money to keep the lights on. It's the advertising reps, circulation specialists, product developers, and data scientists charged with understanding the audience and creating things they will pay for.

The news industry—and especially local news—is desperately struggling to figure out a sustainable business model. Outside of the big national organizations like *The New York Times*, almost no other organization has cracked the code.

Frankly, we need help. And we could use the expertise academics can provide.

Chris Wiggins was hired in 2014 to be the chief data scientist at *The New York Times*. He is also an associate professor of applied mathematics at Columbia University. Beyond helping with data science in the newsroom, his team's work has also helped *The Times* better understand its audience and develop products and strategies to serve it.

Other organizations would kill for that kind of support. So, if you care about news and its role in democracy, step back and think about how your work or expertise might be able to contribute.

Know a thing or two about data? See if your local newsroom needs a hand understanding its audience metrics. Study human behavior? Think about how your expertise might help a newsroom better serve its readers. Advise startups in your spare time? Consider what you can teach news organizations about building and supporting products people love.

We journalists believe we occupy an important role in democracy, and we are all worried about how well our current business model will be able to support that. If you think you can help, a lot of organizations would be glad to have you.

Sharing Is Caring, and Sometimes Can Lead to Academic Bylines

In January 2018, *The New York Times* published a piece called The Follower Factory, which explored an underground economy that traffics in fake social media followers, often patronized by wealthy celebrities hoping to boost their profiles online.

The piece was part of a package that was a finalist for the Pulitzer Prize. And one of the most striking things about it was its byline: three reporters and technologists from *The Times*, alongside one professor, Mark Hansen, from Columbia University.

For journalists, bylines are sacred real estate. For many reporters, having their name at the top of a story is a big reason they come to work in the morning. For a news organization, putting those names front and center represents an imprimatur of trust: these are our people, they adhere to our standards, and you can put faith in the work they have done.

Which is to say, putting an academic's byline at the top of a story is no small thing. But it is also, in some ways, the logical extension of Philip Meyer's work from the 1960s.

Journalists and academics are natural collaborators. They both seek the truth and adhere to stringent professional ethics designed to preserve the integrity of their inquiry. Their jobs demand they be thoughtful, skeptical, inquisitive—always challenging their biases and assumptions in order to get as close as possible to pure, unassailable conclusions.

They also have egos (often big ones) and agendas (often conflicting ones). Sometimes they have tempers (short ones). And despite their natural affinities, sometimes when you put a journalist and an academic on the same project, things go totally sideways.

Don't let it. Be clear when you work with a journalist. Take the time to understand where they are coming from. Understand where your motivations intersect, and where they differ. Build authentic trust and relationships.

Ask questions. Be clear. Leave no room for confusion.

16

Would We Do It Again?

Opportunities in Journalism and Academic Collaboration

Jennifer Moore

It all began with a question: What could happen if all of the storytellers in a region turned their attention to one topic?

For nearly two years, I worked on a university-led public engagement research project called One River, Many Stories.[1] In my role as a journalism professor at the University of Minnesota Duluth, I worked with faculty partners on a grant-funded project to study collaboration and cooperation among journalists and the public in our community. Inspired by public engagement research used in disciplines such as public health, we designed a project to give journalists an opportunity to change their long-held work routines to co-create stories with their competitors as well as community members.

As a study in participatory and engaged journalism, my colleagues and I learned a lot about how universities can work with the public to generate new knowledge. In our case, it was to understand how a community storytelling project could help facilitate innovation and collaboration among journalists and citizens alike. Knowing that stories from the community could offer new and alternative narratives outside of what's reported in the mainstream media, this project was an opportunity to give everyone a platform to tell stories and build trust between journalists and audiences in our media ecosystem in Duluth, Minnesota.

Our original project was a finalist for a Knight Cities Challenge in 2016. While we didn't make the final cut, a scaled-back version of our study was supported by a local nonprofit funded by the Knight Foundation. We were fortunate to have their guidance and trust from the beginning. They were trusting and allowed us to conduct our work free of heavy oversight.

Jennifer Moore, *Would We Do It Again?* In: *Journalism Research That Matters.* Edited by: Valérie Bélair-Gagnon and Nikki Usher, Oxford University Press. © Oxford University Press 2021. DOI: 10.1093/oso/9780197538470.003.0017

Using community engagement strategies as a university faculty member was both rewarding and time-consuming. You are committing to help empower your community members to find and deploy unique solutions to problems. In our case, it was how to help strengthen our media ecosystem through storytelling cooperation and collaboration. Like news organizations across the country, the greater Duluth media market is negotiating the impact of shrinking audiences and decreasing revenue streams. With fewer newsroom staff to report important stories, and with those still in business doing more with less, we hoped our journalism storytelling experiment could bring about positive change and help foster new opportunities to engage audiences through participation. In the face of a changing media landscape, could our project design—meant to disrupt long-held reporting routines and conventions—convince professional journalists to adopt engaged journalism storytelling strategies? Would collaboration occur?

The research project asked anyone to tell one story about the St. Louis River—an important waterway in our region that has been receiving renewed attention in recent years. There were no barriers to entry, and no story was off limits. Anyone who had something original to say about the St. Louis River and its communities, its history, its people, were invited to participate. We planned to study how we could use our position as university faculty to help facilitate collaboration—not only among competing media organizations but also with public storytellers.

We organized our project into phases. First, to field test, build relationships, and train journalists and community members to work together. We encouraged a big push to publish stories during April 2017. In the final phase we assessed the project by gathering journalists and community participants together to have them help us understand what was learned.

The results of our 18-month research project proved to be both rewarding and surprising. The surprises, at first, were interpreted as disappointments. But looking back I'm proud of the research I did with my colleagues and continue to collaborate with others at my university as a result of what One River, Many Stories afforded me as a public scholar.

Here's what you can expect if you are thinking of taking your scholarship as a university professor in this direction.

Foster your community relationships early and maintain them throughout your project.

The journalism program at the University of Minnesota Duluth already had established relationships with local and regional media organizations. That trust was a key to early buy-in and support. Working alongside a media partner, the digital-first publication *Perfect Duluth Day* was also critical to gain the trust of other journalists in the community. In fact, our media partner is the one who suggested the St. Louis River as the topic for our public engagement research.

Earning the trust of your media community is not all you will need to do. We also engaged early with nonprofit organizations already working in the community, especially organizations that focus attention on the St. Louis River as well as nonprofits that serve vulnerable populations. Like us, you will need them to help you build trust in order to do the work this kind of public research requires. These partnerships will help you encourage participation from people who might otherwise mistrust your project and institutions unfamiliar to them, like journalists and university professors.

Ask for support from community leaders.

This is a must, especially if you're at a public institution of higher education. We had the support of both the current and previous mayors of Duluth, who wrote letters of support on our behalf to our grant funder.

Establish a presence outside of the university (and hire help).

Because we established relationships early with community partners, we were offered a space to work out of at a local nonprofit, Ecolibrium3, that organizes resilience and sustainability work in our community. With their help, we were able to gain the trust of other organizations they worked with, and involved many more community partners in the project.

We also hired administrative support who helped us coordinate partnerships and helped organize many public-facing events to engage audiences with what we were doing, why we were doing it, and how they could participate. It was important to have a contact on the project who was a citizen who could bridge the community with the university.

Allow your civic partners to co-create knowledge with you (e.g., let go of the idea that you're in charge).

Mobile phones allow anyone with the capacity to be a reporter. To that end, we organized several "skills sessions" as public events where journalists and other experts talked about everything from photography to covering controversial topics. We hosted these events across town and at different times of the day, hoping to capture a wide range of participants. Journalists have always worked with their audiences, but now they were using them to help gather photos and videos to help report news. We hoped our skills sessions could make that process more collaborative.

Include your students. They are, after all, the future of journalism.

A number of students had meaningful experiences working alongside media professionals and were able to apply what we're teaching them. Our grant allowed for five students to be placed as interns to help with the project. One class of journalism students worked with a middle school and designed a project to teach the journalism skills they were learning so they could report stories in their own stories. Other students were encouraged and participated in the storytelling project, bringing a college student's perspective to the riverway in ways mainstream journalists and others did not.

Harness the power of social media early and often.

We asked people to publish and share their stories widely. So we could curate and archive stories on the project's web site, onerivermn.com, we asked participants to share their work on social media networks and use the hashtags #OneRiverMN and #ChiGamiiziibi (the Ojibwe name for the St. Louis River).

Publish your research with a general audience as your first audience.

You are conducting public scholarship. That means you have to make your work not only accessible to a general audience, but also package it in a way where people will actually want to read it. We hired a graphic design colleague early on, to create a visual identity for One River, Many Stories that included logos, web presence, and so on. We maintained a website throughout the project and updated it regularly with our own content, including blog posts and interviews with participants. We also wrote and published a beautiful, full-color final report (you can find a PDF version online at onerivermn. com).

We also took many opportunities to talk about our research project with the public. We presented our work in professional and community settings before, during, and after the project ended. We published pieces of our research in both scholarly and popular publications.

Invite your university colleagues. You might be surprised what happens.

Had you told me that an original documentary-style play would be written, produced, and staged by a theater colleague and go on to win national awards in his discipline, I would not have believed you.

My colleagues and I held an information session early in the process and invited the entire campus to talk to us. We didn't know if anyone would attend. A lot of people who did attend didn't really get what we were doing. However, one colleague in particular not only got it but created what is easily the most memorable outcome of this community-engaged research. The play *One River* sold out every night it was staged and won numerous regional and national awards for screenwriting, acting, and stage production. The play made the journalism produced reach audiences in a completely different way—packaged as performance. Colleagues from our education college also contributed content and had their students participate by telling stories through art education.

Prepare for the unexpected.

This cannot be overstated. We did not expect the level of engagement and participation that One River, Many Stories received from individuals and groups seemingly far afield from the profession of journalism. It's fair to say that the scientists, playwrights, art teachers, musicians, and poets not only surprised us but also outpaced the level of participation from the journalism community. While journalists and news organizations in our community overwhelmingly supported the project, it became clear that financial and structural constraints didn't allow them to step outside their codified routines to collaborate in ways we attempted to facilitate. They participated in the project but didn't breach their long-held roles as gatekeepers of knowledge. Instead, it was the artists, scientists, and others with storytelling skills who participated in ways the journalism community could not and did not.

The *One River* play previously mentioned is one example of what was unforeseen. Others include an EPA ecologist who partnered with a cartographer to create a 50-foot map of the 192-mile riverway. That map was displayed alongside the work of a Native American photographer commissioned by the Duluth Art Institute to document the indigenous communities who live along the river and still depend on it today. Wisconsin Public Radio hosted a storytelling contest featuring stories and poetry about the river. Winners read their poetry and short stories in front of an audience for later broadcast.

What did we learn? Participation encouraged learning. Unexpected partnerships formed. And journalistic routines are tough to change. If you consider how journalists and their audiences can work together, imagine the possibilities. By inviting the public to tell stories alongside working journalists, a wide range of stories were told that mainstream journalists don't often tell. In our assessment with participants, we were told that participation in the project caused many to gain a new understanding and renewed concern for the river.

Our strategy to get early buy-in, plant ourselves in the community, find partners to help us reach audiences beyond our capacity as faculty, and let go of control paid off and helped build trust. At the end of the project we heard overwhelmingly from both journalists and participants (those people who Jay Rosen has now famously called "the people formerly known as the audience") wanted another community project to be planned and organized.

If your institution is like mine, public engagement is increasingly being recognized as an important avenue for research. Faculty at research institutions are uniquely positioned to do this kind of public-engaged scholarship. It's a powerful way to make our work serve the mission of the institutions where we work and the constituencies we serve. I'd go even further to argue that it is *our moral duty* as scholars to perform acts of public scholarship to help sustain and enrich the community we live in.

My colleagues and I hoped that One River, Many Stories could serve as a model for university–community public engagement. I thrive on collaboration and understand that it's part of my job in my role as faculty at a public institution to do community-engaged research. Working alongside my journalism colleagues and using our training as scholar-teachers to help our community was a remarkable and rewarding experience. We made a lot of mistakes along the way and made adjustments when we could. But we also created opportunities for ourselves and others to work outside of disciplinary boundaries.

To read more about One River, Many Stories, go to onerivermn.com. You can see many of the stories published and download a copy of the Final Report.

Note

1. This essay is based on research that appears in Jennifer E. Moore and J.A. Hatcher, "Disrupting Traditional News Routines through Community Engagement: Analysis of the One River, Many Stories Media Collaboration Project," *Journalism Studies* 20, no. 5 (2019): 749–764, and published in the technical report, J.A. Hatcher. and J.E. Moore,. "One River, Many Stories: Final Report" (Duluth: Duluth News Tribune, 2017). Distributed through the Knight Foundation.

17

What Journalism Researchers
Should Be Doing

Derek Willis

With all the ways of communicating
We can't get in touch with who we're hating.
Hüsker Dü, "Turn on the News" (1984)

Let's begin with this unfortunate irony: as communicators, journalism scholars and working journalists often fail to understand each other. We publish, we move on to other things, and we certainly complain to our colleagues.

It's entirely fair for an academic to say, "Well, you're journalists, so you should be able to find and interpret what we publish." But very few reporters cover journalism as an industry the way that we cover other topics, and almost all who do are at national news organizations. The distance between academic research and the average local news organization—whatever that means today—is so large that neither can effectively see the other on a sustained basis.

It's too easy to hold onto the idea that while the pace of doing journalism has increased during the past 25 years, the pace of academic research about journalism has not. To blame the academy for its publishing schedule is to deflect attention from where it belongs: on what is actually changing within journalism, why it is changing, and what that means for journalists. Those sweeping changes give both scholars and practitioners an opportunity to build the kind of relationship in which we both listen to and learn from each other.

Broadly speaking, the fundamentals of journalism are well understood by those who study and teach it. But at the margins—in particular the

Derek Willis, *What Journalism Researchers Should Be Doing* In: *Journalism Research That Matters.* Edited by: Valérie Bélair-Gagnon and Nikki Usher, Oxford University Press. © Oxford University Press 2021.
DOI: 10.1093/oso/9780197538470.003.0018

newer ways of doing journalism—the understanding of what we're doing and what impact that has on newsrooms and the profession at large is too often missing. And those who do journalism would benefit from that knowledge.

That doesn't mean that the research itself is absent; there are interesting studies being published all the time. But interesting is not always the same as useful, and the disconnect has become, among many professionals (and especially those working in areas that are not uniformly taught at colleges and universities), so vast that there is scarcely any relationship at all.

The explosion of the ways of producing and publishing journalism feeds into this, as do changes in career paths and the hollowing-out of local and regional news organizations. We're in the midst of rapid and significant changes, which can make research seem outdated and backward looking, but it's exactly the time to dig in.

There's little question that professionals could use the insights of independent, peer-reviewed research. When news organizations try something new, they often make mistakes, and learning from them becomes an exercise in peer and self-criticism. Those are not without value, but they are done with the goal of fixing the immediate problem, not necessarily understanding the systems that helped to generate it.

Such research efforts could start with an ongoing look at the very definition of news. Given the varied methods of publishing, the ability to address the interests of niche audiences, and the breakdown of a coherent hierarchy of news organizations, the question "what is news?" has a lot of potential answers. Given that we're seeing existing news organizations wither and new ones arise, journalism research could provide a more stable foundation to those building the next generation of news.

Another area to look at is news behavior. For some of the largest news organizations, or those chasing a digital readership that overlaps with the giants, there has been an increase in the volume and tempo of publishing. A handful of times over the past few years I've taken a snapshot of just how many things—articles, videos, slideshows—that *The New York Times* or *The Washington Post* has published in a day or a week. It's a lot. There's little doubt in my mind that changing the volume and pace of publishing has a real impact on a news organization. We should know what those impacts are, not just on those organizations but the ones who take their cues from them. Counting things may not feel like the greatest example of academic inquiry, but it is something that few newsrooms are doing in a way that focuses on newsroom effects rather than audience. Certainly, that knowledge isn't widely shared across newsrooms.

When newsrooms change how they publish, that has implications for career paths. Those of us who have worked in journalism for 20 years can feel as if our job histories have little relevance to today's environment. Many of the opportunities that were available to less experienced journalists in 1995 don't exist now; for those that remain, often there are fewer of them. There have to be effects and lessons that newsroom leaders can learn from this shift. As journalists, we're pretty good about reporting on things that happen. We're not as good at reporting on things that used to happen but don't now. Research could help us understand not just what we're missing but how that has changed how we work.

What I'd love to see is more longitudinal survey research that follows individuals or organizations over time. Reporters and editors leave, and often take the lessons they've learned with them. News organizations should capture this, but we mostly don't. That's an opportunity for scholars, who, in devoting sustained attention, could provide useful insights to newsrooms but also could close the gulf that separates too many journalists from the people who study their work. The work of OpenNews, a nonprofit organization that connects journalists to their peers to learn from each other, might serve as a framework. While not publishing academic research, OpenNews publishes lessons that newsrooms can examine and learn from, and does so in a way that strengthens ties in the industry.

Social media isn't uncharted territory for journalism research, either, and there have been really interesting studies about the social networks of journalists, among other things. What would help newsrooms is having greater definition and evaluation of the ways that they engage readers—the patterns and habits that have been built intentionally or otherwise—which understandably differ depending on the news organization. Given the different ways that newsrooms are using social platforms for journalism, it's worth an independent look at how those are working, especially for smaller news organizations. *The New York Times* will always be worthy of study, but the difference between *The Times* and all but a handful of its peers is, if anything, wider than it used to be.

Speaking of *The Times*, I'd personally be interested in knowing whether the agenda-setting impact assigned to it, demonstrated by decades of research, still exists and, if so, how it has changed. Maybe that's just me, but if journalism challenges conventional wisdom, journalism research should, too.

The behavior of readers gets a fair amount of attention, particularly from efforts like Medill's Local News Initiative. We need much more of this kind of research. News organizations may rightfully think they are offering their audiences more convenience by publishing on multiple platforms and via individual products, but there are a lot of unknowns about how people consume the news. Among them is how the platform environment informs the credibility of a story or publisher. To be clear: there are studies and experiments that have been done in this area. What news organizations could use is more detailed research focused on the many small ways that trust can be gained or shed. Research that generated specific conclusions for particular types of news organizations would be very useful.

The technological changes within journalism, while not unknown, deserve more scrutiny. While there are some academic programs that actually create new tools and software for doing journalism—a useful effort—there is a need for research that examines how newsrooms use tools. That includes the standards for ethical use, the ways that tools can limit or shape the kinds of stories done, and how those tools change the behavior of reporters. Right now, the best reviews we get are from each other at professional conferences or online. The contents of the main listserv devoted to what we used to call "computer-assisted reporting" have, as near as I can tell, never been the subject of an academic study, yet it contains one of the best histories of how reporting tools (and the people who use them) have changed over the past two decades.

I've worked for two nonprofit journalism organizations in my career, including my current employer, and while this model isn't particularly new, the variations of it are. A lot of academic attention to these organizations has focused—rightly—on their funding, and that work should continue. It's also important that we learn more about how these organizations work differently than their for-profit colleagues, and where they overlap and don't. Many of these efforts involve collaborations with for-profit news organizations, academic institutions, and other "non-traditional" journalism partners. These collaborations deserve more study because they can be a marked departure from the norm, compared to our traditional understanding of how journalism is done.

Many of the Journalism Studies I read go at least some of the way toward achieving the goals I've described here. And that's the frustrating part, because as much as I understand the need to place a series of events or behaviors in the proper theoretical context, as a working journalist I'm left wanting something more, something that I can act on. Such conclusions may be an awkward fit in some research (or even inappropriate). But for journalism research to matter more to newsrooms, it has to speak to how they do their jobs not in the theoretical sense but in concrete ways they can recognize and apply.

Finally, even incredibly useful research won't be seen by practitioners if it's only accessible behind pay-walled journals or discussed at conferences where a journalist would need to spend hundreds of dollars to attend. I know that this complaint is not original, but it is important—and it can be solved. In my area of political data journalism, there has been an explosion not just of publicly available research but of sites hosted by news organizations devoted to explaining and discussing it (think Mischiefs of Faction or The Monkey Cage). We need journalism researchers to come up with creative ideas about the different ways they can spread their knowledge. Sue Robinson is a great example with her guides for community outreach.

Come to think of it, that's one problem that scholars and practitioners share. Maybe we can figure it out together.

Conclusion: Betrothed or Belligerent

What Type of Engagement Do We Need?

Matt Carlson

Introduction

For journalism researchers and working journalists, much of the talk about how to confront the trials of the present moment revolves around the notion of engagement. This has resulted in a breadth of understandings and practices such that no fixed meaning exists.[1] To address this ambiguity, a starting place is to recognize engagement to be a semantically promiscuous word. Since its inception in the English language, it has carried with it a degree of vagueness that allows it to take on a variety of meanings in a variety of contexts. Thinking about these differences can help us step back and examine how we use it in the realm of journalism. It also helps us work against the dismissal of engagement as a buzzword employed both in the news industry and among researchers, to instead ask what engagement gets us when thinking about journalism at a time when there is an extraordinary amount of thinking about journalism going on.

First, when we invoke the word "engagement" in the abstract, we often conjure an image of the promise of marriage that follows a formal proposal. In this sense, engagement is a relationship state predicated on the promise of an eventual wedding that will in turn produce the new state of marriage. In this sense, you and your betrothed enter into an engagement. Yet nearly a century before this meaning of engagement became popular, engagement meant "a battle or fight between armies or fleets." This may well describe wedding planning for many couples, but this bellicose meaning persists in contemporary military usage to mark the point at which combatants actually fight. In a softer usage, the idea of engaging someone or something suggests a level of intensity and engrossment.

Matt Carlson, *Conclusion: Betrothed or Belligerent* In: *Journalism Research That Matters*. Edited by: Valérie Bélair-Gagnon and Nikki Usher, Oxford University Press. © Oxford University Press 2021. DOI: 10.1093/oso/9780197538470.003.0019

Looking across these definitions, we see two sets of opposing meanings. The first, more overt one, is the divide between engagement as harmonious versus engagement as conflictual. In the matrimonial sense, at least as contemporarily understood, engagement is ideally a willing partnership jointly entered into with the promise of formally coming together in the future. In its military sense, the goal is to triumph by defeating the other. In these senses, engagement can indicate either extreme amity or enmity, depending on the context.

But there is also a second division in the usage of engagement that distinguishes between engagement as promise and as action. Looking back further into the etymological history reveals a meaning of engagement as the making of a pledge. In J.L. Austin's sense,[2] pledges function as a particular type of speech act that not only has meaning but also consequences for those involved. For relationships, an engagement is a pledge to get married. But engagements are also agreed-upon plans. Conversely, engagement can also indicate the undertaking of action. A war is not a speech act, but an intense material struggle. It is a set of actions designed to have lethal consequences. Engagement then functions on a spectrum marked by a pledge to do something on one end and the doing of a thing on the other.

The dual dueling meanings—engagement as accord versus discord and promise versus action—provide a starting point to engage with engagement in the context of journalism that promotes a range of approaches available to scholars. At first glance, the more amicable definition may seem to fit. But, on a basic level, a growing interest in engagement rests on the recognition that the current model doesn't fully work. Accenting engagement—whether in reference to story formats and frames, sourcing practices, or business models—signals an intensity of focus to identify and ameliorate with the hope of finding something that works better.

What, then, is the role of the journalism scholar? Are we betrothed to the journalists we study, or are we belligerents? The answer lies in seeing engagement as connection at a distance in a way that this term is not a contradiction, but a situational asset. We are in a place to critique news, not out of hostility but rather out of a longing to see improvement. The question that animates this volume is how to use research to challenge journalists to improve their practices in particular and concrete ways. This involves an outward view fixed on journalistic practices, but it also suggests the need for an internal gaze on the forces that shape what journalism scholarship looks like.

To be engaged in journalism, scholars need to be engaged with looking at their own practices.

Engaging Engagement

Confronting the inadequacies of journalistic practice in this present technological, economic, and cultural moment is the main goal of many of this book's chapters. Authors take up engagement in its different iterations to point to what needs fixing. Perhaps most worrisome, in Chapter 7, Edgerly draws on current research about news audiences to warn of the high number of news avoiders. No matter what interventions journalists take, an inability to get news in front of audiences negates the power of journalism as an institution. Attracting audiences is difficult work, as is generating revenue within the news industry at a time when advertising dollars have alarmingly migrated to Google and Facebook—two organizations that do not produce any news content. This is about more than diversifying revenue streams; it gets to foundational questions about what the news business ought to look like now that advertising streams have turned into trickles. In Chapter 14, Kilgo also challenges journalists to confront the difficulties of the present context but moves beyond the news to the epidemic of unarmed Black men being killed by police officers. Sadly, this occurs often enough for the reporting to adopt familiar routines. Even as journalists cover protests and raise awareness, their failure to engage systemic inequalities curtails the effectiveness of the news coverage. These chapters all engage journalism by laying bare its shortcomings and asking journalism to do better to connect to its digital audiences, find revenue, and acknowledge how it covers injustice.

But critique is not reserved for journalists. Engagement also means turning inward to examine journalism research and the state of the academy. The authors that do this tackle the inertia of university research and its entrenched reward system that prioritizes academic-facing work above industry- or public-facing work. The latter two may be valued, but usually only after the first has been established. This is not to discount academic-facing work as unworthy; journalism research—and communication research generally—has long struggled to be taken as seriously as its social science and humanities siblings. At the same time, the challenges offered by authors in this book deserve attention. Both Weber (Chapter 3) and Toff (Chapter 4) point to the uphill battle for university-produced research to make it outside the university.

Toff shows that intermediaries between the news industry and journalism research—Columbia Journalism Review, Nieman, and Poynter—rarely act as vehicles for circulating academic journalism research (even though these get a lot of attention when shared). Weber looks at the policy realm to lament the dearth of journalism research within media-related policy debates, especially compared with other disciplines. Intentions are not enough, and Toff and Weber each indicate the need for resources to systematize translation efforts to broker research to industry and policy audiences.

Other authors push journalism researchers to adapt to the changing world in which we live and work. In Chapter 13, Ekdale calls for reflection on the many ways in which scholars and scholarship reinforces ethnocentrism by perpetuating a Western European/North American view of the world. This is not a new charge, but an urgent one to address in an era of global media flows. The internationalization of the field will help, but only through sustained efforts. Relatedly, Palmer in Chapter 5 looks specifically at international news reporting to show the inequalities of who gets featured in research. Well-known foreign correspondents working for Western news outlets get attention at the expense of the lesser-known local staff who do much of the work on the ground. This is beginning to change as digital media make distant workers more visible and accessible.

Changing news practices and the changing news landscape also demand improvements in how academics study and map journalistic flows. In Chapter 2, Holcomb looks back over a decade of local news studies conducted both by academics and nonprofit research organizations to assess its progress. These studies have provided ample insights both on where news sources are within a community and how information flows between them. But we also need to revisit what we've learned to push this work forward. Ng (Chapter 8) looks at the rise in collaborative journalism projects and sharing of code across news organizations. Although collaboration has always occurred in journalism—as with pack journalism—digital media provide new tools for journalists to work with, which leads to new tools for academics to keep up with these innovations.

Finally, several authors looked at engagement through a focus on how we teach—and teach about—journalism. As the technologies of news production and circulation change, so too does the teaching of media literacy. In Chapter 6, Tully calls for news literacy to be positioned in a more central way and to be refitted for the present media environment. Her vision of literacy includes thinking about how to teach participation and not just passive reception. Boyles in Chapter 12 more specifically argues for increasing education around data literacy to better train journalists to work with newly available tools. Pushing this training requires moving past a sense of how things have been done traditionally.

And, not to omit marital bliss, engagement has increasingly meant the marriage of journalism education with news outlets. There have always been blurry lines between journalism education and the profession, particularly with personnel moving in both directions. Internships have been a place for learning-by-doing for the student journalist. But a combination of factors emerging from declines in newsroom resources, coupled with increased access to digital tools and publishing platforms, allow for classwork to become published work. In Chapter 11, Mourão and Shin show how students can engage communities through their coursework, which helps develop a sense of efficacy while providing news coverage in areas left out by journalists.

Future Engagement

Contemporary journalism is in a strange state. One the one hand, it is imperiled by structural changes that challenge its basic models of revenue generation, media changes that dilute audience attention, and political changes that question its veracity. Dangers are everywhere. On the other hand, journalism has never been better. Journalists have more tools to gather, create, and share news; news audiences can participate in new ways, and our access to news is unparalleled. Innovations abound. What role does thinking about engagement have in this scenario?

One answer is that engagement is, ultimately, about forging connections. This view privileges a more harmonious definition of engagement to stress a desire for connection. This is partly the legacy of the mass communication era; for a long time, the industrial production of news meant little feedback from audiences except in their roles as consumers who purchase a subscription or tune into a program. The public journalism movement in the 1990s arose from dissatisfaction with this arrangement as it attempted to insert the audience into news in novel ways.[3] Notably, many journalists found this to be controversial. The explosion of digital technologies has not completely upended traditional journalism, but it has encouraged greater communication. Disenchantment with journalism along with a high media choice environment creates pressure to connect with audiences more substantially than in the past.

If engagement is about the forging of connections, then the question that must be addressed before we go on with our endeavors is a basic one: What are our goals as journalism scholars? Are they more transient goals about keeping up with the current moment to address political, economic, technological, and cultural shifts? This is engagement as a reaction to change, an effort to keep pace with the world. Or are our goals more foundational than this? In the miasma of media change, is engagement is about tracking back to Carey's basic argument that journalism is not just information transmission but about crafting shared meanings?[4] This communitarianism lurks within thinking of engagement, if it is not explicitly stated.

Rather than try to resolve dissonant meanings, it serves us well to attend to engagement as a complicated term that can at once encompass accord and conflict, promise and action. It behooves us to define its meaning to make its use intelligible, but also to recognize the space it affords us as we take up our positions.

Notes

1. Regina G. Lawrence, Daniel Radcliffe, and Thomas R. Schmidt, "Practicing Engagement: Participatory Journalism in the Web 2.0 Era," *Journalism Practice* 12, no. 10 (2018): 1220–1240.
2. J.L. Austin. *How to Do Things with Words* (Oxford: Oxford University Press, 1962).
3. Tanni Haas, *The Pursuit of Public Journalism* (New York: Routledge, 2007).
4. James W. Carey, *Communication as Culture* (London: Routledge, 1992).

Bibliography

Abbott, Jim. (2005). *Newspaper in Education: A Guide for Weekly and Community Newspapers.* Washington, DC: Newspaper Association of American Foundation.

Abernathy, Penelope. (2016). "The Rise of a New Media Baron and the Emerging Threat of News Deserts." Center for Innovation and Sustainability in Local Media, University of North Carolina at Chapel Hill, https://www.usnewsdeserts.com/wp- content/uploads/2016/09/07.UNC_RiseOfNewMediaBaron_SinglePage_01Sep2016-REDUCED.pdf.

Abernathy, Penelope M. (2020). "The Local News Landscape in 2020: Transformed and Diminished." UNC Hussman School of Journalism and Media,. https://www.usnewsdeserts.com/reports/news-deserts-and-ghost-newspapers-will-local-news-survive/the-news-landscape-in-2020-transformed-and-diminished/.

Ajzen, Icek. (2002). "Perceived Behavioral Control, Self-Efficacy, Locus of Control, and the Theory of Planned Behavior." *Journal of Applied Social Psychology*, no. 32 (4): 665–683.

Ajzen, Icek. (2011). "The Theory of Planned Behavior: Reactions and Reflections." *Psychology & Health* 26, no. 9: 1113–1127.

Alexander, Michelle. (2010). *The New Jim Crow: Mass Incarceration in the Age of Colorblindness* (New York: The New Press).

Alfter, Brigittee. (2019). *Cross-Border Collaborative Journalism: A Step-by-Step Guide* (New York: Routledge).

Ali, Christopher. (2017). *Media Localism: The Policies of Place* (Urbana-Champaign, IL: University of Illinois Press).

Allern, Sigurd, and Ester Pollack. (2017). "Journalism as a Public Good: A Scandinavian Perspective." *Journalism* 20, no. 11; 1423–1439.

American Society of News Editors. (n.d.). "ASNE History," https://www.asne.org/asne-history.

Ananny, Mike. (2013). "Press–Public Collaboration as Infrastructure: Tracing News Organizations and Programming Publics in Application Programming Interfaces." *American Behavioral Scientist* 57, no. 5: 623–642.

Anderson, C.W. (2010). "Journalistic Networks and the Diffusion of Local News: The Brief, Happy News Life of the 'Francisville Four.'" *Political Communication* 27, no. 3: 289–309.

Anderson, C.W. (2016). "News Ecosystems," in *The SAGE Handbook of Digital Journalism*, eds. C.W. Anderson, et al. (London: SAGE Publications).

Anderson, C.W., Emily Bell, and Clay Shirky. (2012). *Post-Industrial Journalism: Adapting to the Present* (New York: Tow Center for Digital Journalism, Columbia University).

Appelgren, Ester. (2018). "An Illusion of Interactivity: The Paternalistic Side of Data Journalism." *Journalism Practice* 12, no. 3 (2018): 308–325.

Arceneaux, Kevin, and Martin Johnson. (2013). *Changing Minds or Changing Channels? Partisan News in an Age of Choice.* (Chicago: University of Chicago Press, 2013.).

Ashley, Seth, Adam Maksl, and Stephanie Craft. (2017). "News Media Literacy and Political Engagement: What's the Connection." *Journal of Media Literacy Education* 9, no. 1: 79–98.

Association for Education in Journalism and Mass Communication. (n.d.). "AEJMC History,." http://www.aejmc.org/home/about/aejmc-history/.

Aufderheide, Patricia, and Charles M. Firestone. (1993). "Media Literacy: A Report of the National Leadership Conference on Media Literacy" (Queenstown, MD: Aspen Institute), https://files.eric.ed.gov/fulltext/ED365294.pdf.

Austin, J.L. (1962). *How to Do Things with Words* (Oxford: Oxford University Press).

Ba-Quy Vuong, et al. (2008). "On Ranking Controversies in Wikipedia: Models and Evaluation." *WSDM '08: Proceedings of the 2008 International Conference on Web Search and Web Data Mining* (February): 171–182.

Barge, Kevin J., and Pamela Shockley-Zalabak. (2008). "Engaged Scholarship and the Creation of Useful Organizational Knowledge." *Journal of Applied Communication Research* 36, no. 3: 250–251.

Barker, Derek. (2004). "The Scholarship of Engagement: A Taxonomy of Five Emerging Practices." *Journal of Higher Education Outreach and Engagement* 9, no. 2: 123–137.

Barnett, Steven, and Judith Townend. (2015). "Plurality, Policy and the Local." *Journalism Practice* 9, no. 3: 332–349.

BBC. (2020). "A New Era for Public Service Reporting,." https://www.bbc.co.uk/lnp/.

Beckett, Charlie, and Robin Mansell. (2008). "Crossing Boundaries: New Media and Networked Journalism." *Communication, Culture & Critique* 1, no. 1: 92–104.

Bennett, W. Lance, Regina G. Lawrence, and Steven Livingston. (2008). *When the Press Fails: Political Power and the News Media from Iraq to Katrina* (Chicago: University of Chicago Press).

Benton, Joshua. (2018). "That Politico Article on 'News Deserts' Doesn't Really Show what it Claims to Show," *Nieman Journalism Lab,* April 9, 2018, https://www.niemanlab.org/2018/04/that-politico-article-on-news-deserts-doesnt-really-   show-what-it-claims-to-show.

Berglez, Peter, and Amanda Gearing. (2018). "The Panama and Paradise Papers. The Rise of a Global Fourth Estate." *International Journal of Communication* 12, https://ijoc.org/index.php/ijoc/article/view/9141.

Bergstrom, Andrea M., Mark Flynn, and Clay Craig. (2018). "Deconstructing Media in the College Classroom: A Longitudinal Critical Media Literacy Intervention." *Journal of Media Literacy Education* 10, no. 3: 113–131.

Bernholz, Lucy, Chiara Cordelli, and Rob Reich. (2016). "On the Agenda-Setting and Framing Influence of Foundations Relative to Social Challenges," in *Philanthropy in Democratic Societies: History, Institutions, Values,* eds. Rob Reich, Chiara Cordelli, and Lucy Bernholz (Chicago: University of Chicago Press).

Berrett, Charles, and Cheryl Phillips. (2016). *Teaching Data Journalism and Computational Journalism* (New York: Columbia University School of Journalism and Stanford University).

Blom, Robin, and Lucinda D. Davenport. (2012). "Searching for the Core of Journalism Education: Program Directors Disagree on Curriculum Priorities." *Journalism & Mass Communication Educator* 67, no. 1: 70–86.

Bloom, Nicholas, Luis Garicano, Raffaella Sadun, and John Van Reenen. (2014). "The Distinct Effects of Information Technology and Communication Technology on Firm Organization." *Management Science* 60, no. 12: 2859–2885.

Boczkowski, Pablo J. (2005). *Digitizing the News: Innovation in Online Newspapers.* (Cambridge, MA: MIT Press).

Boczkowski, Pablo J. (2010). *News at Work: Imitation in an Age of Information Abundance.* (Chicago: University of Chicago Press).

Boczkowski, Pablo J., and Zizi Papacharissi. (2018). *Trump and the Media* (Cambridge, MA: MIT Press).

Boczkowski, Pablo J., and Ignacio Siles. (2014). "Steps toward Cosmopolitanism in the Study of Media Technologies." *Information, Communication & Society* 1, no. 5: 560–571.

Bogenschneider, Karen, and Thomas J. Corbett. (2010). "Family Policy: Becoming a Field of Inquiry and Subfield of Social Policy." *Journal of Marriage and Family* 72, no. 3: 783–803.

Bond, Paul. (2016). "Leslie Moonvies on Donald Trump." *Hollywood Reporter,* February 29, 2016, https://www.hollywoodreporter.com/news/leslie-moonves-donald-trump-may-871464.

Boyd, Danah M. (2017). Did Media Literacy Backfire? https://points.datasociety.net/did-media-literacy-backfire-7418c084d88d.

Boyles, Jan Lauren. (2016). "The Isolation of Innovation: Restructuring the Digital Newsroom through Intrapreneurship." *Digital Journalism* 4, no. 2: 229–246.

Boyles, Jan Lauren. (2017). "Laboratories for News? Experimenting with Journalism Hackathons," *Journalism,* Preprint, 1–17, https://doi.org/10.1177/1464884917737213.

Boyles, Jan Lauren. (2020). "Deciphering Code: How Newsroom Developers Communicate Journalistic Labor." *Journalism Studies* 21, no. 3: 336–351.

Braun, Joshua, and Jessica L. Eklund. (2019). "Fake News, Real Money: Ad Tech Platforms, Profit-Driven Hoaxes, and the Business of Journalism." *Digital Journalism* 7, no. 1: 1–21.

Brenan, Meg. (2019). "Americans' Trust in Mass Media Edges Down to 41%." Gallup, https://news.gallup.com/poll/267047/americans-trust-mass-media-edges-down.aspx.

Brownson, Ross C., Graham A. Colditz, and Enola Knisley Proctor. (2018). *Dissemination and Implementation Research in Health: Translating Science to Practice* (City: Oxford University Press).

Bucay, Yemile, Vittoria Elliott, Jennie Kamin, and Andrea Park. (2017). "America's Growing News Deserts." *Columbia Journalism Review,* Spring 2017, https://www.cjr.org/local_news/american-news-deserts-donuts-local.php.

Bulger, Monica, and Patrick Davison. (2018). "The Promises, Challenges, and Futures of Media Literacy." Data & Society Research Institute. Available from https://datasociety.net/library/the-promises-challenges-and-futures-of-media-literacy/.

Bunce, Mel. (2010). "'This Place Used to Be a White British Boys' Club': Reporting Dynamics and Cultural Clash at an International News Bureau in Nairobi." *The Round Table* 99, no. 410 (2010): 515–528.

Bunce, Mel. (2011). "The New Foreign Correspondent at Work: Local-National 'Stringers' and the Global News Coverage of Darfur." Oxford: Reuters Institute for the Study of Journalism, http://openaccess.city.ac.uk/id/eprint/3600/1/The_new_foreign_corre-spondent_at_work.pdf.

Burns, Niels, and Maureen Brugger. (2012). *Histories of Public Service Broadcasters on the Web.* (London: Peter Lang).

Cardin, Benjamin. (2009). "Senator Cardin Introduced Bill That Would Allow American Newspapers to Operate as Non-Profits," March 24, 2009, https://www.cardin.senate.gov/newsroom/press/release/senator-cardin-introduces-bill-that-would-allow-american-newspapers-to-operate-as-non-profits.

Carey, James W. (1974). "The Problem of Journalism History," *Journalism History* 1, no. 1 (1974): 3, https://search.proquest.com/docview/1300125488?accountid=14553.

Carey, James W. (1992). *Communication as Culture: Essays on Media and Society*, (New York: Routledge, 1992).

Carey, James W. (1996). "Afterword: The Culture in Question," in *James Carey: A Critical Reader*, eds. Eve Stryker Munson and Catherine A. Warren, (University of Minnesota Press, 1996):, 308–340.

Carey, James W. (2000). "Some Personal Notes on US Journalism Education." *Journalism* 1, no. 1 (2000): 12–23.

Carlson, Jake, and Lisa R. Johnston. (2015). *Data Information Literacy: Librarians, Data, and the Education of a New Generation of Researchers, Vol. 2.* (West Lafayette: Purdue University Press), 2015.

Carlson, Matt. (2017). *Journalistic Authority: Legitimating News in the Digital Era* (New York: Columbia University Press).

Carlson, Matt, and Seth C. Lewis, eds. (2015). *Boundaries of Journalism: Professionalism, Practices and Participation* (London, New York: Routledge).

Carlson, Matt, Sue Robinson, Seth C. Lewis, and Daniel A. Berkowitz. (2018). "Journalism Studies and Its Core Commitments: The Making of a Communication Field." *Journal of Communication* 68, no. 1: 6–25.

Carson, Andrea, and Kate Farhall. (2018). "Understanding Collaborative Investigative Journalism in a 'Post-Truth' Age." *Journalism Studies* 19, no. 13: 1899–1911.

Chan, Joseph M., and Lee, Chin-Chuan. (1984). "The Journalistic Paradigm on Civil Protests: A Case Study of Hong Kong," in *The News Media in National and International Conflict*, eds. Andrew Arno and Wimal Dissanayake (Boulder: Westview Press), 183–202.

Chesebro, James W., and Deborah J. Borisoff. (2007). "What Makes Qualitative Research Qualitative." *Qualitative Research Reports in Communication* 8, no. 1: 3–14.

Clayton, Katherine, et al. (2019). "Real Solutions for Fake News? Measuring the Effectiveness of General Warnings and Factcheck tags in Reducing Belief in False Stories on Social Media." *Political Behavior*. Online first, https://doi.org/10.1007/s11109-019-09533-0.

Cole, Stephen. (1983). "The Hierarchy of the Sciences?" *American Journal of Sociology* 89, no. 1: 111–139.

Coleman, Gabriella. (2012). *Coding Freedom: The Ethics and Aesthetics of Hacking* (Princeton: Princeton University Press).

Columbia Journalism Review. (n.d.). "Mission Statement," https://www.cjr.org/about_us/mission_statement.php.

Constantaras, Eva. (2016). "Data Journalism Should Thrive on Cross-Border Collaborations—Why Doesn't It?" *Source*, OpenNews, February 16, 2016, https://source.opennews.org/articles/data-journalism-should-thrive-cross-border-collabo/.

Couldry, Nick. (2013). "Why Media Ethics Still Matters" in *Global Media Ethics: Problems and Perspectives*, ed. Stephen J.A. Ward (Chichester: Wiley-Blackwell), 13–29.

Cowan, Geoffrey, and David Westphal. (2010). "Public Policy and Funding the News." *USC Annenberg School for Communication & Journalism Center on Communication Leadership & Policy* 3.

Craft, Stephanie, Seth Ashley, and Adam Maksl, A. (2017). "News Media Literacy and Conspiracy Theory Endorsement." *Communication and the Public* 2, no. 4: 388–401.

Craft, Stephanie, Seth Ashley, and Adam Maksl. (2016). "Elements of News Literacy: A Focus Group Study of How Teenagers Define News and Why They Consume It." *Electronic News* 10, no. 3: 143–160.

Crawford, Kate, Kate Miltner, and Mary L. Gray. (2014). "Critiquing Big Data: Politics, Ethics, Epistemology." *International Journal of Communication* 8: 1663–1672.

Curry, Alexander L., and Natalie Jomini Stroud. (2019). "The Effects of Journalistic Transparency on Credibility Assessments and Engagement Intentions." *Journalism.* Online first, https://doi.org/10.1177/1464884919850387.

Curtin, Patricia A., and Scott R. Maier. (2001). "Numbers in the Newsroom: A Qualitative Examination of a Quantitative Challenge." *Journalism & Mass Communication Quarterly* 78, no. 4: 720–738.

Cusatis, Christine, and Renee Martin-Kratzer. (2010). "Assessing the State of Math Education in ACEJMC-Accredited and Non-Accredited Undergraduate Journalism Programs." *Journalism & Mass Communication Educator* 64, no. 4: 355–377.

Dabbish, Laura, Colleen Stuart, Jason Tsay, and Jim Herbsleb. (2012). "Social Coding in GitHub: Transparency and Collaboration in an Open Software Repository." *CSCW '12: Proceedings of the ACM 2012 Conference on Computer Supported Cooperative Work* (February): 1277–1286.

Dailey, Larry, Lori Demo, and Mary Spillman. (2005). "The Convergence Continuum: A Model for Studying Collaboration Between Media Newsrooms." *Atlantic Journal of Communication* 13, no. 3: 150–168.

Davis, Peter, and Philippa Howden-Chapman. (1996). "Translating Research Findings into Health Policy." *Social Science & Medicine* 43, no. 5: 865–872.

de Burgh, Hugo. (2003). "Skills Are Not Enough: The Case for Journalism as an Academic Discipline." *Journalism* 4, no. 1: 95–112.

Deeming, Christopher. (2013). "Addressing the Social Determinants of Subjective Wellbeing: The Latest Challenge for Social Policy." *Journal of Social Policy* 42, no. 3: 541–565.

Dennis, Everette E., and Ellen Ann Wartella. (1996). *American Communication Research: The Remembered History* (New York: Routledge).

Deuze, Mark. (2008). "Understanding Journalism as Newswork: How It Changes, and How It Remains the Same." *Westminster Papers in Communication & Culture* 5, no. 2: 4–23.

Dienlin, Tobias, et al. (2020). "An Agenda for Open Communication." *Journal of Communication,* Preprint, 1–26, https://doi.org/10.1093/job/jqz052.

D'Ignazio, Catherine, and Rahul Bhargava. (2016). "DataBasic: Design Principles, Tools and Activities for Data Literacy Learners." *The Journal of Community Infomatics* 12, no. 3: n.p.

Dobkin, Bethami A. (1992). *Tales of Terror: Television News and the Construction of the Terrorist Threat* (New York: Praeger).

Doctor, Ken. "Newsonomics: The Newspaper Industry is Thirsty for Liquidity as it Tries to Merge its Way out of Trouble." *Nieman Journalism Lab,* April 18, 2019, https://www.niemanlab.org/2019/04/newsonomics-the-newspaper-industry-is-thirsty-for-liquidity-as-it-tries-to-merge-its-way-out-of-trouble/.

Donalson, J. (2017). "Impossible Trident," The Illusions Index, July 2017, https://www.illusionsindex.org/i/impossible-trident.

Dourish, Paul, and Edgar Gómez Cruz. (2018). "Datafication and Data Fiction: Narrating Data and Narrating with Data." *Big Data & Society* 5, no. 2: 1–10.

Dunwoody, Sharon, and Robert J. Griffin. (2013). "Statistical Reasoning in Journalism Education." *Science Communication* 35, no. 4: 528–538.

Durkin, Jessica, and Tom Glaisyer. (2010). "An Information Community Case Study: Scranton." New America Foundation, May 2010, https://ecfsapi.fcc.gov/file/7020450503.pdf.

Edelman. (2019). "Trust Barometer." Retrieved from https://www.edelman.com/trust-barometer.

Edgerly, Stephanie. (2015). "Red Media, Blue Media, and Purple Media: News Repertoires in the Colorful Media Landscape." *Journal of Broadcasting & Electronic Media* 59, no. 1: 1–21.

Edgerly, Stephanie. (2018). "A New Generation of Satire Consumers? A Socialization Approach to Youth Exposure to News Satire" in *Political Humor in a Changing Media Landscape: A New Generation of Research,* eds. Jodi C. Baumgartner and Amy B. Becker (New York: Lexington Books), 253–272.

Edgerly, Stephanie, Esther Thorson, and Weiyue Cynthia Chen. (2017). "News Use Repertoires and News Attitudes During the 2016 Presidential Election." (Conference paper, The Future of Journalism, Cardiff, UK, September 14–15, 2017).

Edgerly, Stephanie, Kjerstin Thorson, Esther Thorson, Emily K. Vraga, and Leticia Bode. (2018). "Do Parents Still Model News Consumption? Socializing News Use Among Adolescents in a Multi-Device World." *New Media & Society* 20, no. 4: 1263–1281.

Edgerly, Stephanie, Emily K. Vraga, Leticia Bode, Kjerstin Thorson, and Esther Thorson. (2018). "New Media, New Relationship to Participation? A Closer Look at Youth News Repertories and Political Participation." *Journalism & Mass Communication Quarterly* 95, no. 1: 192–212.

Ess, Charles. (2014). *Digital Media Ethics,* 2nd ed. (Cambridge, UK: Polity).

Ettema, James S. (2007). "Journalism as Reason-Giving: Deliberative Democracy, Institutional Accountability, and the News Media's Mission." *Political Communication* 24, no. 2: 143–160.

European Union. (2019). "Media Freedom and Investigative Journalism - Call for Proposals," The European Commission, 2019, https://ec.europa.eu/digital-single-market/en/news/media-freedom-and-investigative-journalism-call-proposals.

Evans, S.K. (2018). "Making sense of innovation: Process, product, and storytelling innovation in public service broadcasting organizations." *Journalism Studies* 19 no. 1: 4–24.

Fannin, Mike. (2018). "We Need Each Other. So Let's Keep the Conversation Going." *The Kansas City Star,* August 26, 2018, https://www.kansascity.com/news/local/article217302265.html.

Ferand, Tom. (2019). "Plain Dealer Lays off a Third of Unionized Newsroom Staff." *Plain Dealer,* April 1, 2019, https://www.cleveland.com/news/2019/04/plain-dealer-lays-off-a-third-of-unionized-newsroom-staff.html.

Ferrier, Michelle. (2014). "The Media Deserts Project: Monitoring Community News and Information Needs using Geographic Information System Technologies." Presented at the AEJMC Midwinter Conference, University of Oklahoma, February 28–March 1, 2014.

Fink, Katherine, and Michael Schudson. (2014). "The Rise of Contextual Journalism, 1950s–2000s." *Journalism* 15, no. 1: 3–20.

Franks, Suzanne. "Reporting Africa: Problems and Perspectives." (2005). *Westminster Papers in Communication and Culture* 2, no. 0: 129–135.

Franks, Suzanne. (2010). "The Neglect of Africa and the Power of Aid." *International Communication Gazette* 72, no. 1: 71–84.

Freedman, Des, and Daya Kishan Thussu, eds. (2012). *Media and Terrorism: Global Perspectives* (Los Angeles, CA: SAGE Publications).

Freelon, Deen. (2013). "ReCal OIR: Ordinal, Interval, and Ratio Intercoder Reliability as a Web Service." *International Journal of Internet Science* 8, no. 1: 10–16.

Freelon, D., Charlton D. McIlwain, and Meredith Clark. (2016). *"Beyond the Hashtags: #Ferguson, #Blacklivesmatter, and the Online Struggle for Offline Justice."* Center for Media & Social Impact, American University.

Friedland, Lewis, et al. (2012). "Review of the Literature Regarding Critical Information Needs of the American Public." Submitted to the Federal Communications Commission by the University of Southern California Annenberg School for Communication & Journalism in collaboration with the University of Wisconsin–Madison https://www.fcc.gov/news-events/blog/2012/07/25/review-literature-regarding-critical-information-needs-american-public.

Galant, Debbie. (2013). "Media Deserts with Michelle Ferrier, Elon University" https://www.elon.edu/u/news/2013/04/15/michelle-ferrier-presents-media-deserts-hyperlocal-online-news-research/.

Gans, Herbert J. (2004). *Deciding What's News: A Study of CBS Evening News, NBC Nightly News, Newsweek, and Time* (Chicago: Northwestern University Press).

Garfield, Joan. (2002). "The Challenge of Developing Statistical Reasoning." *Journal of Statistics Education* 10, no. 3: 1–12.

George, Cherian, Yuan Zeng, and Suruchi Mazumdar. (2019). "Navigating Conflicts of Interest: Ethical Policies of 12 Exemplary Asian Media Organisations." *Journalism* : 1464884919832188.

Gesualdo, Nicole, Matthew S. Weber, and Itzhak Yanovitzky. (2020). "Journalists as Knowledge Brokers." *Journalism Studies* 21, no. 1: 127–143.

Gieryn, Thomas F. (2006). "City as Truth-Spot: Laboratories and Field-Sites in Urban Studies." Social Studies of Science 36, no. 1: 5–38.

Gillmor, Dan. (2009). "Toward a (New) Media Literacy in a Media Saturated World" in *Journalism and Citizenship: New Agendas in Communication*, ed. Zizi Papacharissi (New York: Routledge), 1–12.

Glickhouse, Rachel. (2019). "Here's what ProPublica learned about managing a collaboration across hundreds of news organizations." Nieman Lab, https://www.niemanlab.org/2019/12/heres-what-propublica-learned-about-managing-a-collaboration-across-hundreds-of-news-organizations/.

Gordon, Rich, and Zachary Johnson. (2011). "Linking Audiences to News: A Network Analysis of Chicago News Websites." The Chicago Community Trust. http://journalismaccelerator.com/resources/linking-audiences-to-news-a-network-analysis-of-chicago-websites/.

Gortmaker, Steven L., Boyd A. Swinburn, David Levy, Rob Carter, Patricia L. Mabry, Diane T. Finegood, Terry Huang, Tim Marsh, and Marjory L. Moodie. (2011). "Changing the Future of Obesity: Science, Policy, and Action." *The Lancet* 378, no. 9793: 838–847.

Graves, Lucas. (2016). *Deciding What's True: The Rise of Political Fact-Checking in American Journalism* (New York: Columbia University Press).

Graves, Lucas, and Magda Konieczna. (2016). "Qualitative Political Communication| Sharing the News: Journalistic Collaboration as Field Repair." *International Journal of Communication* 9 (June 2015), https://ijoc.org/index.php/ijoc/article/view/3381.

Gray, Jonathan, Carolin Gerlitz, and Liliana Bounegru. (2018). "Data Infrastructure Literacy." *Big Data & Society* 5, no. 2: 1–13.

Grieco, Elizabeth. (2018). "Newsroom Employment Dropped Nearly a Quarter in Less Than 10 Years, with Greatest Decline at Newspapers." Pew Research Center, July 30,

2018, https://www.pewresearch.org/fact-tank/2018/07/30/newsroom-employment-dropped-nearly-a-quarter-in-less-than-10-years-with-greatest-decline-at-newspapers/.

Grieco, Elizabeth. (2020). "U.S. Newspapers Have Shed Half of their Newsroom Employees since 2008." Pew Research Center, April 20, 2020, https://www.pewresearch.org/fact-tank/2020/04/20/u-s-newsroom-employment-has-dropped-by-a-quarter-since-2008/.

Griffin, Robert J., and Sharon Dunwoody. (2016). "Chair Support, Faculty Entrepreneurship, and the Teaching of Statistical Reasoning to Journalism Undergraduates in the United States." *Journalism* 17, no. 1: 97–118.

Griffiths, Gareth. (2006). "The Myth of Authenticity" in *The Post-Colonial Studies Reader*, eds. Bill Ashcroft, Gareth Griffiths, and Helen Tiffin, 2nd ed. (London, New York: Routledge), 165–168.

Grinberg, Nir, Kenneth Joseph, Lisa Friedland, Briony Swire-Thompson, and David Lazer. (2019). "Fake News on Twitter During the 2016 US Presidential Election." *Science* 363, no. 6425: 374–378.

Gross, Liza. (2019). "Collaboratives: You Have to Want to Be There." Knight Foundation, https://knightfoundation.org/articles/collaboratives-you-have-to-want-to-be-there/

Grzeszyk, Tabea. (2019). "Diversity Matters! How Cross-Border Journalism Calls Out Media Bias." *Journal of Applied Journalism & Media Studies* 8, no. 2: 169–189.

Haas, Tanni. (2007). *The Pursuit of Public Journalism* (New York: Routledge, 2007).

Hamilton, James. (2004). *All the News that's Fit to Sell: How the Market Transforms Information into News*. (Princeton: Princeton University Press, 2004).

Hanitzsch, Thomas. (2007). "Deconstructing Journalism Culture: Toward a Universal Theory." *Communication Theory* 17, no. 4: 367–385.

Hare, Kristen. (2016). "How ICIJ Got Hundreds of Journalists to Collaborate on the Panama Papers," *Poynter*, http://www.poynter.org/2016/how-icij-got-hundreds-of-journalists-to-collaborate-on-the-panama-papers/405041/.

Harlow, Summer, and Thomas J. Johnson. (2011). "Overthrowing the Protest Paradigm? How the New York Times, Global Voices and Twitter Covered the Egyptian Revolution." *International Journal of Communication* 5: 1–18.

Harlow, Summer., Ramón Salaverría, Danielle K. Kilgo, and Victor García-Perdomo. (2011). "Protest Paradigm in Multimedia: Social Media Sharing of Coverage About the Crime of Ayotzinapa, Mexico." *Journal of Communication* 67, no. 3: 328–349.

Hart, Corinne B. (2011). "The 'Elephant in the Room': Using Emotion Management to Uncover Hidden Discourses in Interprofessional Collaboration and Teamwork." *Journal of Interprofessional Care* 25, no. 5: 373–774.

Hartford Gunn Institute. (1995). "Educational Telecommunications: An Electronic Land Grant for the 21st Century." *Current*, October 22, 1995, https://current.org/1995/10/educational-telecommunications-an-electronic-land-grant-for-the-21st-century/.

Hasebrink, Uwe, and Hanna Domeyer. (2012). "Media Repertoires as Patterns of Behavior and as Meaningful Practices: A Multimethod Approach to Media Use in Converging Media Environments." *Journal of Audience & Receptions Studies* 9, no. 2: 757–779.

Hatch, Richard A. (1967). *Some Founding Papers of the University of Illinois* (Urbana: University of Illinois Press).

Heinrich, Alfred. (2011). *Network Journalism: Journalistic Practice in Interactive Spheres* (New York: Routledge).

Heravi, Bahareh. (2019). "3WS of Data Journalism Education: What, where and who?" *Journalism Practice* 13, no. 3: 349–366.

Hermida, Alfred. (2012). "Tweets and Truth: Journalism as a Discipline of Collaborative Verification." *Journalism Practice* 6, no. 5–6: 659–668.

Hesse-Biber, Sharlene Nagy. (2013). *Feminist Research Practice: A Primer.* 2nd ed. (Thousand Oaks: SAGE Publications).

Hewett, Jonathan. (2015). "Learning to Teach Data Journalism: Innovation, Influence and Constraints." *Journalism* 17, no. 1: 119–137.

Hindman, Matthew. (2018). *The Internet Trap: How the Digital Economy Builds Monopolies and Undermines Democracy* (Princeton: Princeton University Press).

Hobbs, Renee. (2011). "The State of Media Literacy: A Response to Potter." *Journal of Broadcasting & Electronic Media* 55, no. 3: 419–430.

Howison, James, Andrea Wiggins, and Kevin Crowston. (2011). "Validity Issues in the Use of Social Network Analysis with Digital Trace Data." *Journal of the Association for Information Systems* 12, no. 12: 767–797.

Hutchins, Corey. (2014). "FCC Revamps Controversial Study of TV Newsrooms." *Columbia Journalism Review*, February 14, 2014, https://archives.cjr.org/united_states_project/fcc_revamps_controversial_study_of_tv_ne wsrooms.php.

Institute of Communications Research. (1948). Brochure, p. 3, https://www.slideshare.net/NikkiUsher1/icr-original-brochure-1948.

Iyengar, Shanto. (1994). *Is Anyone Responsible?: How Television Frames Political Issues* (Chicago: University of Chicago Press).

Jenkins, Joy, and Lucas Graves. (2019). "Digital News Report: Case Studies in Collaborative Local Journalism." The Reuters Institute for the Study of Journalism, http://www.digitalnewsreport.org/publications/2019/case-studies-collaborative-local-journalism/.

Jeon, Doh-Shin, and Nikrooz Nasr. (2016). "News Aggregators and Competition among Newspapers on the Internet." *American Economic Journal: Microeconomics* 8, no. 4: 91–114.

Jewell, Christopher J., and Lisa A. Bero. (2008). "Developing Good Taste in Evidence: Facilitators of and Hindrances to Evidence-Informed Health Policymaking in State Government." *The Milbank Quarterly* 86, no. 2: 177–208.

Johansson-Sköldberg, Ulla, Jill Woodilla, and Mehves Çetinkaya. (2013). "Design Thinking: Past, Present and Possible Futures." *Creativity and Innovation Management* 22, no. 2: 121–146.

John S. and James L. "Informing Communities: Sustaining Democracy in the Digital Age," 2009. https://www.aspeninstitute.org/publications/informing-communities-sustaining-democracy-digital-age/

Journalism Grants. (2020). "What Are the Application Criteria?" Journalism Grants, The Innovation in Development Reporting Grant Programme, https://innovation.journalismgrants.org/eligibility.

Juergensmeyer, Mark, ed. (2014). *Thinking Globally: A Global Studies Reader* (Berkeley: University of California Press).

Kahne, Joseph, and Benjamin Bowyer. (2017). "Educating for Democracy in a Partisan Age: Confronting the Challenges of Motivated Reasoning and Misinformation." *American Educational Research Journal* 54 (1): 3–34.

Kahne, Joseph, Nam-Jin Lee, and Jessica Timpany Feezell. (2012). "Digital Media Literacy Education and Online Civic and Political Participation." *International Journal of Communication* 6: 1–24.

Kayser-Bril, Nicolas. (2017). "Collaboration–One Tool among Many," in *Global Teamwork: The Rise of Collaboration in Investigative Journalism*, ed. R. Sambrook (Oxford: Reuters Institute for the Study of Journalism), 59–63.

Kiesow, Damon. (2018). "Newspapers Are Failing the Product Solution Stack Test." *Medium*, March 11, 2018, https://medium.com/media-stack/newspapers-are-failing-the-product-solution-stack-test-e8362a0482ca.

Kiesow, Damon. (2018). "What It Takes to Shift a News Organization to Reader Revenue." *American Press Institute*, October 2, 2018, https://www.americanpressinstitute.org/reader-revenue/what-it-takes-to-shift-a-news-organization-to-reader-revenue/.

Kilgo, Danielle K., Summer Harlow, Victor García-Perdomo, and Ramón Salaverría. (2018). "From #Ferguson to #Ayotzinapa: Analyzing Differences in Domestic and Foreign Protest News Shared on Social Media." *Mass Communication and Society* 21, no. 5: 606–630.

Kilgo, Danielle K., Rachel R. Mourão, and George Sylvie. (2019). "Martin to Brown: How Time and Platform Impact Coverage of the Black Lives Matter Movement." *Journalism Practice* 13, no. 4: 413–430.

Kilgo, Danielle K., and Summer Harlow. (2019). "Protests, Media Coverage, and a Hierarchy of Social Struggle." *The International Journal of Press/Politics* 24, no. 3: 508–530.

Kittur, Aniket, Bongwon Suh, Bryan A. Pendleton, and Ed H. Chi. (2007). "He Says, She Says: Conflict and Coordination in Wikipedia." *CHI '07: Proceedings of the SIGCHI Conference on Human Factors in Computing Systems* (April 2007): 453–462.

Knight Foundation, John S. and James L. (2009). "Informing Communities: Sustaining Democracy in the Digital Age." https://www.aspeninstitute.org/publications/informing-communities-sustaining-democracy-digital-age/

Knight, Kevin. (2017). "Question 52. The Angels in Relation to Place." New Advent, http://www.newadvent.org/summa/1052.htm#article3. [Original Source: *The Summa Theologiæ of St. Thomas Aquinas* (Second and Revised Edition, 1920)].

Koltay, Tibor. (2011). "The Media and the Literacies: Media Literacy, Information Literacy, Digital Literacy." *Media, Culture & Society* 33, no. 2 (2011): 211–221.

Koltay, Tibor. (2016). "Data Governance, Data Literacy and the Management of Data Quality." *International Federation of Library Associations Journal* 42, no. 4: 303–312.

Koltay, Tibor. (2017). "Data Literacy for Researchers and Data Librarians." *Journal of Librarianship and Information Science* 49, no. 1: 3–14.

Kreiss, Daniel. (2016). "Beyond Administrative Journalism: Civic Skepticism and the Crisis in Journalism" in *The Crisis of Journalism Reconsidered: Democratic Culture, Professional Codes, Digital Future*, eds. Jeffrey C. Alexander, Elizabeth Butler Breese, and María Luengo (Cambridge, UK: Cambridge University Press), 59.

Kreiss, Daniel, and J. Scott Brennen. (2016). "Normative Theories of Digital Journalism," in the *Sage Handbook of Digital Journalism Studies*, eds. Alfred Hermida, C.W. Anderson, David Domingo, Tamara Witschge (New York: Sage), chapter 20, 299–314.

Ksiazek, Thomas B., Edward C. Malthouse, and James G. Webster. (2010). "News-Seekers and Avoiders: Exploring Patterns of Total News Consumption Across Media and the Relationship to Civic Participation." *Journal of Broadcasting & Electronic Media* 54, no. 4: 551–568.

Kumar, Deepa. (2012). *Islamophobia and the Politics of Empire* (Chicago: Haymarket Books).

Lacy, Stephen. (1992). The financial commitment approach to news media competition, Journal of Media Economics 5, no. 2: 5–21.

Lanosga, Gerry, and Jason Martin. (2018). "Journalists, Sources, and Policy Outcomes: Insights from Three-Plus Decades of Investigative Reporting Contest Entries." *Journalism* 19, no. 12: 1676–1693.

Lavis, J., M. Wilson, K. Moat, A. Hammill, J. Boyko, J. Grimshaw, and S. Flottorp. (2015). "Developing and Refining the Methods for a 'One-Stop Shop' for Research Evidence About Health Systems." *Health Research Policy and Systems* 13:.

Lawrence, Regina G., Daniel Radcliffe, and Thomas R. Schmidt. (2018). "Practicing Engagement: Participatory Journalism in the Web 2.0 Era," *Journalism Practice* 12, no. 10: 1220–1240.

Lee, Nam-Jin, Dhavan V. Shah, and Jack M. McLeod. (2013). "Processes of Political Socialization: A Communication Mediation Approach to Youth Civic Engagement." *Communication Research* 40, no. 5: 669–697.

Levendusky, Matthew. (2013). *How Partisan Media Polarize America* (Chicago: University of Chicago Press).

Lewandowsky, Stephan, Ullrich K.H. Ecker, and John Cook. (2017). "Beyond Misinformation: Understanding and Coping with the "Post-Truth" Era." *Journal of Applied Research in Memory and Cognition* 6, no. 4: 353–369.

Lewis, Seth C. (2018). "The Gap Between Journalism and Research is Too Wide." *Nieman Journalism Lab,* December 2018, https://www.niemanlab.org/2018/12/the-gap-between-journalism-and-research-is-too-wide/.

Lewis, Seth C. (2012). "From Journalism to Information: The Transformation of the Knight Foundation and News Innovation," *Mass Communication and Society* 15, no. 3: 309–334.

Lewis, Seth C., and Nikki Usher. (2014). "Code, Collaboration, and the Future of Journalism." *Digital Journalism* 2, no. 3: 383–393.

Lewis, Seth C., and Nikki Usher. (2016). "Trading Zones, Boundary Objects, and the Pursuit of News Innovation: A Case Study of Journalists and Programmers." *Convergence: The International Journal of Research into New Media Technologies* 22, no. 5: 543–560.

Lichterman, Joseph. (2017). "Howard University Decides it Won't Sell WHUT in Spectrum Auction" *Current,* February 17, 2017, https://current.org/2017/02/howard-university-decides-it-wont-sell-whut-in-spectrum-auction/.

Lichterman, Joseph. (2019). "These Chicago News Orgs Worked Together to Create a Collaborative Voting Guide." The Lenfest Institute for Journalism, https://www.lenfestinstitute.org/solution-set/these-chicago-news-orgs-worked-together-to-create-a-collaborative-voting-guide/.

Lima, Antonio, Luca Rossi, and Mirco Musolesi. (2014). "Coding Together at Scale: GitHub as a Collaborative Social Network." *8th International AAAI International Conference on Weblogs and Social Media, ICWSM 2014.*

Lombard, Matthew, Jennifer Synder-Duch, and Cheryl Campanella Bracken. (2002). "Content Analysis in Mass Communication: Assessment and Reporting of Intercoder Reliability." *Human Communication Research* 28, no. 4: 587–604.

Lotz, Amanda. (2014). *The Television Will Be Revolutionized* (New York: NYU Press).

Lowrey, Wilson. (2012). "Journalism Innovation and the Ecology of News Production: Institutional Tendencies." *Journalism & Communication Monographs* 14: 214–287.

Lugo-Ocando, Jairo, and An Nguyen. (2017). *Developing News: Global Journalism and the Coverage of "Third World" Development* (London, New York: Routledge).

Lunn, Pete, and Frances Ruane. (2013). *Using Evidence to Inform Policy* (Dublin: Gill & Macmillan).

Madden, Mary, Amanda Lenhart, and Claire Fontaine. (2017). "How Youth Navigate the News Landscape." *Data & Society*, https://datasociety.net/output/how-youth-navigate-the-news-landscape/.

Maier, Scott R. (2003). "Numeracy in the Newsroom: A Case Study of Mathematical Competence and Confidence." *Journalism & Mass Communication Quarterly* 80, no. 4: 921–936.

Maksl, Adam, Stephanie Craft, Seth Ashley, and Dean Miller. (2017). "The Usefulness of a News Media Literacy Measure in Evaluating a News Literacy Curriculum." *Journalism and Mass Communication Educator* 72, no. 2: 228–214.

Malik, Momin M., Sandra Cortesi, and Urs Gasser. (2013). *The Challenges of Defining 'News Literacy.'* (Cambridge: Berkman Center Research).

Mandinach, Ellen B., and Edith S. Gummer. (2013). "A Systemic View of Implementing Data Literacy in Educator Preparation." *Educational Researcher* 42, no. 1: 30–37.

Mare, Admire, ed. (2018). "Conflict Sensitive Journalism: A Practical Handbook for Journalists in Southern Africa," https://www.nust.na/sites/default/files/documents/Final%20Handbook%2015%20Oct%202019%20.pdf.

Martin, Justin D. (2017). "A Census of Statistics Requirements at U.S. Journalism Programs and a Model for a 'Statistics for Journalism' Course." *Journalism & Mass Communication Educator* 72, no. 4: 461–479.

Martínez de la Serna, Carlos. (2018). "Collaboration and the Creation of a New Journalism Commons," *Columbia Journalism Review*, March 30, 2018, https://www.cjr.org/tow_center_reports/collaboration-and-the-journalism-commons.php/.

Marwick, Alice E. (2018). "Why Do People Share Fake News? A Sociotechnical Model of Media Effects." *Georgetown Law Technology Review* 474, no. 2: 474–512.

Marwick, Alice E., and Rebecca Lewis. (2017). "Media Manipulation and Disinformation Online." Data & Society Research Institute, https://datasociety.net/library/media-manipulation-and-disinfo-online/.

Masullo, Gina M., Alex Curry, and Kelsey Whipple. (2020). "Building Trust: What Works for News Organizations," https://mediaengagement.org/research/building-trust.

Mayer, Joy. (2019). "Knight Commission Report Calls for 'Radical Transparency' in Journalism. Trusting News Can Help." Last modified February 5, 2019, https://medium.com/trusting-news/knight-commission-report-calls-for-radical-transparency-in-journalism-trusting-news-can-help-95e3a7bd044f.

McCall, Vivian. (2019). "News Outlets Call University Of Illinois Policy A Reporter Gag Order." will.radio.tv.online, November 14, 2019, https://will.illinois.edu/news/story/news-outlets-call-university-of-illinois-policy-a-reporter-gag-order.

McDonald, Nora, and Sean Goggins. (2013). "Performance and Participation in Open Source Software on GitHub," *CHI EA '13: CHI '13 Extended Abstracts on Human Factors in Computing Systems* (April 2013): 139–144.

McLeod, Douglas M., and James K. Hertog. (1999). "Social Control, Social Change and the Mass Media's Role in the Regulation of Protest Groups" in *Mass Media, Social Control and Social Change: A Macrosocial Perspective*, eds. David Demers and Kasisomayajula Viswanath (Ames: Iowa State University Press), 305–330.

Mickelson, Roslyn Arlin, Martha Cecilia Bottia, and Richard Lambert. (2013). "Effects of School Racial Composition on K–12 mathematics outcomes: A Metaregression Analysis." *Review of Educational Research* 83, no. 1: 121–158.

Mihailidis, Paul, and Samantha Viotty. (2017). "Spreadable Spectacle in Digital Culture: Civic Expression, Fake News, and the Role of Media Literacies in 'Post-Fact' Society." *American Behavioral Scientist* 61, no. 4: 441–454.

Mindich, David T.Z. (2005). *Tuned Out: Why Americans Under 40 Don't Follow the News* (Oxford, UK: Oxford University Press).

Mitchell, Amy, and Rick Edmonds. (2014). "News Organization Partnerships and Collaborations." Pew Research Center, December 4, 2014, https://www.journalism. org/2014/12/04/journalism-partnerships/.

Morel, Richard Paquin, and Cynthia Coburn. (2019). "Access, Activation, and Influence: How Brokers Mediate Social Capital among Professional Development Providers." *American Educational Research Journal* 56, no. 2: 247–288.

Mourão, Rachel R., Danielle K. Kilgo, and George Sylvie. "Framing Ferguson: The Interplay of Advocacy and Journalistic Frames in Local and National Newspaper Coverage of Michael Brown." *Journalism*, 22, no. 2 (2018). doi: 10.1177/1464884918778722.

Moseley, Charles, Harold Kleinert, Kathleen Sheppard-Jones, and Stephen Hall. (2013). "Using Research Evidence to Inform Public Policy Decisions." *Intellectual and Developmental Disabilities* 51, no. 5: 412–422.

Mourão, Rachel R., Danielle K. Kilgo, and George Sylvie. (2018). "Framing Ferguson: The Interplay of Advocacy and Journalistic Frames in Local and National Newspaper Coverage of Michael Brown." *Journalism*, doi: 10.1177/1464884918778722.

Murrell, Colleen. (2015). *Foreign Correspondents and International Newsgathering: The Role of Fixers* (New York; London: Routledge).

Musgrave, Shawn, and Matthew Nussbaum. (2018). "Trump Thrives in Areas that Lack Traditional News Outlets," *Politico*, https://www.politico.com/story/2018/04/08/ news-subscriptions-decline-donald-trump-voters-505605.

Nadler, Anthony. (2018). "Nature's Economy and News Ecology." *Journalism Studies* 20, no. 3: 1–17.

National Research Council. (2012). "Using Science as Evidence in Public Policy." eds. Kenneth Prewitt, Thomas A. Schwandt, and Miron L. Straf, 122. (Washington, DC: The National Academies Press, 122.

Napoli, Philip M. (2015). "Social Media and the Public Interest: Governance of News Platforms in the Realm of Individual and Algorithmic Gatekeepers." *Telecommunications Policy* 39, no. 9: 751–760.

Napoli, Philip, Sarah Stonbely, Kathleen McCollough, and Bryce Renninger. (2015). "Assessing the Health of Local Journalism Ecosystems," prepared for the Democracy Fund, the Geraldine R. Dodge Foundation, and the John S. and James L. Knight Foundation, June, 2015, http://mpii.rutgers.edu/wp-content/uploads/sites/129/2015/ 06/Assessing-Local-Journalism_Final-Draft-6.23.15.pdf.

Napoli, Philip M., et al. (2017). "Local Journalism and the Information Needs of Local Communities." *Journalism Practice* 11, no. 4: 373–395.

Napoli, Philip, Ian Dunham, and Jessica Mahone. (2020). "Assessing News Media Infrastructure: A State-Level Analysis." News Measures Research Project. https:// futureoflocalnews.org/portfolio-item/assessing-news-media-infrastructure-a- state-level-analysis/.

National Research Council. (2012). "Using Science as Evidence in Public Policy." eds. Kenneth Prewitt, Thomas A. Schwandt and Miron L. Straf (Washington, DC: The National Academies Press), 122.

Newman, Nic, et al. (2020). "Digital news report," Reuters Institute, http://www. digitalnewsreport.org/.

Nguyen, An, and Jairo Lugo-Ocando. (2015). "The State of Statistics in Journalism and Journalism Education–Issues and Debates." *Journalism* 17, no. 1: 3–17.

Nielsen, Rasmus Kleis. (2018). "No One Cares What We Know: Three Responses to the Irrelevance of Political Communication Research." *Political Communication* 35, no. 1: 145–149.

Nielsen, Rasmus Kleis, Frank Esser, and David Levy. (2013). "Comparative Perspectives on the Changing Business of Journalism and Its Implications for Democracy." *The International Journal of Press/Politics* 18, no. 4: 383–391.

Nieman Journalism Lab. "About Nieman Lab," https://www.niemanlab.org/about/.

Nisbet, Matthew C., and Declan Fahy. (2015). "The Need for Knowledge-Based Journalism in Politicized Science Debates." *The ANNALS of the American Academy of Political and Social Science* 658, no. 1: 223–234.

Nordenstreng, Kaarle, and Daya Kishan Thussu, eds. *Mapping BRICS Media* (London, New York: Routledge).

Northwestern University Local News Initiative (n.d.), https://localnewsinitiative.northwestern.edu/.

Nutley, Sandra M., Isabel Walter, and Huw T.O. Davies. (2007). *Using Evidence: How Research Can Inform Public Services* (Chicago, IL: Policy Press).

O'Brien, Daniel, Christian-Mathias Wellbrock, and Nicola Kleer. (2020). "Content for Free? Drivers of Past Payment, Paying Intent and Willingness to Pay for Digital Journalism–A Systematic Literature Review." *Digital Journalism*, Online First, 1–30. 0.1080/21670811.2020.1770112.

Oliver, Kathryn, Simon Innvær, Theo Lorenc, J. Woodman, and J. Thomas. (2014). "A Systematic Review of Barriers to and Facilitators of the Use of Evidence by Policymakers." (2014). *BMC Health Services Research* 14.

OpenNews. (2020). Community Partners Inc., https://communitypartners.org/project/opennews.

Ordway, Denise-Marie. (2018). "Polarizing the Network: The Most Interesting New Digital and Social Media Research." *Nieman Journalism Lab*, November 20, 2018, https://www.niemanlab.org/2018/11/polarizing-the-network-the-most-interesting-new-digital-and-social-media-research.

Örnebring, Henrik. (2019). "Journalism Cannot Solve Journalism's Problems," *Journalism* 20, no. 1: 226–228.

Orton, L., F. Lloyd-Williams, D. Taylor-Robinson, M. O'Flaherty, and S. Capewell. (2011). "The Use of Research Evidence in Public Health Decision Making Processes: Systematic Review." *PLoS ONE* 6(7)

Palinkas, L.A., A.R. Garcia, G.A. Aarons, M. Finno-Velasquez, I.W. Holloway, T.I. Mackie, L.K. Leslie, and P. Chamberlain. (2016). "Measuring Use of Research Evidence: The Structured Interview for Evidence Use." *Research on Social Work Practice* 26(5), 550–564.

Palmer, Jerry, and Victoria Fontan. (2007). "'Our Ears and Our Eyes': Journalists and Fixers in Iraq." *Journalism: Theory, Practice & Criticism* 8, no. 1: 5–24.

Palmer, Lindsay. (2016). "'Being the Bridge': News Fixers' Perspectives on Cultural Difference in Reporting the 'War on Terror.'" *Journalism* 19, no. 3: 314–332.

Palmer, Lindsay. (2018). *Becoming the Story: War Correspondents since 9/11* (Urbana: University of Illinois).

Palmer, Lindsay. (2019). *The Fixers: Local News Workers and the Underground Labor of International Reporting* (New York: Oxford University Press).

Pangrazio, Luci, and Neil Selwyn. (2019). "'Personal Data Literacies': A Critical Literacy Approach to Enhancing Understandings of Personal Digital Data." *New Media & Society* 21, no. 2: 419–437.

Papacharissi, Zizi. (2015). "The Unbearable Lightness of Information and the Impossible Gravitas of Knowledge: Big Data and the Makings of a Digital Orality." *Media, Culture & Society* 37, no. 7: 1095–1100.

Paterson, Chris. (2011). *The International Television News Agencies: The World from London* (New York: Peter Lang).

Pedelty, Mark. (1995). *War Stories: The Culture of Foreign Correspondents* (New York: Routledge).

Perrin, Andrew, and Monica Anderson. (2019). "Share of U.S. Adults Using Social Media, Including Facebook, Is Mostly Unchanged Since 2018." *Pew Research Center*, April 10, 2019, https://www.pewresearch.org/fact-tank/2019/04/10/share-of-u-s-adults-using-social-media-including-facebook-is-mostly-unchanged-since-2018/.

Pettit, Becky. (2012). *Invisible Men: Mass Incarceration and the Myth of Black Progress* (New York: Russell Sage Foundation). (2019).

Pew Research Center———. (2010). "How News Happens,." https://www.journalism.org/2010/01/11/how-news-happens/.

Pew Research Center———. (2015). "Local News in a Digital Age," https://www.journalism.org/2015/03/05/local-news-in-a-digital-age/.

Pew Research Center———. (2018). "Newspapers Fact Sheet," https://www.journalism.org/fact-sheet/newspapers/.

Pew Research Center———. (2018). "News Use Across Social Media Platforms 2018," https://www.journalism.org/2018/09/10/news-use-across-social-media-platforms-2018/.

Pew Research Center. (2019). "Share of U.S. Adults Using Social Media, Including Facebook, is Mostly Unchanged Since 2018." April 10, 2019, https://www.pewresearch.org/fact-tank/2019/04/10/share-of-u-s-adults-using-social-media-including-facebook-is-mostly-unchanged-since-2018/.

Picard, Robert. (2011). *The Economics and Financing of Media Companies* (New York: Fordham University Press).

Picard, Robert, Valérie Bélair-Gagnon, and Sofia Ranchordás. (2017). "The Impact of Charity and Tax Law/Regulation on Not-for-Profit News Organizations." Reuters Institute for the Study of Journalism and University of Oxford Information Society Project, Yale Law School, https://reutersinstitute.politics.ox.ac.uk/sites/default/files/2017-11/The%20impact%20of%20charity%20and%20tax%20law%20regulation%20on%20not%20for%20profit%20news%20organisations.pdf.

Pickard, Victor. (2019). "The Violence of the Market." *20th Anniversary Special Issue: The Challenges Facing Journalism Today* 20, no. 1: 155,. https://doi.org/10.1177/1464884918808955.

Pingree, Raymond J., et al. (2018). "Checking Facts and Fighting Back: Why Journalists Should Defend their Profession," *PloS one* 13, no. 12: e0208600, https://journals.plos.org/plosone/article?id=10.1371/journal.pone.0208600.

Poole, Robert. (2018). "If You Can Afford a Plane Ticket, Thank Deregulation." *Reason*, June 2018, https://reason.com/2018/05/26/if-you-can-afford-a-plane-tick/.

Popper, Nathaniel. (2009). "Good Morning, Postville! An Unlikely Thorn in Agriprocessors' Side," *Columbia Journalism Review*, March/April, https://archives.cjr.org/feature/good_morning_postville_1.php.

Potter, W. James. (2019). *Media Literacy* (9th ed.) (Thousand Oaks: Sage).

Poynter. (n.d.). "Mission & Vision," https://www.poynter.org/mission-vision/.

Poynter. (n.d.). "Poynter is a Thought Leader," https://www.poynter.org/poynter-thought-leader/.

Pressman, Matthew. (2018). *On Press: The Liberal Values That Shaped the News* (Cambridge: Harvard University Press).

Prior, Markus. (2007). *Post-Broadcast Democracy: How Media Choice Increases Inequality in Political Involvement and Polarizes Elections* (New York: Cambridge University Press).

Pybus, Jennifer, Mark Coté, and Tobias Blanke. (2015). "Hacking the Social Life of Big Data." *Big Data & Society* 2, no. 2: 1–10.

Rao, Shakuntala. (2011). "The 'Local' in Global Media Ethics." *Journalism Studies* 12, no. 6: 780–790.

Rao, Shakuntala, and Seow Ting Lee. (2005). "Globalizing Media Ethics? An Assessment of Universal Ethics Among International Political Journalists." *Journal of Mass Media Ethics* 20, no. 2–3: 99–120.

Rao, Shakuntala, and Herman Wasserman. (2015). *Media Ethics and Justice in the Age of Globalization* (London: Palgrave Macmillan).

Rave, Jodi. (2018). "American Indian Media Today." Democracy Fund, November 2018, https://www.democracyfund.org/publications/american-indian-media-today.

Reese, Stephen D. (2016). "The New Geography of Journalism Research: Levels and Spaces." *Digital Journalism* 4, no. 7: 816–826.

Richie, Beth. (2012). *Arrested Justice: Black Women, Violence, and America's Prison Nation* (New York: New York University Press).

Robinson, Sue. (n. d.). Community Outreach https://suerobinson.org/co/.

Robinson Sue. (2018). *Networked News, Racial Divides: How Power and Privilege Shape Public Discourse in Progressive Communities* (New York: Cambridge University Press).

Robinson, William I. (2005). "What is a Critical Globalization Studies? Intellectual Labor and Global Society" in *Critical Globalization Studies*, eds. Richard P. Appelbaum and William I. Robinson (New York: Routledge), 11–18.

Rogers, Everett M. (2001). "The Department of Communication at Michigan State University as a Seed Institution for Communication Study." *Communication Studies* 52, no. 3): 234–248.

Rogers, Everett M. (1994). *A History of Communication Study: A Biographical Approach* (New York, Toronto: The Free Press, Maxwell Macmillan Canada, Maxwell Macmillan International).

Rosenstiel, Tom. (2009). "Where the News Comes From—and Why it Matters." Pew Research Center, September 25, 2009, https://www.pewresearch.org/2009/09/25/where-the-news-comes-from-and-why-it-matters/.

Royal, Cindy, et al. (ForthcomingYear). "Product Management in Journalism and Academia." *Journalism and Mass Communication Quarterly* 97, no. 3: 597–616.

Royal, Cindy. (2019). "PhDigital Bootcamp: 2019 Evaluation Assessment." July 24, 2019, http://phdigitalbootcamp.com/report/PhDigital_evaluation_report_final2019.pdf.

Rubin, Alan M. (2009). "The Uses-and-Gratifications Perspective on Media Effects" in *Media effects: Advances in Theory and Research*, eds. Jennings Bryant and Mary Beth Oliver (New York: Routledge), 165–184.

Said, Edward W. (1978). *Orientalism* (New York: Pantheon Books).

Schaffer, Jan. (2010). "Exploring a Networked Journalism Collaborative in Philadelphia," J-Lab: The Institute for Interactive Journalism. http://www.j-lab.org/publications/exploring-a-networked-journalism-collaborative-in-philadelphia/.

Schmidt, Christine. (2018). "Ten Newsrooms, 4 Countries, Thousands of Kids: ProPublica Launches a Project to Find Immigrant Children." Nieman Lab, https://www.niemanlab.org/2018/06/seven-newsrooms-4-countries-thousands-of-kids-propublica-launches-project-to-find-immigrant-children/.

Schneider, Pat. (2018). "Q&A: Sue Robinson Wants White Reporters to Change the Way They Report." *Madison.com*, January 28, 2018, https://madison.com/news/local/education/university/q-a-sue-robinson-wants-white-reporters-to-change-the/article_345954f7-996f-5c75-9fde-10c32f72cf66.html.

Schrock, Andrew, and Gwen Shaffer. (2017). "Data Ideologies of an Interested Public: A Study of Grassroots Open Government Data Intermediaries." *Big Data & Society* 4, no. 1: 1–10.

Schrøder, Kim Christian. (2015). "News Media Old and New." *Journalism Studies* 16, no. 1: 60–78.

Schudson, Michael. (1981). *Discovering the News*. (New York, Basic Books, 1981).

Schudson, Michael. (2001). "The Objectivity Norm in American Journalism." *Journalism* 2, no. 2: 149–170.

Segev, Elad. (2015). *International News Flow Online: Global Views with Local Perspectives* (New York: Peter Lang).

Seo, Soomin. (2016). "Marginal Majority at The Postcolonial News Agency." *Journalism Studies* 17, no. 1: 39–56.

Shahin, Saif, Pei Zheng, Heloisa A. Sturm, and Deepa Fadnis. (2016). "Protesting the Paradigm: A Comparative Study of News Coverage of Protests in Brazil, China, and India." *The International Journal of Press/Politics* 21, no. 2: 143–164.

Shanahan, Elizabeth A., Mark K. McBeth, Paul L. Hathaway, and Ruth J. Arnell. (2008). "Conduit or Contributor? The Role of Media in Policy Change Theory." *Policy Sciences* 41, no. 2: 115.

Shoemaker, Pamela J., and Timothy P. Vos. (2009). *Gatekeeping Theory* (New York: Routledge).

Shome, Raka, and Radha S. Hegde. (2002). "Postcolonial Approaches to Communication: Charting the Terrain, Engaging the Intersections." *Communication Theory* 12, no. 3: 249–270.

Siebert, Fred S., Theodore Peterson, and Wilbur Schramm. (1984). *Four Theories of the Press: The Authoritarian, Libertarian, Social Responsibility and Soviet Communist Concepts of What the Press Should Be and Do* (Urbana-Champaign: University of Illinois Press).

Singer, Jane B. (2014). "User-Generated Visibility: Secondary Gatekeeping in a Shared Media Space." *New Media & Society* 16, no. 1: 55–73.

Sjøvaag, Helle, and Elrik Stavelin. (2012). "Web Media and the Quantitative Content Analysis: Methodological Challenges in Measuring Online News Content." *Convergence* 18, no. 2: 215–229.

Smyrnaios, Nikos, Sophie Chauvet, and Emmanuel Marty. (2017). "The Impact of CrossCheck on Journalists & the Audience Learning the Lessons from a Collaborative Journalism Project Fighting Disinformation Online During the French Presidential Election," hal-0198555, November 2017, http://hal.univ-grenoble-alpes.fr/hal-01985555.

Spivak, Gayatri Chakravorty. (1988). "Can the Subaltern Speak?" in *Marxism and the Interpretation of Culture*, eds. Cary Nelson and Lawrence Grossberg (Urbana: University of Illinois Press), 271–313.

Stites, Tom. (2011)."Layoffs and Cutbacks Lead to a New World of News Deserts", *Nieman Journalism Lab*, Retrieved from https://www.niemanlab.org/2011/12/tom-stites-layoffs-and-cutbacks-lead-to-a-new-world-of-news-deserts/.

Stonbely, Sarah. (2017). "Comparing Models of Collaborative Journalism." Center for Cooperative Media, https://centerforcooperativemedia.org/new-research-comparing-models-collaborative-journalism-released-sept-29/.

Stroud, Natalia J. (2011). *Niche News: The Politics of News Choice* (Oxford: Oxford University Press).

Stryker Munson, Eve, and Catherine A. Warren. (1996). "Introduction" in *James Carey: A Critical Reader*, eds. Eve Stryker Munson and Catherine A. Warren (University of Minnesota Press), 5.

Sylvie, George. (2018). *Reshaping the News: Community, Engagement, and Editors* (New York: Peter Lang).

Tal, Samuel-Azran, and Tsahi Hayat. (2017). "Counter-Hegemonic Contra-Flow and the Al Jazeera America Fiasco: A Social Network Analysis of Al Jazeera America's Twitter Users." *Global Media and Communication* 13, no. 3: 267–282.

Tandoc, Edson C. Jr., Richard Ling, Oscar Westlund, Andrew Duffy, Debbie Goh, and Zheng Wei Lim. (2018). "Audiences Acts of Authentication in the Age of Fake News: A Conceptual Framework." *New Media & Society* 20, no. 8: 2745–2763.

Tandoc, Edson C., and Ryan J. Thomas. (2015). "The Ethics of Web Analytics." *Digital Journalism* 3, no. 2: 243–258.

Tandoc, Edson C. Jr., Zheng Wei Lim, and Richard Ling. (2018). "Defining 'Fake News': A Typology of Scholarly Definitions." *Digital Journalism* 6, no. 2: 137–153.

Taneja, Harsh, and James G. Webster. (2015). "How Do Global Audiences Take Shape? The Role of Institutions and Culture in Patterns of Web Use." *Journal of Communication* 66, no. 1: 161–182.

Tech Transparency ProjecT. (2019). "Google's Media Takeover." Google Transparency Project, Campaign for Accountability, October 9, 2019, https://www.techtransparencyproject.org/articles/googles-media-takeover.

Thung, Ferdian, Tegawende F. Bissyande, David Lo, and Lingxiao Jiang. (2013). "Network Structure of Social Coding in GitHub." *2013 17th European Conference on Software Maintenance and Reengineering* (March 2013): 323–326. https://ieeexplore.ieee.org/document/6498480

Thussu, Daya Kishan. (2007). "The 'Murdochization' of News? The Case of Star TV in India." *Media, Culture & Society* 29, no. 4: 593–611.

Torney-Purta, Judith, and Jo-Ann Amadeo.. (2011). "Participatory Niches for Emergent Citizenship in Early Adolescence: An International Perspective." *The Annals of the American Academy of Political and Social Science* 633, no. 1: 180–200.

Tseng, Vivian. (2012). *The Uses of Research in Policy and Practice* (Washington, DC: Society for Research in Child Development).

Tuchman, Gaye. (1978). *Making News: A Study in the Construction of Reality* (New York: Free Press).

Tully, Melissa, Adam Maksl, Stephanie Craft, Emily K. Vraga, and Seth Ashley. (2019). "Understanding Critical News Consumption: Theorizing and Measuring News Literacy." Paper Presented at the 2019 Future of Journalism Conference, Cardiff, UK.

Tully, Melissa, and Emily K. Vraga. (2017). "Effectiveness of a News Media Literacy Advertisement in Partisan Versus Nonpartisan Online Media Contexts." *Journal of Broadcasting & Electronic Media* 61: 144–162.

Tully, Melissa, and Emily K. Vraga. (2018). "A Mixed-Methods Approach to Examining the Relationship Between News Media Literacy and Political Efficacy." *International Journal of Communication* 12: 766–787.

Tully, Melissa, Emily K. Vraga, and Leticia Bode. (2020). "Designing and Testing News Literacy Messages for Social Media." *Mass Communication and Society* 6: 22–46.

Tully, Melissa, Emily K. Vraga, and Anne-Bennett Smithson. (2020). "News Media Literacy, Perceptions of Bias, and Interpretation of News." *Journalism* 21: 209–226.

Twelfth International Conference on Grey Literature, Prague, 2010, http://www. textrelease.com/gl12conference.html.

University of Missouri., (n. d.)., "The J-School Legacy," https://journalism.missouri.edu/ the-j-school/the-j-school-legacy/.

Usher, Nikki———. (2014). *Making News* at The New York Times. (Ann Arbor: University of Michigan Press, 2014).

Usher, Nikki———. (2016). *Interactive Journalism: Hackers, Data, and Code.* (Urbana: University of Illinois Press, 2016).

Usher, Nikki———. (2017). "Does Anyone Care about Journalism Research? (No, Really)." *Poynter*, April 5, 2017, https://www.poynter.org/newsletters/2017/does-anyone-care-about-journalism-research-no-really/.

Usher, Nikki. (2018). "Re-Thinking Trust in the News: A material approach through 'Objects of Journalism.'" *Journalism Studies* 19, no. 4 (2018): 564–578.

Usher, Nikki, Jesse Holcomb, and Justin Littman. (2018). "Twitter Makes it Worse: Political Journalists, Gendered Echo Chambers, and the Amplification of Gender Bias." *The International Journal of Press/Politics* 23, no. 3: 324–344.

Van Aelst, Peter, and Stefaan Walgrave. (2016). "Information and Arena: The Dual Function of the News Media for Political Elites." *Journal of Communication* 66, no. 3: 496–518.

van der Haak, Bregtje, Michael Parks, and Manuel Castells. (2012). "The Future of Journalism: Networked Journalism," *International Journal of Communication* 6, http:// ijoc.org/index.php/ijoc/article/download/1750/832.

Van Duyn, Emily, and Jessica Collier. (2019). "Priming and Fake News: The Effects of Elite Discourse on Evaluations of News Media." *Mass Communication and Society* 22, no. 1: 29–48.

Verweij, Peter, and Elvira van Noort. (2014). "Journalists' Twitter Networks, Public Debates and Relationships in South Africa." *Digital Journalism* 2, no. 1: 98–114.

Vraga, Emily K., and Melissa Tully. (2015). "Media Literacy Messages and Hostile Media Perceptions: Processing of Nonpartisan Versus Partisan Political Information." *Mass Communication and Society* 18: 422–448.

Vraga, Emily K., and Melissa Tully. (2016). "Effective Messaging to Communicate News Media Literacy Concepts to Diverse Publics." *Communication and the Public* 1: 305–322.

Vraga, Emily K., Melissa Tully, Adam Maksl, Stephanie Craft, and Seth Ashley. (2021). "Theorizing News Literacy Behaviors." *Communication Theory*, 31(1), 1–21.

Vraga, Emily K., Melissa Tully, and Hernando Rojas. (2009). "Media Literacy Training Reduces Perception of Bias." *Newspaper Research Journal* 30, no. 4: 68–81.

Wahl-Jorgensen, Karin. (2013). "The Strategic Ritual of Emotionality: A Case Study of Pulitzer Prize-Winning Articles." *Journalism* 14, no. 1: 129–145.

Wahl-Jorgensen, Karin. (2016). "The Chicago School and Ecology: A Reappraisal for the Digital Era." *American Behavioral Scientist* 60, no. 1: 8–23.

Wahl-Jorgensen, Karin, and Thomas Hanitzsch, eds. (2009). *The Handbook of Journalism Studies* (New York: Routledge).

Waldman, Steve, and the Working Group on Information Needs of Communities. (2011). "The Information Needs of Communities: The Changing Media Landscape in a Broadband Age," July, 2011, https://transition.fcc.gov/osp/inc-report/The_Information_Needs_of_Communities.pdf.

Ward, Vicky, Allan House, and Susan Hamer. (2009). "Knowledge Brokering: The Missing Link in the Evidence to Action Chain?" *Evidence & Policy: A Journal of Research, Debate and Practice* 5, no. 3: 267–279.

Wartella, Ellen. (1987). *A History of the Institute of Communications Research.* https://media.illinois.edu/icr.

Washington, Laura. (2011). "The Paradox of our Media Age and What to Do About It." *In These Times,* April 5, 2011, http://inthesetimes.com/article/7151/the_paradox_of_our_media_ageand_what_to_do_about_it.

Wasserman, Herman. (2011). "Global Journalism Studies: Beyond Panoramas." *Communicatio* 37, no. 1: 100–117.

Wasserman, Herman. (2011). "Towards a Global Journalism Ethics Via Local Narratives." *Journalism Studies* 12, no. 6: 791–803.

Weaver, David., A., and Joshua M. Scacco. (2013). "Revisiting the Protest Paradigm: The Tea Party as Filtered through Prime-Time Cable News." *The International Journal of Press/Politics* 18, no. 1: 61–84.

Weber, Matthew S., et al. (2019). "Connecting the Dots: Digital Subscriptions," News Media Alliance, https://www.newsmediaalliance.org/release-new-study-reveals-connection-entertainment-news-media-subscriptions/.

Weber, Steve. (2004). *The Success of Open Source* (Cambridge: Harvard University Press).

Weinberg, Steve. (2008). *A Journalism of Humanity: A Candid History of the World's First Journalism School* (Columbia: University of Missouri Press).

Wihbey, John, and Mark Coddington. (2017). "Knowing the Numbers: Assessing Attitudes among Journalists and Educators about Using and Interpreting Data, Statistics, and Research." *International Symposium on Online Journalism* 17: 5–24, https://isoj.org/wp-content/uploads/2017/04/isoj_journal_v7_nl_2017.pdf.

Yanovitzky, Itzhak, and Matthew Weber. (2019). "Analysing Use of Evidence in Public Policymaking Processes: A Theory-Grounded Content Analysis Methodology." *Evidence & Policy: A Journal of Research, Debate and Practice* 16, no. 1: 65–82.

Yanovitzky, Itzhak, and Matthew S. Weber. (2018). "News Media as Knowledge Brokers in Public Policymaking Processes." *Communication Theory* 29, no. 2: 191–212.

Yarnall, Louise, J.T. Johnson, Luke Rinne, and Michael Andrew Ranney. (2008). "How Post-Secondary Journalism Educators Teach advanced CAR Data Analysis Skills in the Digital Age." *Journalism & Mass Communication Educator* 63, no. 2: 146–164.

Zamith, Rodrigo. (2019). "Transparency, Interactivity, Diversity, and Information Provenance in Everyday Data Journalism." *Digital Journalism* 7, no. 4: 470–489.

Zelizer, Barbie. (2004). *Taking Journalism Seriously: News and the Academy.* (Thousand Oaks, CA: Sage).

Zelizer, Barbie. (2006). "Journalism and the Academy," in *The Handbook of Journalism Studies,* eds. Karin Wahl-Jorgensen and Folker Hanusch (London, New York: Routledge), 29–41.

Zelizer, Barbie. (2007). "Introduction: On Finding New Ways of Thinking About Journalism." *Political Communication* 24: 111–114.

Zelizer, Barbie. (2016). "Communication in the Fan of Disciplines." *Communication Theory* 26, no. 3: 213–235.

Zion, Lawrie, and David Craig, eds. (2015). *Ethics for Digital Journalists: Emerging Best Practices* (New York; London: Routledge).

Index

For the benefit of digital users, indexed terms that span two pages (e.g., 52–53) may, on occasion, appear on only one of those pages.

Tables and figures are indicated by *t* and *f* following the page number